NOW YOU'RE

COOKING

FOR COMPANY

NOW YOU'RE
COOKING
FOR COMPANY

EVERYTHING A BEGINNER

NEEDS TO KNOW TO

HAVE PEOPLE OVER

BY ELAINE CORN

An Astolat Book, Harlow & Ratner, Emeryville, CA

FOR DAVID AND ROBERT

Special thanks to: Kathleen Abraham, Hilary Abramson,
Ellie Brecher, Martha Casselman, Darrell Corti, Vivienne Corn,
my students at Draeger's, Barbara Fitzpatrick, Rebecca Green,
Cindy Indorf, Moe Kalisky, Robin Kline, Christi Landis,
Ronni Lundy, Andrea London, Patricia Murakami,
Marcie Rothman, John Ruden...and Elaine, Jay, and Dan.

Library of Congress Cataloging-in-Publication Data

Corn, Elaine
   Now you're cooking for company : everything a beginner needs to
know to have people over / by Elaine Corn.
      p.   cm.
   "An Astolat book."
   Includes index.
   ISBN 1-883791-03-0
   1. Entertaining. 2. Cookery. 3. Menus. I. Title.
TX731.C665 1996
642'.4—dc20   96-18683
                                                         CIP

Design: McClain Design
Typesetting: Classic Typography
Production: Dave Granvold

Printed in Singapore
10 9 8 7 6 5 4 3 2 1

Harlow & Ratner
5749 Landregan Street
Emeryville, CA 94608

CONTENTS

INTRODUCTION

So you'd like to invite some company over. Sounds like fun. Having folks over has no equal in making and keeping friends. There is simply nothing like it to bond people. If you're new at cooking, you probably have some doubts. Could your recipes stand up to the food you've had at your friends' homes? What would you make? How do you "design" a menu when you've never done it before? It's been so long since an invited guest crossed your threshold that you'd certainly have to clean the house. You'd have to clean again after the company leaves. Well, maybe.

I'm convinced that the real problem for most beginning cooks is a simple case of procrastination, brought on by an exaggerated sense of risk. As I see it, if you keep waiting until you think you've got cooking for company completely learned, it's going to be a long time before you make that first phone call to invite a friend or relative over.

Now, it's true that having folks over means feeding them. No matter whose home you go to, anywhere in the world, you get something just for walking in the door. Usually it's simple — a wedge of cheese, a dish of olives, a plate of cookies, a cup of coffee. (Notice the lack of themes and set design.) Simple is good, and it's the logical place for a beginner to start. Just because you once got invited to a banquet doesn't mean in return you have to stage one too.

It took me a long time to learn the lesson of simplicity. I used to be a run-amok party-giver. Back in the 1970s in Texas I had 80 people to my one-bedroom duplex for freshly slain deer and gallons of beer. Back in the 1980s when I lived for a while in Louisville, I had 80 people for country ham, mint juleps, and so much cole slaw that I had to mix it in my bath tub. (The recipe to this day is known as Bathtub Slaw, and no, if you're wondering, you can't mix enough sliced cabbage to fill a bathtub with your clothes on.)

Nearly twenty years later I believe I've discovered the secret of having people over: Friends

4

like casual evenings or afternoons where little is demanded of them. And they'll come on your terms. If your terms are steaks on the grill with salad and beer, those are great terms (please invite me!). Anyone new to entertaining should take this seriously. Steak, salad, and beer may not seem like much, but it's a menu to be proud of and which is sure to please.

What's important is getting started. Having just one small party will bring about radical change in how you approach this area of your life. Just getting a couple of people together at your house has its own built-in element for rein-forcement. What seems daunting the first time will be easy the next. You'll be ready for a larger group, although you may never stage a really big party. You'll know your comfort level when you reach it.

To assure your success, give a little thought to whom you're teaming up for the few hours they'll be at your house. I've invited friends with only one thing in common—they knew me. The house filled up with two doctors, two lawyers, a chef, a cosmetics retailer, an office-machine sales-person, three newspaper reporters, a realtor, a dietitian, a pharmacist, and random neighbors. Well, the lawyers found each other. A reporter talked to the doctors about a story she was work-ing on. The cosmetics retailer wanted to cook. The dietitian liked my neighbors who made crafts.

I've also had people over who all were in the same line of work. This can be a lot of fun. But be careful. It can descend into boring one-note con-versation.

And remember just one more thing: There's a distinction between having a Dinner Party and having people over. If you never call it "Dinner Party" you'll feel a lot better about making food for you to eat with some people you like.

1

YOUR FRIENDS AWAIT

THE TWELVE
IMMORTAL CHORES

EIGHT STEPS TO ACHIEVING YOUR HOSTING POTENTIAL

Before you cook for company, it's important to prepare yourself both psychologically and physically. The following steps will help you to get in the mood and functioning efficiently. Feel comfortable with these, and soon you'll be inviting people in on impulse and getting ready so calmly, it will seem automatic.

1. PRACTICE

Make a recipe at least once, better yet twice, before you show off. Exceptions to this rule are pieces of meat that are too expensive and too large to make only for yourself.

2. DON'T COMPARE THE DINNER YOU'RE MAKING TO OTHER DINNERS

Your style of feeding company will be different from what your friends or parents do. Enjoy the elaborate settings and butler-passed hors d'oeuvre when you're someone else's guest. When you first begin having company to your own house, the following are all you'll need for true accomplishment:

- A couple of recipes that came out great.
- Well-fed friends who appreciate what you've achieved—even overcome.
- Satisfaction in knowing that making a meal for someone else is a nice thing to do and is a wholesome use of your time.

3. ORGANIZE

In *Now You're Cooking* I emphasized the importance of learning to organize your ingredients before you use them, and to set them up conveniently near your mixing bowl or the stove. It is just as important to organize the various activities that lead to having folks spend a few hours eating in your house. Organization is as .

important for three guests as it is for 30. Read more about how to fit a style of organization to your personality on page 14.

4. USE YOUR KITCHEN CABINETS AS BULLETIN BOARDS

The back-and-forth nature of your physical relationship with a recipe means it's got to be near you and it's got to be easy to read. Take the books, magazines, or newspaper clippings with the recipes you'll be making to a copy machine. If the recipe's type is small, here's your chance to enlarge it (the better to prevent skipped ingredients and missed instructions). Tape the copies to the cabinets or kitchen wall near your work area. This puts the recipes within immediate sight. In addition, your kitchen won't be burdened by a stack of books, and the recipes will be in a form that invites scribbling. If you've made a "to do" list, tape that on the wall, too.

5. READ THE RECIPES ALL THE WAY THROUGH

Skipping this step is the number 1 reason recipes end in ruination. As flexible as I am through most of the cooking processes, this is one inviolate rule. You've got to know what's going to happen to your ingredients, how you'll be spending your time, and if a dish will take 5 minutes or an overnight marinade. A recipe is not a murder mystery with a surprise ending.

6. GET A FEEL FOR THE ZEN OF MENUS

At first be less concerned with such elusive concepts as balancing taste and contrasting texture. Instead, concentrate on grouping recipes according to what is quick, what is a make-ahead, and what is—here come the most dreaded words in cooking—last minute. The elusive elements seem to pull together on their own. Two recipes are perfectly in sync if one is an entree that bakes while you give your complete attention to making the other, a salad. A third recipe, dessert, might be ready and waiting in the refrigerator.

You'll learn that recipes don't have to done at the same time, only available at the same time. For more about timing the courses in a meal, see page 15.

7. LET HUMAN NATURE BE

Don't be surprised to find women talking to women and men talking to men. Sometimes the world works that way. Forcing the man-woman-man-woman seating arrangement is a little outdated, too. I'd rather introduce people who share interests, regardless of gender.

8. REMEMBER THE LAW OF POPULATION

The more people you have, the less food you need per head. This is an absolute for a buffet.

THE EIGHT IMMORTAL CHORES
In *Now You're Cooking* I devoted eleven pages to THE EIGHT IMMORTAL CHORES, the basic skills every new cook must learn before real cooking begins. I call them "immortal" because no short cut or machine has found a way to kill them off.

They are so important for every beginning cook to know that I am repeating them here, in a shorter form. Four more chores specific to company follow these.

ONE-HAND HOLD, FOR SLICING

TWO-HAND HOLD, FOR CHOPPING, MINCING

THE FIRST IMMORTAL CHORE

CHOP AN ONION

You'll need a sharp knife with a blade at least 6 to 8 inches long and a cutting board. Hold the onion with your fingertips curled under. Notice a flat barrier forms across the fingers between the first and second knuckles. This area is a guide for the knife to lean on.

To keep the onion from rolling, cut it in half through the poles, leaving part of the root (hairy end) attached to each half. Peel the papery skin from the onion. Place the halves cut side down.

Make slices with the knife tip aimed at the onion's root. Cut to but not through the root.

Turn the knife blade parallel to the counter, steady the top of the onion with your palm, and make 2 or 3 horizontal cuts, cutting to but not through the root.

Finally, go back to the top of the onion and slice down through the grid you've made. You've made diced onion.

If you want smaller pieces, hold the knife in your dominant hand and rest the palm of your other hand on top of the blade. Lift the handle up and down, keeping the point in place so it pivots on the board. Move the knife in a fan shape all over the onion until the pieces are as small as you need.

THE SECOND IMMORTAL CHORE

MINCE GARLIC

Detach as many cloves as you need from the head of garlic. Whack a clove with the flat side of a knife blade, a jar, or a skillet; the peel will burst and release the clove inside. Cut off the brown root tip.

With a sharp paring knife, cut the clove into lengthwise slivers. Cut across the slivers with slices close together to make small pieces.

Switch to a chef's knife and rock it back and forth, as in chopping an onion (above) until the pieces are very fine. Gather the garlic into a small pile with the knife's blade as you go.

CUT CELERY AND CARROTS

Celery: Break off a rib of celery from the bunch. Cut off the dirty white parts, then wash the rib well. Trim off the leaves. Lay the celery on a cutting board round side down.

With the tip of a paring knife, make 3 lengthwise cuts completely down the rib. Cut across them to make small pieces.

Carrot: Halve the carrot lengthwise. With flat sides down, cut each half into a number of strips. Cut across the strips.

THE FOURTH IMMORTAL CHORE

SEED AND CHOP TOMATOES

Cut the tomato in half through its equator, using a serrated knife. Hold one half in your palm, over the garbage can or sink. Gently squeeze, then flick the seeds out. Repeat with the other half.

Cut the tomato as you would an onion (see page 10).

THE FIFTH IMMORTAL CHORE

SLICE MUSHROOMS

If the mushrooms are nice and white, wipe them clean with a paper towel. If they're dirty, rinse them.

Cut off the stems flush with the caps. Set the caps flat on a cutting board and slice them as thick or thin as you want. To chop, rock a chef's knife over the slices, as in chopping an onion (page 10).

GENTLY SQUEEZE
THE TOMATO HALF

WASH LETTUCE

Separate as many leaves as you're going to use from a head of lettuce. Wash the leaves individually under running water. Dry the leaves in a salad spinner or roll the leaves up in a clean kitchen towel to dry them. Spin-dried lettuce will keep 1 week in a zip-style freezer-quality bag with the air pressed out, in the refrigerator.

PEEL POTATOES

Brace the potato on the edge of the sink with one hand and hold a vegetable peeler in the other hand. In quick flicks away from you, peel off pieces of skin directly into the sink. Rotate the potato as you go, not the peeler. If the potato gets gritty, rinse it off. To keep potatoes white, set them in a bowl of cold water after peeling, but for no more than a few hours.

CHOP PARSLEY

Pull off the leaves from the thicker stems. Rinse the leaves in a strainer under cold water. Drain on a cloth or paper towel, then put the leaves on a cutting board.

Move a chef's knife up and down over the leaves using the 2-hand hold, as in chopping an onion (see page 10). After the first cuts, gather the parsley into a small pile and keep cutting until you have fine, little pieces.

CLEAN THE HOUSE

Cleaning a house which isn't ordinarily guest-ready can be daunting. You have to approach housework like chopping onions. Not many people like to chop onions, but little cooking will happen if you don't do it.

HAVING PEOPLE OVER: FOUR MORE IMMORTAL CHORES
I asked a number of beginning cooks why they don't invite friends in more often. The first reason everyone gave was the untidiness of their homes. The second reason was that they were unwilling to do anything about it. Worrying about cooking the meal was third. So overwhelming was the anxiety about cleaning that it immediately became an Immortal Chore. Other important chores behind the scenes get you organized, time the courses in a meal, and straighten up after your company leaves.

HOUSE CLEANING DON'TS:

DON'T clean the same day as the party. Anyone who tries to clean, set the table, shop, and cook all on the same day will be exhausted by the time the fun is supposed to begin. Instead, clean the day before and set the table. You'll wake up to a house just about ready to throw open its doors and you'll be freed of the fear of anyone showing up early.

DON'T clean rooms no one will see. Some of us like to show off our homes with short tours to all the nooks. I've even led friends to my first walk-in closet, I was so proud of it. You can still leave most of the house open for viewing even if you close the doors to a few unruly bedrooms.

DON'T rule out other ways to get your house clean:

1. Hire help

A one-shot cleaning service may be worth the money. Not only will you avoid cleaning altogether, but the time you would have spent doing it will open up for cooking. I predict one of three things will happen:

- You'll enjoy having a housekeeper so much that you'll hire one to show up bi-monthly or weekly to keep your place clean. This is a healthy way of giving up and solving the problem.
- You'll always regard cleaning as a last-minute blast from a maid service.
- You'll learn to do the cleaning yourself and to stay on top of it, because it will save you money.

2. Superficial cleaning

This is done by you—quickly. Clear tables and countertops of clutter. Vacuum and dust. Close doors to unavailable rooms. This works for people who know who they are and make no excuses for the fact that a certain lack of order comes with the evening.

HERE ARE
SOME LIST TOPICS:

- Who's coming?
- The menu
- Ingredients
- Everything else—pick what applies:
  Candles
  Napkins—cloth or paper
  Paper cups
  Ice
  Music (playing a new CD makes you feel as if you've just arrived at your own party)
  Fireplace logs
  Flowers
  Wine or beer
  Bottled water
  Soda for kids (Oh, who am I kidding? Grown-ups drink these, too.)
  Coffee and tea, sugar and cream
  Plastic garbage bags

DON'T FORGET EQUIPMENT
What baking pans, pots, utensils, and serving platters are called for in your recipes? Do you have them? Do you have enough of them?

GET AS ORGANIZED AS YOUR PERSONALITY ALLOWS

If you are naturally organized like my mother, The Queen of Lists, you will have no problem organizing yourself to have company. Personally, I get by with one list. It's a combo menu-shopping list (although once at the store the menu expands dramatically from impulse buys).

Lists derive their styles from the personalities behind them. Mine have a few arrows shooting off to circled reminders and huge parentheses grouping things—it's my shorthand and it's what I understand. A list can be an impulse on a napkin. Sometimes it's on the back of a discarded print-out from the computer. It doesn't matter if your list is in chronological order of how you'll approach your goal, or if it's a set of multiple lists.

The ultra-organized might feel best with a Things To Do group of lists that go day-by-day. The lists will transport you in an orderly way from maybe a week out, and keep you on track each day until you pull it all together The Day Of. In addition you'll have a separate shopping list. The Day Of will get its own final things-to-do list.

If you're a list sloth, my suggestion is to make lists only for areas where you are weakest. I'm always so focused on the food that I forget the frills—candles, bottled water, paper napkins and disposable cups (if we'll be outside or having kids), and ice. Ice is a Thing To Do if you have an ice maker; get it going and save each batch in plastic containers. Ice is a Thing To Buy if you don't.

Finally, if you can handle only one list, make it for the menu. It is inevitable that you will then make a list for the ingredients.

LEARN TO TIME THE COURSES IN A MEAL

This is the topic most mysterious for people new to cooking. How can three kinds of food all be done at the same time?

The answer is: They don't have to be done at the same time. They only have to be available at the same time.

Two new ways to think about how food gets to the table should help.

WHAT'S HOT, WHAT'S NOT

Change every precept you have of how hot or how cold food has to be when it comes to the table. Food can be too hot for human consumption. Food that is too hot burns the tongue, roof of the mouth, and mouth lining. Food that is too hot can't be tasted as well as food that is—how did Goldilocks put it?—just right. That point of not too hot and not too cold is best described as from body temperature up to 115 to 120 degrees. If food is too hot or too cold, all you feel is the sensation of the temperature.

Soup is not much of an exception. Yes, hot soup should be hot, but not so hot that it scalds. I always think of my grandfather slurping deadly hot soup, which is how he insisted it be served. He schluhped the soup off a huge spoon in order to pull in air with each swallow. This particular sound isn't something you want to hear when you have company. For you, this is good news. After a pot of soup boils you still don't have to serve it. It will stay within an appropriate "hot" temperature range for probably 10 minutes.

Cold Food Is Cool

If food is to be served cold, our first tendency is to think ice cold. Food that is too cold won't hurt you, like food that is too hot. It's just hard to taste it. Next time you go to a buffet, make a point of noticing the temperature of the food. It will probably be just cool or at room temperature. Fish served "cold," for example, is actually cool. Some dishes, such as salads and marinated vegetables, taste best with that cold edge from the refrigerator warmed up a little. Room temperature is the best temperature for serving most dishes billed as "cold." Serving at room temperature shouldn't scare you at all. Four hours at room temperature is regarded as safe. If the food has any acid in it or on it, such as a salad dressing containing vinegar or lemon juice, chances of spoilage grow slimmer.

Keeping Your Cool With Hot Foods

Let's say the basic plate of food for dinner has three components—meat and two vegetables. If you've baked the meat, it will stay hot for quite a while after it comes out of the oven. The length of time depends on how big the meat is and how long it was hot in the oven. A turkey? You've got a good hour to let it sit on the countertop waiting for its edible companions. In most large pieces of meat a phenomenon takes place that actually increases the internal temperature 5 to 10 degrees for a short period of time.

Baked chicken? It will stay hot out of the oven probably 15 or 20 minutes if you cover the finished dish with foil. That's plenty of time to make two vegetables via sauté pan, microwave, steamer, or broiler. Sautéed fish filets, despite a comparatively short time spent in a skillet, will give you 10 to 15 extra minutes once they're out of the skillet and on a serving platter. Besides, most sautéed meat has to wait for the pan juices to be turned into sauce. If you doubt that sautéed fish (or chicken breasts, veal scallops, pork chops, or even zucchini) could stay hot this long, cover them with foil. Even if the dish cools a little, it will be pleasantly hot for eating. In addition, the boiling-hot pan juices will be poured over any of these meats, making them hot again.

THE MENU AS BALLET

Think of a menu as something like a ballet. In the making, it has tension and relaxation. You'll find yourself moving and thinking quickly during one part of the preparation and twiddling your thumbs while a pot simmers slowly or bakes in the oven. If you think you'll be nervous, emphasize more make-ahead dishes. Many of the recipes in this book have make-ahead options.

Planning Ahead

Take a look at your menu. You may love all the recipes individually, but do they relate—and I don't mean by taste, culture, or era? It's to your advantage that the recipes relate to each other in timing. One recipe cooks slow in the oven while another is a quickie on top of the stove. Miraculously, they're ready together.

For example, soup, cole slaw, meat, a vegetable, and dessert may sound unworkable. Look again. The soup is made ahead. It's cold in the refrigerator, and all it needs is reheating. Does the microwave sound like a good place? The cole slaw was made three days ago. The meat is in the oven. The vegetable might be sautéed, broiled, or microwaved, and dessert is strawberries and cream. You cut and sugared the strawberries maybe yesterday, but certainly before you got the meat in the oven. What will your life be like when everyone comes? The cole slaw will be on the table. The soup will be in a pot reheating over low heat on the stove (or you'll do the microwave suggestion). The meat will be just about done. The vegetable will be prepped (washed and chopped and ready to be cooked). The strawberries lie in wait in the refrigerator. In short, when your house gets crowded, you go to the kitchen and ... and ... cook a vegetable. Now that's what I call great timing!

Avoiding the Pitfalls

Mentally take yourself through the paces of the menu you've planned. Ask yourself some of these questions:

Will you need to sauté two things at once on top of the stove? The technique "sauté" implies quick cooking over high heat. This is code for last minute. You need to watch a sauté. So, especially because you'll have guests in the house, change one of the sautés to a recipe that can be made ahead, baked, served cold, or grilled outdoors. One sautéed dish you can easily handle.

Are you baking more things than will fit in one oven? My mother's double-oven fetish is logical to me now. She used to have stacking double ovens. Now she's got a new set-up—one oven under the range and one over the range. They are like two children; she loves them both the same. I always thought because she's such a good cook that she deserved to have two ovens. In truth, the person with only one oven must become the better cook.

The one-oven cook has to make menus that outwit a shortage of oven space. If one baked recipe can be made ahead, the one-oven kitchen can succeed in producing a menu with two or more baked dishes. It works again if the recipes bake in the same temperature range at the same time. Between 325 degrees and 375 degrees you can combine the baking of meats, vegetables, various casseroles, and certain egg dishes. For baking cakes, cookies, and pies, the oven must give itself up completely to the required temperature for the best results.

If you have one oven, I suggest menus with a baked dish—chicken, beef, lamb, ham—buttressed by a salad and perhaps a vegetable made in a separate pan that can roast along with the meat, such as potatoes au gratin or baked carrots. Dessert is an obvious make-ahead, or one that won't need the oven when the meat is in it.

Don't forget your extra burner—your microwave oven. If you don't want to bake the carrots, get them chopped and in a bowl with some brown sugar and salt, cover with plastic wrap and microwave them.

What kind of chopping is in your menu? How many onions will you have to chop? Depending on your skills, one onion could take nearly 5 minutes to peel and chop. Ask yourself the same question about garlic, tomatoes, mushrooms, celery, carrots, and potatoes. Lots of books and teachers try to help by advising you to chop all the onions and garlic ahead of time and store them in zip-style plastic bags. Will you? As long as I've cooked, I've never gotten it together to do this. If you are the chop-and-Ziploc type, you can subtract time off your prep on The Day Of.

What recipes need overnight in the refrigerator? For example, marinating meats (although a few hours is usually sufficient).

What recipes are complete make-aheads? Salad greens can be washed, spin-dried, torn, and put in zip bags with the air pressed out up to a week ahead. Other make-aheads are:

Dips and spreads
Soup
Marinated salads or cole slaw
Cake
Cookies

THE TWELFTH IMMORTAL CHORE

CLEAN UP

Dirty dishes, lipstick stains, and dried-up food. Just part of the glamour of hosting. The minute you pick up even a couple of wine glasses, body language signals a close to the get-together. It's possible some of your guests will help you clear the table. I always accept. We bond, you know, over the sink together. We have a good talk. But it would be rude to expect it. This is your party. You're having it with the understanding that you'll be the one cleaning up.

WHAT KIND OF CLEANER-UPPER ARE YOU?

I divide clean-up personalities into three types:

The Hate-It Personality. My only advice is to either hire help or follow the style of one of the other two types.

The Immediate Clean-up Personality. You believe there's nothing like waking up to a house so clean no one would guess a bash happened there the night before.

The Morning-After Personality. You leave the mess and make demands on no one. In the morning, you jump out of bed anxious to start cleaning and actually relax during this time alone.

Whether you want to get it over with or will deal with it later, you can still streamline the clean-up.

CLEAN-UP, STAGE ONE: FOOD

(A must for Immediate or Morning-After types)

1. Hang a big plastic garbage bag somewhere in your kitchen—stretched over a drawer, punched with a hole and hung on a knob. All party trash will go in this bag.

2. Using your tray, take ketchup bottles, mustard bottles, the butter dish—everything that must be returned to the refrigerator. With one swing of the refrigerator door, these items will be returned.

3. Return to the scene and clear food that must be wrapped or stored for later use. On this trip, load the tray with serving platters holding uneaten food, bowls of salsa or olives, uneaten crackers and dip. Once back in the kitchen, wrap leftover food and get it in the refrigerator, and return crackers, olives, etc. to their original jars, containers, or boxes. Put them all away.

4. Morning-After option: Anything that looks like a soaker (pots or pans with food stuck or burned on) fill with very hot tap water and dishwashing liquid until morning.

CLEAN-UP, STAGE TWO: SILVERWARE AND GLASSES

1. For those whose dishwasher comes with a claim that pre-washing isn't necessary, take it at its word. Put the dirty silverware directly into the dishwasher.

2. For everyone else, have ready a tub or extra sink full of hot water with dishwashing soap. Swish handfuls of silverware in this water, then transfer them to the dishwasher. If you don't have a dishwasher, rinse on the spot and let dry in the dish drainer while you head back to the scene with your tray for the glassware.

3. Bring all the wine glasses and water glasses to the kitchen. You can probably get away with pouring the undrunk beverages down the drain

and placing the glassware directly in the dish-washer without rinsing. If there's a stubborn-looking lipstick blot or dried wine on the bottom, rinse first.

Plates, Other Platters, Bowls

1. Return to the scene and stack all the plates, bowls, cups and saucers. Carry as much in one trip as you can, but don't force it. These are the easiest trips, so if your load becomes heavy, best to make two lighter loads. As you clear, if no one is still seated at the table, you may decide to designate one plate a garbage plate. Scrape all the food from the other plates onto it and set the garbage plate on top. If you'll be running the dishwasher soon, take these just-collected dishes directly to the dishwasher, and fill it up.

2. If paper napkins have been used, grab them now. If cloth napkins and placemats have been used, bundle them for the laundry.

CLEAN-UP, STAGE THREE: KITCHEN

1. You might have to run two cycles in the dishwasher. While the dishwasher runs, tackle anything left on your countertops or in your sink. Morning-Afters can finish washing soakers tomorrow. Leave hand-washed items to dry in a dish drainer. They'll be shinier than if you took the time to dry them with a towel.

2. Wipe your countertops. Take out the garbage. If there's time, empty the dishwasher and put the clean dishes away.

3. Walk away. Smile.

2

STOCKING UP

EQUIPMENT

THE PANTRY

WHAT YOU'LL NEED MORE OF
SILVERWARE

If you don't have enough silverware to last the meal, you might want to invest in some add-on flatware.

Let's say you have 8 forks and 8 people come over. For a buffet, you'll have few problems. Everyone will eat everything at the same time and with the same utensils. But if you're seated at the table and salad is its own course, afterwards you'll have no clean forks left for eating the entree. With flatware so inexpensive at so many stores, it's a simple matter to have separate forks for each course.

If you find yourself with not enough forks, the best thing to do is to wash them and set them out again as you're bringing the next course to the table. Don't make everyone keep their dirty forks. (Doesn't this annoy you if it happens at a restaurant?)

GLASSWARE

You might get by on a short supply of dishes and silverware, but I draw the line at glassware. A glass almost never ends up where it started. People stray from the wine glass originally in their hand. I've seen women search for lost goblets by trying to match lipstick stains. Doubt and good graces usually lead most guests to conclude that the only way to keep drinking is with a new glass. You, as host, will pay for the inconvenience of not having enough glasses because you'll be the one picking up lost ones and washing and drying them instead of concentrating on cooking and making folks feel comfortable.

There is no shortage of stores selling inexpensive drinking glasses, wine glasses and goblets, coffee cups and disposable cups. Tip: January and February are the best glassware clearance months.

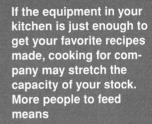

If the equipment in your kitchen is just enough to get your favorite recipes made, cooking for company may stretch the capacity of your stock. More people to feed means

• You'll need more of some of equipment

• You'll need bigger versions of certain cookware

6-inch regular or
   non-stick skillet
10-inch cast iron skillet
Spatula (pancake turner)
Tongs
Pot holders
Paper towels

8-inch or 9-inch glass
   or non-stick square
   baking pan
Oblong baking dish,
   9×13-inch (sometimes
   9×12) glass, or non-
   stick if you like
Big roasting pan with
   handles
Flat rack that fits inside
   the 9×13-inch baking
   dish
Bulb baster
Thick pot holders
Instant-read thermometer
Aluminum baking sheet,
   10×15-inch with sides
   (also called jelly roll
   pan)
9-inch pie plate, glass

The broiler rack and pan
   that came with your
   oven
Shallow baking pan with
   low sides and a rack
   set inside
Tongs
Long-handled spatula
Oven mitts that cover
   your forearms
Skewers—long metal
   ones are best
Aluminum foil
Bulb baster

Here's a quick survey of other equipment you'll need more of:

KNIVES

A few more very sharp knives. If you don't already have a chef's knife, now is the time to get one.

MEASURING DEVICES

Glass measuring cups (for liquids). Pyrex, Anchor Hocking, and Fire King are durable glass and microwavable. Having more will save you from washing the same one every time a measuring cup is called for.

Measuring cup sets (for dry ingredients). Keep a few sets within reach. You won't have to wash one every time you need it.

COOKWARE

Cookie sheets, or baking sheets (sometimes called jelly roll pans). Besides needing them for making cookies, you can slip them under baking casseroles to catch spills and give an added layer of insulation.

Broiler pan. If the one that came with your stove is black and sticky, treat yourself to a new porcelain pan with a fitted steel broiler rack, for under $20. These fit the broilers of standard gas or electric ovens.

TOOLS AND GADGETS

More **rubber spatulas.**
Extra **oven thermometer** (if you've got two ovens).
Extra **instant-read thermometer.**
Extra **timer.**

OTHER EQUIPMENT

A second **salad spinner.**
Cake cooling racks (or "grids") or just a bigger one, for cooling cookies or for setting hot baking dishes to cool.

DISHES

Corn-on-the-cob dishes and extra prongs.

Oval platters. Bold designs, colorful patterns, solid colors, and brave white always set food off nicely. Many are dishwasher-safe and can be had for as low as $12.

FOR CLEAN-UP AND STORAGE

A **lightweight tray** makes clean-up quick.

Plastic storage tubs with lids for leftovers. A variety of sizes will speed your clean-up and keep order in your refrigerator. Put leftovers in the smallest container that will hold them.

Plastic dish tub that you can use as a busing tub, just like in restaurants, or as an extra soaking sink during clean-up.

Utensil holder. Now that you'll be owning more equipment, get a spinning plastic holder with compartments. Or go to the thrift-antique-junk store for any kind of decorative can or crock. Use one for whisks, one for wooden spoons, and one for metal utensils.

Extra rubber gloves. You never know if this is what will convince a friend to help.

Dish towels. I keep a few tucked away to use when company comes. My real stash of dish towels is clean but looks dirty.

WHAT YOU'LL NEED BIGGER

COOKWARE

Cast iron skillet—10½-inch diameter.

Wide, heavy **non-stick skillet**—12-inch diameter.

Bigger pots. Choose a material that won't discolor vegetables (stainless steel, enamel-covered cast iron, non-stick surfaces). If you don't have a 4-quart saucepan, that is a pot with one handle and high sides, get one for soup and wilting leafy greens.

Roasting pan. The sides should be short, no higher than 1½ inches. Roasters with high sides block heat from the bottom portions of the meat.

FOR BOILING:
Dutch oven—4½ to 8 quarts
Big soup pot/stock pot— taller than it is narrow, up to 9 to 12 quarts
Lids for the Dutch oven and stock pot
Colander
Strainer

Stainless steel soup pot, taller than it is round. Aluminum is durable and reasonably priced, but stainless steel has a clean health record.

OTHER EQUIPMENT

Cutting board. If you're still chopping onions on a round board the size of a plate, get yourself a big board 14 by 20 inches or 12 by 18 inches. The polyethylene ones cost between $10 and $15, depending on thickness.

Rubber spatulas. Consider a spoonula, a cross between a big rubber spatula and a big rubber spoon, an excellent scraper.

Big cooling rack that's 10 by 15 inches and will fit inside a jelly roll pan of the same dimensions. Good for retaining the crispness of fried foods made ahead but kept warm in the oven.

FOR MEASURING AND MIXING

Mixing bowls. Nested bowls of glass or stainless steel can be used to mix just about anything and won't react to highly acidic ingredients, such as vinegar.

Measuring "bowls." The best ones are plastic with a spout and often a handle, for mixing, stirring, and pouring.

FOR SERVING

Salad bowl. Tired of serving salad in your biggest pot? A big glass or wooden bowl is in order.

Salad serving spoon and fork.

Serving platters. One big platter can serve a variety of appetizers or many courses at the same time in a small space, and with only one thing to wash.

Serving bowls. Get some good-looking pottery bowls for the buffet to serve salad, mashed potatoes, soup.

EXTRAS THAT WILL HELP YOU COOK MORE FOOD

Electric or butane burner. If you have a four-burner stove, a single electric or butane burner, often called a "fifth burner" (before we started calling the microwave the fifth burner) will immediately expand your heating power. A Max Burton butane burner costs about $40 and is used widely by chefs and caterers when they travel from their kitchens. Because it is non-electric it truly can be used anywhere. It uses a canister of fuel about the size of a can of hair spray, and these can be purchased at the store where the burner is sold. A Toastmaster electric "buffet" range costs about $25, and provided you can place it near an outlet, is a big help. That big pot of soup that will be bubbling away for a couple of hours can be set on an electric burner away from the usual action, freeing up your work space and stove top.

Crock pot. Also good for keeping foods just warm enough to taste good on a buffet.

Good-looking **oven-to-table cookware.** Why bake in a baking dish so ugly you can't bring it to the table? You can't go wrong with the reasonably priced white ovals, squares, and rectangles from Corning or Pyrex-Crown Corning.

EXTRAS YOU NEVER THOUGHT YOU NEEDED

Table and chairs. If you don't have a dining table or enough chairs, this is the era for you. We are in the middle of a furniture renaissance. For about $200, you could have a trendy bleached-looking farmhouse table with chairs and an extra leaf. I've seen a table and four chairs for the same price in dark wood with forest-green chairs and in pine with matching pine chairs. I'm talking about extremely low-cost starter sets. You might also consider a pedestal base with a round or rectangle of glass set over it. Even if you don't

Champagne
Scotch, Bourbon, Gin,
  Vodka
Martini fixings
Bloody Mary fixings
White wine
Sherry
Beer—good beer,
  preferably local
Bottled water, bubbly
  or still
Unsalted macadamia nuts
Unsalted cashews
Variety olives—stuffed,
  herbed, garlicked
Salsas—Pick them up
  on trips.
Mustards
Mayonnaise
Jars of Italian roasted
  red peppers or real
  Hungarian pimientos
Artichoke hearts
Cheese and crackers

*BRUNCH AND
BREAKFAST*
Maple syrup—look for
  medium amber, Grade A
Local honey
Exotic jams and jellies—
  pick these up on
  vacations.

*FOR SALADS AND
SALAD DRESSINGS*
Really fine olive oil
Walnut oil
Company vinegars—
  rice, balsamic, red
  wine, fruit (such as
  raspberry), sherry
  from Spain
Mustards—Dijon, dark
  grainy, herb, honey
Boxed croutons
Chunk of parmesan—
  for grating

like the table top, it won't matter if you use a tablecloth.

Storage space. As your kitchenware accumulates, where will you put it all? Pegboard and hanging pot racks open up enormous cabinet space previously a tangle of pans. You can add open shelves on a spare place on the wall. You could also buy an inexpensive baker's rack for stacking dishes. Really big pots not used much stay in the garage. If you are anxious to cook for company, you'll probably be buying a couple of big pots, too (see page 25). I have a friend who economizes on space by keeping the good silver under a bed inside her biggest roaster. These two needs usually happen together, so it's actually a convenient spot for pulling them out in one motion.

THE PANTRY

The opposite of a stocked pantry is shopping. I don't like unnecessary shopping. Aren't we the folks who use time, precious time—or lack of it—as an excuse to not cook at all? Your slush fund of extra time is somewhere between your house at that grocery store.

My sister-in-law shops every day. It's her way of leaving work behind. When the professional part of her day ends, the second part kicks in with a visit to a supermarket on the way home. For her it's like therapy. For me, it would end in therapy. I'll do anything to avoid impromptu shopping, including sending my husband and praying that the 10 years between now and my son's driver's license passes quickly.

You can see that I haven't mastered the ultimate in pantry quality-of-life. My kitchen doesn't have lots of storage space, let alone a true pantry. And so I, too, must shop.

To combat the call of the supermarket I've improvised pantries where possible throughout the house, and you can, too. The garage houses extras of paper towels, ketchup, soft drinks, sacks of various flours and sugar bought at discount stores. I take small replenishments back to the kitchen when they're needed. An interior closet has a good stable temperature for wine, my homemade jams, and a stash of baking chocolates (their atmospheric requirements are about the same).

THE COMPANY PANTRY

In *Now You're Cooking,* I explained what I consider the you-gotta-have-its for a basic pantry, including such items as oils, vinegars, mustards, herbs and spices, pastas, rices, etc. And I strongly urged beginning cooks to get rid of the demons in your pantries—those processed foods that make us dependent on others for things we can make better ourselves: Dried soup mixes. Cake mixes. Rice mixes that take longer to cook and make you stir more than plain long-grain rice.

So how do you plan a pantry for company?

You don't. The pantry food you need for company is the same as you ought to have around all the time. This is the food that becomes dinner when you have to cook on the spur of the moment or when you can't get to the store. It's the extras—fancy mustards, olives brought back from a trip, local honey, nuts, and great cheeses that give you less to think about when company shows up. What if some friends walked in your door now? Is there anything in the house to feed them?

FOR COOKING
Olive oil—extra virgin
Unsalted butter
Fish stock, fish bouillon, or clam juice
Canned green chilies, whole or diced
Canned chicken stock
Canned beef stock
Canned vegetable stock
Canned whole plum tomatoes, Italian
Canned whole tomatoes, generic
Tomato sauce
Tomato paste in a tube
Dried tomatoes
Nice rice—short, fat Arborio; long, slender Jasmine
Beyond spaghetti— fettuccine, linguine, bow ties, corkscrews (fusilli), medium shells
Frozen corn
Frozen peas
Frozen spinach (emergencies only)

CONDIMENTS
Relishes—Vidalia onion relish, regional chow-chow
Peperoncini—mild-hot pickled Italian peppers
Pickled Italian tomatoes

DESSERTS
Pure vanilla extract—not imitation
Dark brown sugar
Canned pumpkin
Unsweetened chocolate squares
Semi-sweet chocolate squares
Semi-sweet chocolate chips
Hot fudge sauce
Butterscotch or caramel sauce
Maraschino cherries, with stems

Having company implies a visit to the store. You might be clever enough to build a menu with ingredients you know you have around— rice, pasta, or beans; potatoes; canned stock and canned tomatoes; wine. But when the anchors of the menu are in place, the perishables will show up—the meat, fish, chicken, fruit, vegetables, cheese, and bread. There is no question that you'll be buying these fresh. But, having a good back-up pantry will streamline your shopping.

The recipes in this book are direct. They use fresh food, but often that fresh food is mixed with pantry items. For carrot soup, canned chicken stock is combined with carrots you clean and cut yourself. Canned tomatoes go into a sauce you sauté and simmer and stir. Dried herbs flavor Thick White Bean Soup With Chicken Thighs and actually stand up better than fresh herbs would, because the recipe needs long cooking.

The Back-Up Pantry items listed on pages 28 to 30 are foods to keep in your pantry especially for company. Remember that "pantry" includes your refrigerator and freezer. The list deals less with survival than with the survival of the host. These are the little indulgences you have ready to whet appetites. They make people feel comfortable if you're still busy pulling off this thing called company cooking. Many of the foods on this list simply add interest. Some of them make for happy endings.

3

GETTING STARTED

PREP

SET-UP

PREP

The preparation needed to cook for company is exactly like what you'd do to get ready to cook for yourself or your family. Whether you're cooking for one or for 20, you have to get ready. You can't cook chopped mushrooms until you've chopped them. You can't puree carrots for soup until you've chopped them and cooked them. The steps that lead to a finished dish can be boring and may even seem irrelevant. But what got soaked, chopped, drained, cut, or mashed can show up in amazing ways at the table.

Professional cooks refer to the steps that get them ready to cook simply as "prep." Here are some basic rules to help you:

PREP RULE 1:
READ THE ENTIRE RECIPE

I know I've said this before, but it's so important it bears repeating. If you don't know what you'll be doing and what's going to happen to the food, you aren't ready to cook. The recipes in this book are written to prepare you in as many ways as possible at the outset for what will happen to you and the food as you go along. You'll know before you need it what pan or bowl to use. You'll pre-chop vegetables and open cans long before they're summoned. Even so, it's part of the bargain that if you want to make a recipe you've got to become positively intimate with it before you start. The built-in cure for hasty cooks is a flop. Flop once, read evermore! Tip: If you tape all the recipes to the kitchen cabinets, they'll always be in sight and easy to read. Having them in view also helps with the next rule.

PREP RULE 2:
GET THE INGREDIENTS
READY TO USE IN THE RECIPE

When I'm making more than one recipe, I like to get all the ingredients that I'll be using onto the countertop or kitchen table. This collection starts when I return from shopping. Chicken stock, canned tomatoes, the produce, herbs, and spices are unbagged but not put away. In bursts of hyper-organization, I line up the food in the order I'll use it, or group it according to what recipe it goes in. Only food that must be refrigerated or frozen is out of sight. Fresh herbs go in a glass of water, vase-style, for easy plucking and long life out of the refrigerator. It keeps me from constantly opening and closing the refrigerator door.

That's only part of getting ingredients ready. If you see an ingredient listed in the recipe as "1 tablespoon minced parsley," get out the parsley, put it on a cutting board, take a chef's knife to it, mince it as finely as you can, and measure it in a tablespoon. Now you have the ingredient called for. You aren't ready to cook until you do.

PREP RULE 3:
ARRANGE YOUR
PREPARED INGREDIENTS
IN AN ORDERLY WAY

Many recipes in this book tell you to transfer the onions you've just chopped from the cutting board to a dinner plate. Next to the onions you might be placing minced garlic, a bowl of chopped mushrooms, or minced basil. This plate is actually a little tray you can carry to the stove. (I make a point of using a dinner plate because—sorry, this is a sweeping assumption—everybody's got one.) When the recipe calls for the onions, you can push them off the plate into the pan with a knife or spoon. If the ingredients look like they'll slide into one another, use small prep bowls—coffee cups, custard cups, soup bowls, Asian tea cups—to hold them. The only drawback to the bowls is there will be more of them to wash.

PREP RULE 4:
GET AHEAD

When making more than one recipe it's helpful to combine the chores. This is especially relevant in cooking for company. If two recipes you've selected use chopped onions, chop them all in one step. You can keep chopped onion in a zip-bag in the refrigerator as long as 3 days. Treat garlic the same. Peel the cloves and mince all of them at once. Refrigerate what you won't immediately use in a little olive oil. It will keep for a week.

TO SIT DOWN OR TO BUFFET?
You have the option of a sit-down dinner *or* buffet up to the point when you don't have enough chairs for each place setting. After that, you'll be having a buffet.

PLANNING A BUFFET

Set up the flow of your buffet the day or night before. Arrange to have the drinks and food in different spots, if you have room. This prevents the otherwise inevitable human clumping.

How will the buffet flow? If the buffet is on a table, you have several choices.

1. THE DOUBLE LINE

Anchor each of the two corners at one end of the table with a stack of dishes (or paper plates). This is START. Put duplicate plates of food along both sides of the table to force a double line. This speeds up serving and is good for groups of 12 or more. As you're planning things out, put the serving dishes where you think they ought to go as sort of a dress rehearsal, even though you'll come get them when it's time to fill them. Also set out the serving spoons and forks (or tongs). These are easy to forget when you actually do serve. At the end of the line(s) you can put napkins and the silverware. Silverware looks good flat in a basket or upright, pencil-holder-style, in a glass.

2. THE ROUND-ABOUT

Make a round-about with an obvious START marked by a stack of dishes. The napkins and silverware are at START. Put serving bowls and platters all around the table, progressing from appetizers to dessert (unless you're saving dessert for a separate appearance later). If your serving bowls double as work bowls when you cook, take them back to the kitchen and leave a Post-it note on the spot where each one will go when you serve—but take it off before anyone arrives!

3. FAMILY STYLE

For haphazard family style, choose your START and mark it with a stack of dishes. Serving dishes may be set out at random, or proceed from appetizer to entree, or go from cold to kept-hot. This is especially nice if you set out a buffet

34

on a countertop or island in the kitchen. With this arrangement, some dishes, such as chili or soup, can be ladled out straight from the pots they cooked in. Have soup bowls very close, an unspoken code for "use these bowls for soup."

SIT-DOWN BUFFET

If you want a buffet but you want to eat at the table rather than serve from it, you have other choices:

1. SIDEBOARD BUFFET

The buffet is served from a sideboard — or kitchen counter or other piece of furniture — and is carried to the available table. Set the table for exactly the number of guests, or let your guests bring silverware to the table with them and their plate of food.

2. FOOD-ALL-OVER-THE-HOUSE

This is the grazing-style buffet. The table is available for whoever gets there first. Others can have a seat in the livingroom or, yes, a bedroom where dip is out on a cleared bureau. This is a casual arrangement for television events such as Oscar night or the Super Bowl.

A SET TABLE

Set the table the day or night before. You'll wake up comforted that you've got this behind you. It makes the house seem ready, which, of course, it is. Anyone could walk in the door at any time and feel as if a meal were imminent.

First, decide on whether or not to use a tablecloth. A plain wood table with colorful fabric placemats can be very stylish. And it will save you a dry cleaning bill. Don't be misled into thinking that placemats automatically add formality. They can look quite casual, and they perform a job. Placemats made of fabric, plastic, or even polyester muffle sound, like the annoying clanging of silverware and glassware on a naked table.

Tablecloths, on the other hand, can really make the mood. The formality of a white tablecloth from a French jacquard loom is beautiful, but it's just one style. Look at what people are doing for tablecloths: A bedspread or sheet. A swatch of fabric. A kilim rug! And all in sync with a set of dishes that may mix or match. If you have two tablecloths that don't quite fit the table, use both by centering the smaller one on top of the larger one. Avoid anything that's overly large. Tablecloths that sweep the floor may look romantic in magazines, but they're truly annoying around the knees and shoes.

This is going to sound snobby, but a set table ought to have cloth napkins. You don't have to fold them like origami, and you don't need anything more fancy than what you can put in your washing machine.

What goes on the table is up to your style, the size of your table, and whether you'll all be seated or roaming during a buffet. In general, a table can be minimally set with only the place settings. (You won't distract from the minimalist feel if you add candles.) If you like, stock the table with salt, pepper, bread, and butter. Bread is best in a bread basket. You can pass one plate of butter, or put a stick at either end of the table, which also will be passed around. If you have enough little cups, you can put a small tub of butter at each place setting.

ANATOMY OF A PLACE SETTING

The historical arrangements of chorus lines of silverware, stacks of plates and bowls at a single setting, and napkins folded like origami do not suit the times. For a simple meal a bare-bones place setting is sufficient.

Silverware—The handle of each piece of silverware is even with the bottom rim of the plate. Place the fork to the left of the plate, and the knife and spoon to the right of the plate. If there are two or more forks, line them up in the order they'll be used, with the first fork the farthest left. On the other side of the plate the first-used spoon will be farthest on the right. Diners know—or they should—that the outermost utensil is the one to use next.

Plates—Plates go in the center. They can be waiting on the table.

Napkins—The traditional place for a napkin is to the left of the plate, either to the left of the forks or under them. If the place settings are close together, put the napkin under the forks to save space. If plates are on the table, you can center folded napkins on the plates. I've also seen napkins near the spoons.

Glasses—Put them above the knife tip.

Appetizer or bread-and-butter plates—Above the fork.

THE PRESENTATION

I have a friend whose husband likes to cook. But once the cooking is done, he thinks he's done thinking about it. He serves the food at the table in the old bent pots and pans it cooked in.

One of the points I emphasize often to beginners has nothing to do with cooking. It's about what your cooking looks like. Food doesn't have to be fancy to make a good presentation. The food speaks for itself—even a blob of mashed potatoes. It's what the potatoes are on or in that makes them look great. Unfortunately, the pot the potatoes got mashed in, or the sticky glass baking dish a chicken baked in, don't do much to compliment your food—or all the work you put into it.

Especially for company, and even more importantly for buffets, after the food has cooked in your reliable, yet boring or ugly piece of cookware, get it out of there. I'm talking mostly about clear glass baking dishes, metal baking pans, nonstick saucepans or skillets (except for omelets), woks, and plastic mixing bowls. If you have cooked an item in something interesting that also happens to be ovenproof, by all means bring it to the table. You've beaten the system because you got a good presentation without an extra platter to wash. Keep this in mind when you shop for cookware. Colorful pottery and enamel-covered iron baking dishes abound.

Cookware and bakeware can be round or elliptical, oval or square. They're white or clay, patterned or plain.

BE ARTFUL

Serve on pieces that uplift your food. It will show that you care about it, and your company will be awed. (Exceptions are little informalities that provide charm and reality, like ladling chili or mulled wine from the pot keeping them warm on the stove.)

Presentation platters do not have to be expensive. I have found everything from Fiesta ware to Franciscan ware, old Chinese platters, Mexican cazuelas, even odds and ends from Wedgwood and Limoges china at garage sales and thrift stores. Antique stores are full of eclectic bowls, platters, covered casseroles, and dishes made of colored glass. A gourmet store will have the latest in Mediterranean platters; shallow, wide pasta bowls; and maple salad bowls.

Not all of it has to match. Fit serving pieces to the food or mood. If you like Italian pottery, mix up the colors, patterns, and shapes within the species. One way to go about this is to decide on something that's personal. I have a friend who has spent years filling out a set of green Fire King depression glass. For obvious reasons, I collect "corn" things. I may not serve on all of them at the same time—unless we're having a summer corn dinner—but a platter, bowl, or salt-and-pepper pair usually shows up somewhere in a meal.

If you don't have much on hand, the following will improve your presentations immediately, particularly on a buffet:

Two big ovals
Two big rounds
Two medium mixing bowls
Crockery
Porcelain souffle dishes
Colorful small bowls
An offbeat salad bowl, or a really nice expensive
    wooden one

WHAT ABOUT DRINKS?

For more ideas on group beverages beyond wine and beer, see Drinks By the Pitcher, page 296.

The drinks at a get-together can get out of hand. I don't mean that people drink too much. I mean that as hosts we try too hard to please. Try not to feel guilty if you don't have just the right thirst-quencher for everyone. Even at cocktail parties at restaurants, the staff pours one, maybe two, wines. For the non-drinkers, there are mineral waters or soft drinks. If the wine is good and one or two other choices are accessible, you are on strong ground.

At home, too many beverages can create storage problems in your refrigerator, which is far more important for food that needs to stay cold. This is particularly true of multiple packs of soft drinks and beer. I've also found that if people don't feel comfortable helping themselves, you will be the one counted on to continually observe the levels in their glasses, with the expectation that you will also be around to refill when necessary. You are not a sommelier or a bartender, although one of your friends might enjoy the assignment. As host, pouring drinks is only one thing you'll be handling.

WINE AND BEER

For dinner, decide on one or two wines. Have another idea for the drink that will welcome everyone. For instance, you might pour champagne as your guests arrive, then switch to the wines when the meal is served. The wines could be two reds with similar features, such as Merlot from two disparate wineries. You might offer one red wine and one white wine. If you have no idea what to do about wine, there's no one better than a talkative wine retailer (as a rule, this is a redundancy) to help you figure food-and-wine pairings. They love to be asked. They'll also be informed about the explosion of American regional beers.

When everyone first shows up, have the Welcome Wine (Champagne is wine) or cocktail mixings out on a table, with all the glasses you'll need, plus extras. For cocktails, you or a friend can be bartender. For wine, flank the wine bottles with the glasses, and lay out two corkscrews. If it's something that ought to be very cold—Champagne or a white wine such as Riesling—tuck the bottle in a chill bucket filled with ice. (Ice buckets or pails are shaped to keep the ice high on the wine bottle. If you don't have one, use a big bowl or pot.) If you like, be the one to pour a generous first round. Then invite all to keep pouring whatever they want, whenever they want.

The white wine to be served for dinner, if it needs to be cold, can remain in the refrigerator until you're ready to serve it. Don't worry that a white wine didn't get ice cold. Lightly chilled white wine tastes best. Most reds are fine at room temperature. If a red wine is old, open it well ahead of serving so it can "breathe."

Beer, on the other hand, has its priorities. This isn't England, and we like our beer cold. If your group is small enough, leave the beer in the refrigerator. If your group is larger than six, set the beer in a big ice chest, pail, plastic tub, or bucket. Cover with a sack of ice from the grocery store. Put two bottle openers in plain view. Walk away and forget it. This part of the entertainment will take care of itself. For a sit-down dinner, bring the beer to the table along with glasses iced in the freezer.

COFFEE

With today's coffeemakers able to perform their functions with the flick of a switch, it isn't difficult to make exceptional coffee. You can pre-fill the coffeemaker with water and coffee before company arrives. When you and your guests are ready for hot coffee, all that's left is to find that switch. The all-important coffee will be off your mind for the rest of the meal.

Prepare the coffee around 5 or 6 PM if you expect to drink it by 9 PM. For a regular Mr. Coffee-type coffeemaker, fill the chamber with water. Grind the beans fine (or have them ground on the finest setting at the store) and put them in a coffee filter. Assemble all the parts and leave the pot on "Off." As dinner nears its end, make a quick stop in the kitchen, switch the coffeemaker to On and plan on drinking it in 5 to 10 minutes.

If your coffee pot can be programmed to turn on at any hour of the day or night, all you'll have to do is fill it with water and ground coffee beans, and set the timer for the approximate hour you'll pour the coffee.

The only disadvantage to this is that the water won't be sparkling-fresh. Fresh, cold water is the secret to pure-tasting coffee. A few hours won't make too much of a difference. Splurge on your guests and use spring water in your coffeemaker.

As part of pre-dinner Set-Up, have coffee cups or mugs, saucers (if you'll be using them), and sugar (and artificial sweeteners) near your serving area. Get out the creamer but don't fill it until closer to coffee time. For higher style, set out small bowls of brown sugar cubes, white sugar cubes, loose light brown sugar, cinnamon, nutmeg, and cocoa.

You really should offer both regular and decaffeinated coffee. If you have only one coffeemaker, make one of the batches ahead and store it in a thermal carafe. (You can make both ahead, if you wish.) This is also a good idea if you don't have an automatic coffee maker and you don't want to have to brew coffee during your dinner. A thermal carafe will keep coffee hot without keeping it over heat, so your coffee won't taste scorched. You can buy decorative carafes for about $15 to $18. Buy one color for regular coffee, another for decaf. Some guests may want to mix the two in their cup.

The Beans To Buy

Arabica beans are the finest grade. They make coffee that is smooth, rich, and aromatic, regardless of how they're roasted. If there are no specialty coffee stores near you, check at a cafe in your area for beans which can be ground for you.

The Beans Not To Buy

Robusta beans are cheap and the mainstay of major brands that typically sell coffee in cans. Coffee from these beans is bitter and acidic.

HOW TO BREW COFFEE
Except for espresso, the general rule of thumb is:

- 2 level tablespoons ground coffee per cup of water in the coffeepot.
- 1 to 1½ level tablespoons per cup for gourmet coffee ground particularly fine.
- For 8 cups of coffee, use about ½ cup finely ground coffee. If the coffee is too strong, add a little hot water. Next time, reduce the amount of coffee.
- If you are grinding the coffee beans at home, ½ cup beans yields ½ cup finely ground coffee.

People like coffee stronger after dinner than they do the rest of the day. Strong coffee comes from beans ground exceptionally fine. If you use very fresh, high-quality French Roast, and grind it fine, 2 tablespoons per cup may be too much. Experiment with your coffeemaker and the fineness of the grind to get a good strong brew for your guests. Remember that you can't correct weak coffee, but coffee made too strong can be diluted by adding hot water to the pot.

TEA

Not everyone is a coffee drinker. Tea drinking in America is gaining imbibers. As host, be prepared for a couple of tea drinkers in every crowd. All you need is tea, hot water, and a tea pot.

Boil the water in a tea kettle. From there, there are two ways to go:

1. Put a tea bag in a cup or mug. Pour boiling water into the cup. Keep the tea bag in the cup about 3 minutes. Take it out and let your guest add sugar or milk, or drink it straight.

2. Fill your teapot with very hot tap water to warm it. Dump out the hot water and while the pot is still warm put in

> 4 rounded teaspoons of loose tea
> *or* 4 rounded teaspoons of tea leaves inside a tea ball
> *or* 2 tea bags.

Pour in 4 cups of boiling water from the tea kettle, cover the pot, and let it steep 3 minutes (longer for stronger tea, but not much longer or your tea will be bitter). The loose leaves will sink and you will be able to pour clear tea from the spout into tea cups.

Some leaves may accidentally be poured into a cup. Die-hard tea drinkers don't mind. On the other hand, some of the trappings of tea service include individual strainers made of silver or stainless steel, to filter out the loose leaves. Buy some if you want.

As with the mandate for strong coffee after a meal, strong tea is also in order. Black teas are strongest: Earl Grey, English Breakfast, Irish Breakfast, Darjeeling.

Tea drinkers may take their tea black or enhanced. Be prepared with sugar and milk (but not cream — it's too rich) in the English tradition, or with lemon wedges and honey.

PITCHER OF ICED TEA

BEST EQUIPMENT—Clear glass pitcher or other beverage container

Ask for tea in New York and you'll get a pot of hot brewed tea and a tea cup. Ask for tea in Texas and you'll get a pail-size glass of iced tea with free refills.

The iced tea rage in America is underscored by a thirst so great that in some locales tea is swilled like water or cola. It doesn't matter if it's good or bad, strong or weak. When you serve iced tea, be sure it sparkles and shines and is truly refreshing. Otherwise it's just cold tannin.

Iced tea can be made from hot, brewed tea that cools off and is poured over ice. Or it can be made from the start with cold water. I love this cold-water iced tea because it's always sparkling clear—and you don't even have to boil water.

Serves 8

    4 tea bags
    8 cups spring water
    Extras: Lemon wedges, sugar

DO THIS FIRST:

1. Drop the tea bags into a 1-quart pitcher or other container such as a big jar or juice container.

2. Pour the water over the tea bags. Cover the pitcher and refrigerate it 12 hours or overnight.

WRAPPING IT UP:

1. Remove the tea bags.

2. Serve the tea poured over crushed ice or ice cubes. Have handy lemon wedges and sugar.

4

TECHNIQUES PLAIN AND SIMPLE

ROASTING/BAKING

SAUTEING

BROILING

BOILING

GRAVY AND SAUCE

CARVING

If you haven't done much partying at your place, you'll need to figure out how to start. Get-togethers can be easy once you know the bare-bones basics of cooking, including a skeletal food vocabulary. This knowledge will get you through the recipes so you can get on with the fun.

Recipes are written in their own cook-speak. It's a style of communication that may have tripped you up in the past. Reduce, dredge, whisk, blend, marinate—it's all jargon and it's all harmless. Once you become acquainted with how food is cooked, you'll find the jargon helps rather than confuses.

Just remember this: Heat applied to food cooks it. Too much heat overcooks it. Too little heat doesn't get the job done.

Heat defines the way food becomes cooked. You can make food hot in a pan on top of the stove. That's sautéing. You can put food in a hot oven. That's baking or roasting. You can drop the food into a big pot of boiling water (boiling), or slap it on a grill (outdoor broiling). Heat can come from the top, the bottom, or all around. Heat is dry or wet. Heat is fast or slow. Heat goes from warm to fiery-hot.

All the ways you can produce heat and get it to the food are called techniques. One of the most important benefits of understanding various techniques is that you'll become familiar with their timing. Sautéed chicken breasts—hmm, that's about 12 minutes. Ah yes, but baking the same chicken breasts takes 35 to 45 minutes. What does this tell you? It tells you two things. One, different kinds of heat cook food at differ-ent speeds. And two, while something bakes something else can be sautéed. Every time you cook you'll subconsciously wind up your mental clock. This inner timer will develop accuracy and instincts with every recipe you make.

THE MUG SHOT MENTALITY

One technique can cook many foods. Understand-ing this will keep you from making the same five recipes for the rest of your life. I call it the Mug Shot Mentality.

Imagine the camera that takes pictures for your driver's license. The camera doesn't move to do its job. It just clicks as people cycle past.

Now imagine the cam-era is your broiler. Turn it on. Slide a piece of fish through. Click. Do the same thing with a T-bone steak—click—chicken, a lamb chop. The broiler does all the work. It couldn't care less what it's cooking.

The sauté pan oper-ates the same way. Heat butter or oil in a skillet and in no time you could be eating fish, zucchini, pork chops, bananas. The sauté pan just sits there getting hot. You put food in it. The food cooks. Once you under-stand the basic cooking techniques, you'll be able to cook just about anything.

ROASTING

The distinction between roasting and baking may seem confusing. Cookies and cakes "bake" at the same temperatures at which meats successfully "roast." Both baking and roasting happen in the oven with the door shut. Both are easy. Don't worry about the lingo. Whether you call it roasting or baking, your food is serviced by the oven while you tend to the rest of your life. Except for periodic viewing and checking, that's it. The challenge is determining how well things are going each time you take a look.

Roasting and baking are the results of dry heat that surrounds the food. The heat cooks meat from the outside in. Boneless meat is dense throughout and more difficult for heat to penetrate, so it takes a little longer to cook than the same cut with a bone. Meat with a bone cooks faster because after the bone gets hot it acts as a heat source inside the meat.

Vegetables can also be roasted/baked. Look at the popularity of roasted garlic. Okay, it's baked garlic, just the same. The garlic is heated evenly over a rather long period of time until its sugars are drawn out and caramelized, and the pulp turns to paste. Rather than intensifying the flavor, roasting mellows and sweetens it. It's the same for just about any vegetable that is roasted or baked, if the cooking time is long enough to go past a cooked state and into a cooked-caramelized state.

Tips for Roasting/Baking

- Don't roast big meats that you hope to enhance with sauce or gravy in roasting pans that are either glass or grooved on the bottom. Choose materials that can not only take the heat in the oven, but can take even higher heat if placed directly over a burner, which is what happens when you make sauce. Look for stainless steel, enamel-covered cast iron, or anodized aluminum.

- **Preheat the oven.** This is so important. It's not unusual for an oven to take 30 minutes to reach 350°F. Meats that enter the oven chamber before it's truly hot will stew and sweat.

- If you don't want to baste, it's okay.

BAKING/ROASTING LINGO

BAKE—to cook food in dry heat in an oven with the door shut.

BASTE—to spoon juices drawn out during the baking of a roast or dessert all over the food to keep it moist and prevent shrinkage.

DOT—to set small pieces of butter all over the food you're baking.

DRIPPINGS—fat that drips out of the meat onto the bottom of the roasting pan and which can be used to flavor the meat's gravy.

PREHEAT—heat the oven before you use it, so the temperature is as high as it's supposed to be when you start to cook.

RACK—a grate that suspends meats or vegetables above the bottom of the baking dish so they don't stew in their juices and air can circulate under them.

REDUCE HEAT—turn down the heat after the food has cooked a while. This is common if roasting starts out at extremely high heat.

ROAST—same as bake (see above).

TEMPERATURE—the right temperature is important so heat can do its work. Consider having your oven calibrated. In case you ever wondered, a moderate oven is 350°F.

TURN—some foods are turned over halfway through baking.

47

REAL BAKED PUMPKIN

BEST COOKWARE — Cookie sheet
HANDIEST TOOL — A big chef's knife

• Pumpkins over 5 pounds are too unwieldy for kitchen use. Besides, smaller pumpkins are sweeter. Look for the ones called sugar pumpkins.

• Your biggest knife is required for a blade long enough to go through the pumpkin's full diameter.

• If you don't have a cookie sheet, use a piece of heavy-duty aluminum foil or the rack from your broiler pan.

• A form of caramelization is taking place during the baking of winter squash. The pumpkin's sugars are drawn out under heat and become concentrated, which intensifies the flavor of the pumpkin.

• Pumpkin pieces may also be boiled, steamed, or microwaved, but they won't have the secondary flavors from the caramelization of the sugars.

• If you use the baked pumpkin pulp for pumpkin pie, you'll probably have some left over. Here is a side dish you can make with about 2 cups of pulp: While the pulp is still hot, put it in a bowl and add 2 tablespoons butter, 2 tablespoons brown sugar, and ¼ teaspoon salt. Mix and mash with a fork until it looks like it's been pureed. You've got yourself a highly nutritious side dish that serves 6.

Pumpkin is a winter squash not much different from the other winter squashes—butternut, acorn, Hubbard, and turban. You can cook pumpkin by boiling or steaming, but roasting enhances its significant inherent sweetness. You can serve baked pumpkin as a side dish, and when you finish this recipe you will have prepared fresh pumpkin for an appearance in Bumpkin Pie, page 254.

Makes 2 to 3 cups puree

  1 small pumpkin (3 to 5 pounds)

DO THIS FIRST:

1. Preheat the oven to 350°F with an oven rack on the bottom. Get out a cookie sheet or large piece of heavy-duty aluminum foil.

DO THIS SECOND:

1. With your biggest chef's knife, halve the pumpkin from the stem end and down. Push hard on the knife, using both hands. Open up the pumpkin. Ignore the seeds for the time being.

2. Lay the pumpkin halves flat side down on the cookie sheet or foil.

3. Bake 1 hour. A knife point should be able to easily pierce the outer skin, which may be wrinkled at the end of the cooking.

WRAPPING IT UP:

1. Cool the pumpkin on the cookie sheet.

2. When it's touchable (about 30 minutes), scrape out the seeds and strings with a big metal soup spoon.

3. Scrape the pulp directly into a bowl and throw the skin away. The pumpkin pulp is ready to become the star ingredient in pumpkin pie.

ROASTED GARLIC

BEST EQUIPMENT—Heavy aluminum foil

Trendy, yes, but easy, delicious, and versatile. You don't even need to wash a dish. Just wrap the garlic in foil and bake it directly on the rack in your oven. You'll get a spreadable paste with a mellowed garlic taste.

Makes ¼ cup to ⅓ cup garlic paste

1 entire head of garlic

DO THIS FIRST:

1. Preheat the oven to 400°F.

2. Slice the hairy root end off the head of garlic, taking about ¼ inch off the head, to expose the cloves.

3. Wrap the garlic in foil. Put the packet directly on the oven rack. Bake 1 hour.

WRAPPING IT UP:

1. Squeeze the roasted cloves out of their skins and throw the skins away.

LET'S TALK

• To roast many heads at a time, wrap them all in the foil and set the package on a cookie sheet or pie plate.

• If you like, roast the garlic without wrapping it. The flat top where you sliced off the root will brown deeply but with no ill effects to the paste inside. This garlic will caramelize. Wrapped garlic steams.

• Simplicity begs for more. Rub olive oil all over the cut surface, then the entire head, before wrapping. You'll definitely be able to taste the olive oil after the garlic is roasted.

• Use roasted garlic plain as a no-fat spread on crackers or toast, or inside omelets, in mashed potatoes, or when you're too lazy to chop garlic. As a spread it's great topped with blue cheese, tomatoes, or olives.

SAUTÉING

Sautéing is my favorite way to cook. It's quick. The food comes out juicy, as seared as you dare. And you often find that butter (or olive oil) and garlic get involved, which is always good.

The word *sauté* is French. It means to jump. Professional chefs move food around a sauté pan, which is a skillet, without the aid of a spoon because they're strong and practiced enough to hold the pan's handle with one hand, and with a flick of the wrist send the food into the air. In mid-jump the food arcs over the pan and comes down to perfectly redistribute itself. It's quite all right to just stir, which is the home version of all this jumping around.

Think of sautéing as uptown frying. Because it's so quick, you'll sauté often. The speed of the sauté means that sautéed recipes in your menu will probably be cooked last. A more leisurely sauté might happen on the way to completing a baked or broiled recipe, such as cooking the filling you'll then stuff into mushrooms.

For most sautéing, the heat is high. When food sautés, you should be able to hear it cook. Non-stick skillets are fine for sautéing as long as they aren't flimsy, but don't expect deep browning.

Not all sautéing is a flash in the pan. Continued low heat over a long period of time is a subset of sautéing. It's called sweating. Sweated vegetables literally release juices into the pan. But if you keep going, the heat dries those juices up to leave you with vegetables that brown deeply and cook enough to intensify the sugars—think raisins—so they're sweeter after cooking than before.

SUGARED NUTS

BEST EQUIPMENT—Heavy skillet, parchment paper (or waxed paper)
BEST TOOL—Wooden spatula

This is in the betcha-can't-eat-just-one category.

Makes 1 cup

> ½ teaspoon salt
> 2 tablespoons sugar
> 2 tablespoons vegetable oil
> 1 cup nice-looking walnut halves

DO THIS FIRST:

1. Line a cookie sheet with waxed paper and have it convenient to the stove.

2. Measure the salt and sugar into tiny cups and place them near the stove.

DO THIS SECOND:

1. Put the oil into a medium-size skillet (it doesn't have to be non-stick). Turn the heat to high.

2. When the oil is hot, add the nuts. Be quick and stir and stir until the nuts smell toasty. It should happen in less than 1 minute; just smell and keep your wits about you.

DO THIS THIRD:

1. With the heat still high, add the salt and stir quickly without stopping.

2. As you stir, reach for the sugar, add it, and keep stirring constantly and fast until the sugar dissolves and the nuts are shiny.

WRAPPING IT UP:

1. Pour the nuts onto the prepared cookie sheet. Let them cool, then break them apart.

2. Line a tin with waxed paper and store the nuts, covered with an airtight lid.

• Parchment paper will provide the most excellent surface for the nuts to fall on, even better than waxed paper. Nothing will stick.

• If you don't have a cookie sheet, place a double thickness of waxed paper (or parchment paper) directly on your countertop.

• The toastiness picked up by your nose depends entirely on the freshness of the nuts. You're in for some disappointment if it takes the full minute for toastiness to come through—a sign the nuts are over the hill with almost no nose volume. If they're really old, you might detect a rancid odor. I can only tell you to regard that batch as good practice, then go out and buy some fresh nuts from a reputable store.

• The quick stirring is important to keep the nuts from sticking and to get them evenly coated.

• You can substitute whole almonds or pecan halves for the walnuts.

CARAMELIZED ONIONS

SAUTE LINGO

BROWN—to sauté in a little butter or oil on both sides until the food is cooked so much it turns brown. Browning may be a preparatory step. It may be the color of the completed dish, or it may be an unfortunate stage of overcooking.

DEGLAZE—a single word that means to loosen the cooked-on drippings in a sauté pan (or roasting pan, see Making Gravy and Sauce, page 67) by adding a liquid and boiling.

PAN-FRY—to cook in a small amount of butter or oil.

REDUCE—to boil down a liquid to drive off water. Reducing condenses the liquid and helps a sauce develop body and thickness.

REDUCE THE HEAT—turn down the heat.

SAUTE—same as pan-fry; to cook in a small amount of butter or oil.

SAUTE PAN—a skillet.

SKILLET—a sauté pan.

SWEAT—cook a long time in a skillet over low heat to pull out juices from vegetables.

BEST COOKWARE—10½-inch cast iron skillet
BEST EQUIPMENT—Chef's knife and cutting board, wooden spoon

Persistent low heat applied over a long period of time will caramelize a vegetable's natural sugars. Onions may seem to be mostly fumes, but the longer they cook the sweeter they become, and the less they sting. Finally, caramelization coats the pieces. Provided you don't rush this and burn them, the onions will also dehydrate somewhat, which will further concentrate their flavor.

Makes 2 cups

> 3 large yellow onions
> 2 tablespoons vegetable oil

DO THIS FIRST:

1. Peel the onions. Cut each in half through the poles. Now slice the halves into half-rings, and leave them on the cutting board.

2. Take the cutting board over to the stove.

DO THIS SECOND:

1. Put the oil in a big skillet (cast iron is best) on the stove. Turn the heat to high.

2. When the oil is very hot, push the onions off the board into the skillet.

3. Wait for them to sizzle. When you can hear them cooking, turn the heat down to medium-low.

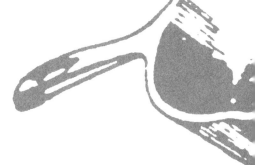

WRAPPING IT UP:

1. Sauté the onions until they're nearly burned, a good 45 minutes. Stir only once in a while at first. As the onions dry up, you'll have to stir more often.

2. In about 15 minutes, you'll notice more moisture in the pan than when you started. The heat is pulling it out of the onions. In 15 more minutes, or thereabouts, the moisture will begin to disappear because the constant heat will evaporate it. *(While the onions cook, clean up the onion skins.)* If you'll be using these onions in California Onion Dip Without Using a Mix (page 107), now's the time to make the main part of the dip.

3. Serve your caramelized onions as a side dish or chop them for the dip recipe.

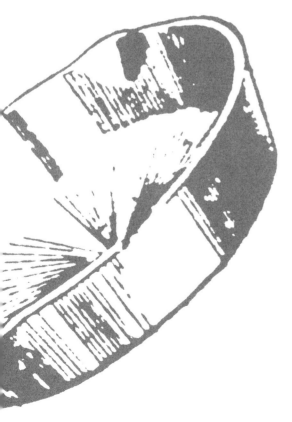

Broiling is upside down grilling. Instead of direct heat coming from underneath food, as it does in your outdoor grill, broiler heat penetrates food from above. You can regulate the intensity of the broiler's effects by adjusting the distance between the food and the broiler element.

Compared to home broilers, an outdoor fire has more choices. You can vary the heat in your grill by varying the amount of charcoal and the way it's arranged. The broiler in your oven has one speed—hot. You turn a knob on your stove to the broiler setting, and that's the intensity you work with. Even so, broiling is easy and quick. It's healthful, too, because fats can drip through a broiler rack. If you line the pan under the rack with foil, there isn't much clean-up.

Broiling is a common technique for entertaining because it's used often to put the finishing touch on hot appetizers. Little bites of food you made ahead, and which lie waiting in the refrigerator, need only a couple of minutes under a pre-heated broiler. Out comes food browned, bubbling, and often crunchy, the broiler's specialty. You won't come close to this perfection with a microwave.

Because of the speed of broiling, entrees you intend to broil should be scheduled near the end of your cooking. Lamb chops, for instance, take about 6 minutes per side. An inch-thick piece of fish takes about 10 minutes, total. Keep these times in mind if you want broiling to be the last thing you do before serving.

WHAT KIND OF BROILER DO YOU HAVE?

In gas stoves the broiler is usually in a lower drawer with a flame in the broiler's ceiling. Leave the drawer closed when broiling with gas. If you have an electric stove, the broiler is the upper heating coil in the oven. When broiling in an electric oven, leave the door ajar. An electric oven's thermostat will turn itself off after it reaches 450°F, in compliance with safety codes.

A FEW TIPS ON BROILING

- Always preheat the broiler.
- If you have time, bring meats to room temperature. They'll cook more evenly from the outside in. Very hot temperatures shock very cold meat and can burn the outside before the heat penetrates the cold, raw interior.
- Get accustomed to the intensity of your broiler so you know how far away from the heat to cook. Generally, the thicker the meat, the farther away from the heat it should be. (But if it's too far, it will take too long to cook and will dry out before it's done.) Thinner pieces of meat and some vegetables can get a little closer.

THE BROILER AS TOASTER

For toasting slices of bread under the broiler all you need is the bread and a swatch of heavy duty foil. Bread broils fast, so keep an eye on it.

BROILING LINGO

BASTE—to spoon or brush juices all over food to keep it moist and prevent drying and shrinkage as it broils.

BROILER ELEMENT/ HEAT SOURCE—in most gas ovens it's the first above the broiler drawer; in an electric range the broiler coil is in the ceiling of the oven.

BROILER PAN—the one that came with your oven and has a broiler rack on top.

BROILER RACK—the one that rests on top of the broiler pan; can also be a cake-cooling rack set on top of a piece of foil.

BROWN—a desirable color for broiled meats, fish, cheese, bread, and vegetables.

CARAMELIZE—what sugars do under intense heat, even sugars in fruits and vegetables and those bound up in meat.

DOT—to place little pieces of butter all over food.

PREHEAT—to warm up the broiler, as you would a grill. Ten to 15 minutes is about right.

TOASTED BREAD ROUNDS WITH TOPPING

• You may have heard these called crostini or bruschette in Italian restaurants. Technically, bruschette are thicker than crostini. We'll just call them toasted bread rounds and not worry how thick they are.

• Depending on the shape of your bread, you might end up calling these toasted bread squares.

• From a 1½-foot-long baguette, which is easy to slice thinly, expect around 50 slices about ¼ inch thick.

• From a 1½-foot-long loaf of bread, such as French sourdough, you'll get between 36 and 48 slices about ⅓ inch thick.

• If your slices from the middle of the loaf are more than 4½ inches wide, cut them in half.

• Rye bread, whole wheat, multi-grain, or herb bread also make delicious toast rounds.

• The timing in this recipe is approximate. It can go up or down depending on how thin or thick your bread is, and how close you've got it to the broiler.

BEST EQUIPMENT — Broiler rack
BEST TOOLS — Cutting board and chef's knife

When company comes, there's nothing like making one thing in less than 2 minutes that immediately feeds 30. These aren't supposed to be Melba-toast crisp, but a little bready in the center. If you think crackers have gotten expensive, being able to make about 50 broiled slices that act like crackers for the cost of a loaf of bread ought to convince you to make your own more often.

Serves up to 30

> 1 loaf French bread
> Melted butter or olive oil
> Grated Parmesan cheese
>
> *Optional toppings:*
> Plain roasted garlic cloves spread thinly (page 49)
> Ricotta Cracker Spread (page 112)
> Tzadziki (page 108)
> ½ cup roasted garlic mixed with 2 tablespoons crumbled gorgonzola

DO THIS FIRST:

1. Preheat the broiler, but take the broiler pan and rack out.

2. Slice the loaf of bread into as many rounds as you'll need. Lay the slices on the broiler rack. (You may have to do this in batches.)

DO THIS SECOND:

1. Broil the slices about 2 inches from the broiler element until the tops are golden, about 45 seconds.

2. Take the pan out of the broiler. Turn the pieces of bread over. Dab them with butter or olive oil, and sprinkle with cheese. Return the pan to the broiler for 30 seconds more, until the cheese is bubbly.

WRAPPING IT UP:

1. Take the toasts off the pan with tongs. If they look oily, drain them on paper towels.

2. Serve the toasts with any of the optional toppings.

STUFFED MUSHROOMS

• Slightly older mushrooms whose caps have detached from the stems and opened a little to reveal the gills are actually easier to stuff than very fresh mushrooms.

• The mushrooms go on the cookie sheet tops down. Yes, they will slide a bit.

• You can buy bread crumbs in the store in boxes or bagged in deli departments. Seasoned bread crumbs work fine in this recipe.

• If you have a food processor, you can make bread crumbs at home. Rip up bread and run the pieces in a food processor until they're fine crumbs. Two slices of bread equal about 1 cup of crumbs.

• Whole wheat, sourdough, rye bread (no crust, it's too tough) or buttermilk bread all will develop into great stuffing.

• As you fry the crumbs, they'll absorb the butter. That's the idea and you're doing it right.

• The mozzarella won't have a chance to melt completely while it's in the skillet. It will finish melting as you stir it in.

BEST COOKWARE—Cookie sheet
BEST EQUIPMENT—Mixing bowl, box grater
BEST UTENSIL—Spoon

My friend Hilary Abramson is the one by whom I judge the beginner-ness of recipes. These stuffed mushrooms are so easy that Hilary was making them before she became a self-confessed beginner. Her primary motivation for even attempting such a recipe was no different than yours soon will be. She couldn't wait to eat them.

Makes about 30

> 30 mushrooms
> 1 cup bread crumbs
> 1 teaspoon minced garlic, or scoop it from a jar
> 2 tablespoons chopped parsley
> 2 eggs
> 1 teaspoon salt
> Generous black pepper
> ¾ cup shredded mozzarella
> ½ cup sour cream
> 3 tablespoons butter
> ¼ cup grated Parmesan cheese

DO THIS FIRST:

1. Wash the mushrooms. Snap off the stems. Arrange the mushrooms on a cookie sheet, stem side up. Put the stems on a cutting board.

2. Put the bread crumbs in a big mixing bowl.

3. Chop the stems and add them to the bowl.

4. Mince the garlic and add it to the bowl.

5. Chop the parsley and add it.

DO THIS SECOND:

1. Crack the eggs into a small bowl. Beat them with the salt and pepper, and pour them into the big bowl.

2. Stir with a fork until the eggs disappear into the crumb mixture. You only need to stir 4 or 5 revolutions.

3. Shred the mozzarella. Measure the sour cream. Have both convenient to the stove.

DO THIS THIRD:

1. Put the butter in a medium-size skillet set over medium-high heat. When the butter is foamy, add the bread-crumb mixture, but keep the mixing bowl handy.

2. Sauté and stir all around the pan for about 3 minutes. Keep the heat at medium-high. The crumbs will become more and more separated.

3. Take the skillet off the heat. Stir in the mozzarella and sour cream.

4. Keep mixing until the sour cream is blended in, but the mozzarella is only partially melted. Put the stuffing back in the mixing bowl.

WRAPPING IT UP:

1. Preheat the broiler with the rack 3 to 4 inches from the broiling element.

2. Stuff the mushrooms using a little spoon. Pack the stuffing in, and mound it high. Sprinkle the tops with Parmesan cheese.

3. Broil 5 minutes. The mushrooms will brown nicely. Serve hot or warm.

MAKE-AHEAD OPTION:

1. Wrap the stuffed mushrooms in plastic and refrigerate overnight.

2. Remove them from the refrigerator 1 hour before broiling.

- You can use an equal amount of ricotta cheese in place of sour cream.

- For kick, mince ¼ teaspoon fresh jalapeño, or add ⅛ teaspoon cayenne pepper.

- The stuffing is put back in its mixing bowl to help it cool faster.

- It's a good idea to have a couple of extra mushrooms handy in case you have leftover stuffing. This isn't an exact science, you know. The size of the stems, how much they shrink during sautéing, and the thirst of the bread crumbs all affect how much stuffing you get.

- Unless your mushrooms are small—about one bite big—have plates and forks ready for serving these. I've served them not just on a buffet but right at the table as an appetizer for the seated.

BOILING

Jokes about not knowing how to boil water stop at the end of this sentence. Water in a pot on the stove with the burner on its highest setting will boil. If you're at sea level, this occurs when the water reaches 212°F. (Boiling happens at slightly lower temperatures at higher altitudes.) If you cover the pot, boiling will happen faster. If you let the water boil without a cover, pretty soon it will boil away. Of course you'd ruin the pot, but you'd learn the lesson of how boiling drives off liquid.

Boiling is a stage of cooking, as in "bring to a boil." Boiling has subsets that continue to cook food but without the violence of what cookbooks call a "rolling" boil. Beneath boiling are simmering over low heat so bubbles barely break the surface, and poaching, which is cooler than a simmer.

Soups and many sauces have to be boiled at one stage or another. If the cover is on, the flavors are situating themselves. If the cover is off, boiling drives off the water to leave behind a soup or sauce with more developed flavor. Think of it as a way to concentrate both flavor and consistency. You may not even notice how much the liquid level drops while making soup, but it does, even if it's just a quarter-cup of water that went off into the atmosphere.

When food sits in a vat of boiling liquid, it's the liquid, not the food, doing the boiling. In pasta-making, the water boils around the pasta. Boil pasta in lots of water. It needs room to swim. A Dutch oven filled two-thirds with water is about right. When a pound of pasta goes into a pot with not enough hard-boiling water, it cools the water and makes it lose its boil. The water has to struggle to get its boil back. Waiting for this seems like an eternity. It's really just a minute or two, but for pasta it *is* an eternity. The pasta gets sticky, because it is sitting in a pot full of starch.

A FEW TIPS ON BOILING:

• Boiling often means draining. Keep your colander near the sink, not more than an arm's reach away, not in a cabinet.

• For big vats of water, such as for pasta, bring the water to its boil on high heat.

• Cover the pot of pasta water as it heats up. You'll get to the boil faster, and with a smaller energy bill.

BOILING LINGO

BRING TO A BOIL—to set liquid, or food in a liquid, over medium or high heat and wait for big bubbles to rumble to the surface.

COVER—liquid comes to a boil more quickly if covered; vegetables keep their color if boiled covered during a short cooking time.

DRAIN—to get rid of the water the food cooked in, usually by pouring it through a colander.

MEDIUM BOIL—medium bubbles break the surface and can be maintained on medium heat.

POACH—to cook food in liquid just below a simmer.

REDUCE—to boil a liquid hard enough to drive off water, which decreases its volume.

ROLLING BOIL—big bubbles break the surface over high heat.

SIMMER—to boil on heat low enough so bubbles barely break the surface of the liquid.

SKIM—to take scum off the top of stock with a big spoon.

CHOCOLATE TRUFFLES

- The essential part of a chocolate truffle—the inside—is technically ganache. Ganache was probably an accident of boiling milk or cream (or at least very hot milk or cream) that spilled on stray chocolate. Voila! the mixture cooled, got thick and smooth, and tasted as privileged as the real black fungus from the French region of Perigord.

- Truffles are made to resemble the natural shape and appearance of the French black truffle. They're rolled in cocoa to simulate the dirt that clings to a freshly dug truffle.

- If you're thinking about sneaking the chocolate into your food processor to chop it, don't. The food processor is chaotic and chops chocolate unevenly while at the same time the blade lodges in a piece and whips it around the work bowl. Chopping chocolate is not very pleasant, but the rewards are truly great. Remember, the smaller you chop it, the more evenly it will melt and the smoother your truffles will be.

- By using semisweet chocolate, you skip the use of sugar as an ingredient.

BEST COOKWARE—Small pot
BEST EQUIPMENT—Large stainless steel mixing bowl, chef's knife and cutting board
HANDIEST TOOL—Rubber spatula

I thought you'd enjoy this example of boiling because instead of the expected—soup, rice, pasta—you'll get truffles. Real truffles.

Bringing chocolate to a boil would be like taking it to hell and back. Yet you can manage its melting with boiling cream. The hot cream meets the cool chocolate, and the cool chocolate meets the hot cream, and you end up with a mixture at a temperature somewhere in the middle—a little warmer than body temperature, which is very nice for chocolate.

Makes 2 dozen

> 8 ounces (½ pound) semisweet chocolate
> 1¼ cups heavy cream
> ¼ cup unsweetened cocoa powder

DO THIS FIRST:

1. Get out a big mixing bowl.

2. Chop the chocolate on a big cutting board with a big chef's knife, using the two-hand hold (see page 10). Try to get all the pieces very small and about the same size. This will take at least 5 minutes, maybe 10.

3. Push the chocolate off the cutting board into the bowl. Have the bowl near the stove.

DO THIS SECOND:

1. Pour the cream into a small pot. Set it on a burner, turn the heat to high, and bring the cream to a boil. This will happen fairly quickly, so watch it.

2. Pour the boiling cream over the chocolate. Use pot holders!

3. Immediately start stirring with a rubber spatula until the chocolate has completely melted. There should be no lumps. Swish along the bottom of the bowl to check for grainy-looking chocolate bits. Keep stirring until they're gone and you've got a chocolate sauce that is absolutely smooth.

DO THIS THIRD:

1. Cover the bowl with plastic wrap. Put it in the refrigerator for 3 to 4 hours so the chocolate can thicken and firm up. When it is firm enough to roll into a ball, the truffles can be formed.

2. Meanwhile, spread a piece of waxed paper on a cookie sheet and have it ready on the countertop. *(Clean up the utensils and wash the pot. Clear a workspace on your countertop or a table.)*

WRAPPING IT UP:

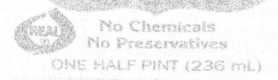

1. Unwrap the cold chocolate and set it next to the cookie sheet. Roll the chocolate into balls about the size of marbles (well, as big a bite as you'd like to have). As you go, line up the balls on the waxed paper.

2. Put the cookie sheet in the refrigerator for about 15 minutes. Meanwhile, measure the cocoa into a little bowl.

3. Use your fingers to roll each truffle in the cocoa, and return it to its spot on the waxed paper. Keep the truffles cold until you're ready to serve them as an after-dinner goodie.

No Chemicals
No Preservatives
ONE HALF PINT (236 mL)

• Heavy cream, sometimes labeled "heavy whipping cream" (one of the great labeling redundancies) is highest in butterfat. A national standard puts it at 36 percent butterfat or more. It stays firm if mixed and refrigerated with more fat, like the cocoa butter in chocolate.

• Whipping cream without the adjective "heavy" is a notch down from "heavy" cream, with 30 to 36 percent butterfat. It will make an acceptable ganache but may take longer to thicken in the refrigerator.

• If the balls of chocolate are loose and soften quickly once on the cookie sheet, put the bowl of chocolate back in the refrigerator and give it a chance to firm up more.

• Cocoa by definition is unsweetened.

• For more about chocolate, see Let's Talk, page 230.

SPAGHETTI WITH GARLIC SAUCE AND MUSHROOMS

BEST COOKWARE—Dutch oven, medium skillet
BEST EQUIPMENT—Colander, strainer
MUST HAVE—Pot holders

Everyone thinks boiling water is easy, so adding noodles to it shouldn't be much of a leap. This is how to make pasta every time. But it takes more than boiling to get a plate of pasta on the table. It needs sauce. This sauce is quick enough to make while the pasta cooks.

Serves 6

Pasta
About 7 quarts water
1 tablespoon salt
12 ounces (¾ pound) spaghetti

Sauce
1 pound fresh white mushrooms
Salt
2 tablespoons minced garlic
¼ cup chopped fresh parsley
¼ cup finely grated Parmesan cheese
½ cup decent olive oil
Lots of black pepper

DO THIS FIRST:

1. Put your colander in the sink (which is clean) to get ready for a hot downpour from a pot of boiling-hot pasta. Get out a platter or large shallow serving bowl.

2. Fill a huge pot two-thirds full of water. Cover. Put it over high heat and bring it to a boil. When steam escapes or the lid rattles, the water is boiling. (While the water is coming to a boil, you can start your sauce.)

DO THIS SECOND:

1. Remove the cover. If you want to add salt, do it now.

2. Add the pasta a little at a time, so the water keeps boiling.

3. Stir, then boil, uncovered, according to the timing on the package directions, until the pasta is firm to the bite—not mushy, yet cooked. (While the pasta cooks, work on your sauce.)

DO THIS THIRD:

1. Snatch a strand of spaghetti from the pot and run it under cold water. Take a bite. Is it soft but with a filament of resistance in the center?

2. If yes, take the pot to the sink and pour the pasta and water into the waiting colander. If no, keep boiling and checking.

WRAPPING IT UP:

1. Slide the drained pasta out of the colander back into its cooking pot.

2. Stir in the sauce.

Garlic Mushroom Sauce

DO THIS FIRST:

1. Snap the stems off the mushrooms, then slice them. Slice the caps into fat slices. Transfer the sliced mushrooms to a medium skillet.

2. Sprinkle with salt. Turn the heat to medium and let the mushrooms cook until they're limp, a good 8 minutes. You'll have to stir them fairly often. They'll shrink to half their original volume.

3. This will give you time to get out a strainer and set it over a bowl. When the mushrooms are done, pour them into the strainer and let the excess liquid drain out.

DO THIS SECOND:

1. Mince and measure the garlic. Chop the parsley and save it in its measuring cup near your serving dish. If you're using a solid piece of Parmesan, grate it now. Otherwise measure the Parmesan, and have it near the parsley.

2. Measure the olive oil and garlic into a medium pot. Turn the heat to low. Stir the garlic while you barely cook it until pale gold—less than 2 minutes. Don't let the garlic burn!

WRAPPING IT UP:

1. The garlic oil will stay hot about 5 minutes while the spaghetti finishes boiling. Mix the garlic oil into the cooked, drained spaghetti. Stir in lots of black pepper. Stir in the mushrooms.

2. Transfer all the spaghetti to your serving dish. Sprinkle with parsley and Parmesan cheese and bring it to the table, where you'll serve it hot.

MAKING GRAVY AND SAUCE

Most of the sauces in this book come from cooking meat beforehand and using what's left in the skillet or roasting pan for the base. Such a sauce is quick and very flavorful. Some might say the difference between sauce and gravy is attitude. It boils down to this:

1. If meat is plain or floured before hitting the pan, the resulting pan juices will make sauce.
2. If flour is added after the meat is cooked in order to thicken the pan juices—that's gravy.

Behind sauce is a holdover from sautéing— deglazing. *Deglaze* is a single word that means to loosen the cooked-on drippings in a sauté pan or roasting pan by adding a liquid and boiling it on the highest heat. When meats cook, their drippings leave a "glaze," which appears as stray bits of food that stick to the bottom of the skillet or baking dish. You think they're burnt, but these nasty-looking particles are the hidden flavor in many sauces—that is, if you can deglaze the pan.

To deglaze, take the finished meat out of the skillet and put it on a serving plate. Immediately add some liquid to the very hot pan (wine, broth, water, vinegar, whatever). The loud sizzling is normal. During this smoky drama, let it boil while you deliberately scrape up the glazey drips from the bottom of the pan. Like a miracle they will dissolve into your emerging sauce.

The longer the liquid boils, the more condensed the flavor will be and the less sauce you'll have. It is not uncommon to end up with half as much sauce as the original volume of liquid. That's why a sauce of this type is called a "reduction."

Gravy is made from pan juices, too, but more importantly, gravy relies on the thickening power of flour. In one respect, gravy can be leaner than sauce. If there is time for the pan juices to cool even 15 minutes in a measuring cup, the fat will separate and rise to the top. It will be quite visible as a yellow layer hanging over the remaining liquid. Once it's cooled, you'll be able to spoon away just about all the fat.

A WORD ON STICKING

If you are a member of the non-stick skillet brigade, please re-read the preceding, about how the meat drippings are supposed to stick. What kind of sauce are you going to get if you're cooking in a pan where nothing sticks? The non-stick skillet industry is turning us into lousy cooks. These tasty bits of residue are supposed to stick! Without them, your sauce will be missing a lot— flavor, color, and body.

That's why I recommend that you buy a set of cast iron pans. The $10 to $15 you'll spend for a set of THREE, including a small, medium, and large, is your best equipment investment. The more you use a cast iron pan the smoother its surface becomes. And you know what? It sort of turns non-stick over time while allowing browning to take place.

To convince yourself of the value of cast iron, go to any auction. A seasoned 10½-inch cast iron skillet of any age, as long as it's still useable, will bring up to $40 or $50. I suggest you start now, so in your old age you'll have something for your heirs. Tell them it's a non-stick skillet.

TIPS ON GETTING GOOD PAN JUICES

• Roast meat in a pan just large enough to hold it. If the pan is too big, any juices that are forced from the meat will spread and burn.

• A pan with low sides is better for roasting than a pan with high sides. High sides block heat.

• You'll get more stuck-on browned bits, those glorious specks of flavor that look like mistakes, if you roast the meat without putting it on a rack.

• Put enough salt and pepper on the meat so the resulting juices will already be nicely seasoned.

• Try to roast meat without adding unnecessary liquid. If you notice the meat doesn't have much juice to give, you certainly should add a little water to the bottom of the pan—between ¼ and 1 cup. Much more than that and you'll start steaming the food you're intending to roast, and the resulting juices will be watery and diluted.

A note on why juices may not come out of a cut of beef

Beef is divided into the grades Prime, Choice, and Select based on its marbling—or fat. Prime beef has the most marbling. It is priced the highest and most of it goes to restaurants. Choice is the middle category and what most Americans find in stores. Choice takes in a broad range of marbling, from medium-high to medium-low. The Select grade has the least marbling. This grade of beef was named to reflect perceived health properties of low-fat beef. Select beef with the most marbling is close to the least-marbled beef in the Choice grade, and should have no problem providing you with enough pan juices for making sauce. But on the low end, Select beef has very little fat, and thus gives off little in the way of pan juices. For this reason, beef short on marbling doesn't make much sense for roasting.

A note on fat

People who know how to cook understand that the fat in meat eventually goes away. People who do not know how to cook incorrectly believe that the fat that comes with the meat ends up inside your body. Don't worry, once you let the fat do its primary job of carrying flavor, you can dismiss it, never to have it pass your lips.

That's because when making sauce from roasting pan juices, you'll give all the fat a chance to isolate itself. Once the evil fat is in plain sight, as an obvious white layer on top of the real pan juices, it's as if the fat already knows its fate is to be scooped up in a spoon and swiftly eliminated.

SAUCE FROM THE PAN JUICES FROM ROASTING

• Pan juices and the sauces that spring from them are more like moisteners. Don't expect more than 1 to 1½ cups, total, after you complete this procedure.

• Whatever it's made of, use a roasting pan that's flat on the bottom. A roasting pan with grooves, sloughs, and troughs is impossible to scrape. This happens a lot with graniteware, so beware.

• The fat will react quickly to the cold temperature in the refrigerator, and will rise and float over the pan juices. It will be visible but still thin. Given an hour or two, the fat would form into a solid block which you could lift completely off the juices.

• The meat isn't ready for slicing until it's had a chance to cool down. Premature slicing wastes juices and shreds instead of cleanly slicing the meat. Refrain from messing with the meat for a good 10 minutes.

• Depending on the size of the meat, the internal temperature may rise 5 to 10° before it actually begins to cool. This forces more juices to the surface, and it's your job to collect them. They are intensely flavored.

TECHNIQUE — Boiling
BEST COOKWARE — Pan used to roast the meat
BEST EQUIPMENT — Cutting board, glass measuring cup, whisk
BEST TOOL — Small strainer

After you've roasted a chicken, turkey, prime rib, or loin of pork, you'll undoubtedly notice various remains in the baking pan — juices, fat, and those same glazey stuck-on pieces of food that end up in your skillet after a sauté.

Again, you are looking at the makings of sauce, provided you can deglaze your roasting pan. Because deglazing takes place over a burner on top of the stove, a glass baking dish that would at any other time be a fine piece of cookware for roasting meat in an oven won't survive.

Think ahead. Sauce is imminent. Roast meats in stainless steel, enamel-covered cast iron, graniteware, or other materials which, after handling the roasting, can endure a burner's direct heat.

Makes 1 to 1½ cups

> Pan juices from your meat
> ½ cup water, chicken stock, brandy, or wine
> Salt and pepper, if necessary
> 1 tablespoon butter

DO THIS FIRST:

1. Using tongs or a big fork, hoist your cooked meat up from the roasting pan, and hold it over the pan until valuable juices stop dripping off the meat.

2. Set the meat on a cutting board and leave it alone.

3. Pour anything that moves (liquids and juices) out of the roasting pan into a glass measuring cup, but don't scrape the bottom of the pan. Immediately put the cup in the refrigerator, and put the roasting pan on top of a burner. You'll be cooking in this pan shortly.

DO THIS SECOND:

1. Measure the ½ cup of water, stock, brandy, or port, or The-Wine-You're-Drinking-Now. Have it convenient to the stove.

2. Check the meat. If it's exuding even more pan juices all over the cutting board as it cools, pour the new juices into the waiting roasting pan. Yum, more flavor.

3. In about 5 minutes, take the cup of pan juices out of the refrigerator. You'll be able to see the risen fat. Scoop it off with a spoon and throw it away.

DO THIS THIRD:

1. Pour the juices remaining in the measuring cup into the roasting pan.

2. Turn the burner to high. When you see bubbling, pour in the water (stock, brandy, or wine). Enjoy the show of smoke, a sign that things are going nicely.

3. Use a wooden spatula to scrape the pan clean as the liquid bubbles. Stir and scrape about 30 seconds to 1 minute, until the liquid cleans itself up and about one-third of it has boiled away.

4. Take a taste. If it needs salt or pepper, add it now.

WRAPPING IT UP:

1. Turn off the heat. Add the butter. Use a whisk or spoon and stir all around the pan until the butter disappears into the sauce, which will now have a little more body.

2. Pour the sauce into a little pitcher. (If the sauce still has little pieces of browned bits, and these are annoying to you, pour the sauce through a mini-strainer held over the pitcher.)

• Sometimes after roasting you'll notice gray-white bubbles that were forced from the meat and sort of cooked in place. This is coagulated blood. As gruesome as this is to discuss, blood is a fine emulsifier (thickener) of sauce, but once it's in this form it won't dissolve. If your sauce finishes with these blobs, please strain it.

THICKENED GRAVY

- A huge mystique comes with making gravy. If you have juices from the roasting pan, you have a highly-flavored base that needs only thickening.

- If you want to hurry the rising of the fat, put the pan juices in the refrigerator immediately. Or put the cup of juices in a bowl filled with ice.

- It is very important that the water you use to dissolve the flour into a paste is cold. Hot water will cause the flour to separate into a million tiny balls, which you'll never be able to get rid of. And don't be tempted to just flail dry flour into the boiling juices as a shortcut. You'll see a million more tiny flour balls floating in your never-to-be gravy, none of which will have the slightest power to thicken the gravy. Even straining won't be of much help.

- If your flour paste is smooth from the beginning, the gravy will be smooth. If you start with lumps, you most certainly will end with lumps.

- A good way to combine flour and water is to shake it in a jar.

- How much or little you salted the original roasted meat has a direct bearing on the saltiness of the pan juices. Don't add salt to this gravy without first tasting it. It may not need any salt.

This is also the way to make gravy on Thanksgiving or after you've roasted any other bird or meat.

TECHNIQUE—Boiling
BEST COOKWARE—Medium-size pot
BEST EQUIPMENT—2-cup glass measuring cup, bulb baster, strainer
BEST TOOL—Whisk

Makes about 1 cup

Pan juices from a chicken (or other roasted meat, such as prime rib)
3 tablespoons flour
3 tablespoons cold water
Salt and pepper

DO THIS FIRST:

1. After you take out the roasted chicken to prepare it for serving, empty everything that's left in the pan into a glass 2-cup measuring cup. (If you've roasted vegetables in the bottom of the pan, strain the liquid through a strainer set over the measuring cup to catch the solids. Press on them a little to squeeze out their literal essence.)

DO THIS SECOND:

1. As the chicken cools, keep collecting juices and adding them to the cup.

2. Wait for golden fat to rise to the top. It will become obvious in less than 3 minutes. It will be easy to grab in about 15 minutes.

3. Spoon off as much fat as you can. A bulb baster will suck it up easily.

DO THIS THIRD:

1. After the fat is gone, take a look at how much liquid is left in the measuring cup. Add tap water to bring it up to 1½ to 2 cups. Pour the liquid into a medium-size pot.

2. Turn the heat to high. Bring the pot to a boil, uncovered. Boil until nearly half of the liquid cooks away.

WRAPPING IT UP:

1. Measure the flour and cold water into a coffee cup. Stir them together extremely well with a fork until you make a very smooth paste. (This might be more than you'll need.)

2. Pour the flour paste, a little at a time, into the boiling juices, stirring constantly, until the gravy becomes as thick as you like. You may not have to add all of it.

3. Add salt and pepper to taste.

• At the end of the gravy making, try adding a shot of Cognac, Madeira, or Sherry.

• The amount of gravy you get depends on the amount of pan juices you start with. You'll have enough flour paste to thicken an extra amount.

SAUTEED CHICKEN IN WINE SAUCE

TECHNIQUE — Sautéing
BEST COOKWARE — 10-inch sauté pan
HANDIEST TOOL — Tongs, wooden spatula

The final consistency of sauce is determined by whether the food cooked plain or floured. Food that is floured has the advantage of going in the pan with thickener — the flour — on it. Here chicken breasts are cooked unfloured in a little olive oil. They are no less deserving of sauce, although in this case the sauce is thin and light.

Serves 4

> 4 boneless chicken breasts, skin on or off
> Salt and pepper, to taste
> 1 cup white wine
> 1 tablespoon olive oil
> 1 or 2 pats butter (optional)

DO THIS FIRST:

1. Wash the chicken. Pat it dry with a paper towel and put it on a plate.

2. Sprinkle the breasts generously with salt and pepper and have the plate convenient to the stove.

3. Measure the wine into a measuring cup and have it near the stove, too. Get out a large good-looking serving plate. *This is your last chance to wipe up any mess before you cook and eat.*

DO THIS SECOND:

1. Put the oil in a 10-inch skillet, such as cast iron, and turn the heat to high. When the oil is very hot (it might even ripple) put the chicken in the pan with your hands, skin side down.

2. Let the pan heat up again until the chicken crackles. Now reduce the heat to medium (or medium-high) and keep cooking so the chicken crackles but doesn't burn or stick. Shake the pan a few times to make sure the chicken is loose. Don't move the pieces or pick them up if you don't have to.

3. After 5 or 6 minutes, when the underside is golden brown, flip the breasts over, using tongs. Keep sautéing over even heat for 5 to 6 minutes more.

DO THIS THIRD:

1. When the chicken is nicely browned, get it out of the pan and onto the serving plate.

2. As quickly as possible get back to the skillet, which should still be on the stove. Crank the heat to high. Immediately pour in the wine.

3. The loud sizzling sound is normal. When the smoke clears, you'll be able to see better. Move a wooden spatula across the bottom of the pan and scrape up the little bits of food that have stuck. The boiling action is helping unstick them.

4. Boil the sauce until it looks like about half of it has boiled away—or what you eyeball to be ½ cup. Taste once more for salt and pepper.

5. *Optional:* Take the skillet off the heat. Add the butter and very slowly swirl it in until the sauce is smooth. You'll see the thickening action of a true emulsion happen before your eyes.

WRAPPING IT UP:

1. Pour the sauce over the chicken and serve.

- White wine is specified in the ingredients list to prevent gasps that would have come had I written "white or red wine." Let me settle this: red wine will make a fine sauce for the chicken, if that's what you're drinking now or have in the refrigerator opened and half full. The red-wine version will be darker than the white-wine sauce, but it won't be red. Instead it will be sort of glisteny brown—and delicious.

- If you don't put enough salt and pepper on the chicken when it starts cooking, it will show up in the sauce. That's why our cooking god gives you one more chance at the end to get some salt in the sauce.

- By the time the sauce boils down and you have scraped and scraped, the nasty bits stuck to the pan should be gone. If not, pour your sauce through a little strainer as your pour it over the chicken.

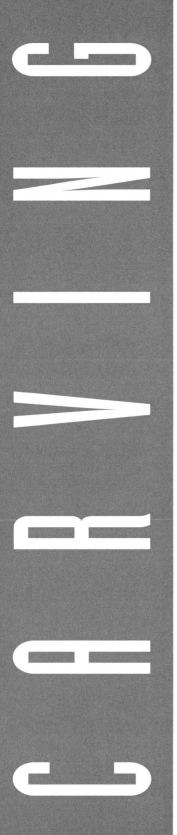

CARVING

Getting a beast out of the oven and to the table in an unbeastly form means you've got to carve it. Too bad carving has always seemed like table art performed by noblemen brandishing heirloom silver and knives only pirates could love. Carving can be easy. And it's not always Dad's job. (Of course, if he likes to do it, let him, even if you end up with a dissection instead of a carving. The job of carving through time has, in fact, switched from men to women and back again to men.) With a sharp knife, a cutting board, and a fork, anyone can take slices off a large piece of meat or cut a turkey down to size.

BONE-IN HAM

If you've roasted (or baked) a bone-in ham, more than likely it's a country ham—Smithfield, Virginia, Kentucky, Tennessee, or Country-Cured. If you did it right, the fat side, where you cut a diamond pattern, is up. Conveniently enough, this the way to situate the ham for slicing.

JUST DO THIS:

1. Wait until the ham has cooled at least 1 hour.

2. With the ham facing you like a sideways log, cut a few slices off the fleshiest end of the log. When you hit bone, stop, and make note of where the bone lies.

3. Now go to the top of the ham and cut diagonally through the skin and meat in the same general direction as the bone. In many recipes this is called "slicing with the bone." Because these hams are salty, the slices are traditionally very, very thin.

A WHOLE CHICKEN

So you think you pulled off the Big Chicken Coup by throwing an entire chicken in the oven without having to cut it up. What could be easier? You barely touched it! Now the chicken is done, and it's in no condition to be served. Not until it's carved. Maybe you'd like a Medieval theme tonight where your friends tear it apart with their hands?

At one end or the other, a chicken's got to be cut. If you buy it already cut for you, you pay on the raw end with cash. If you like the ease of roasting a chicken whole, you pay on the cooked end with carving. Getting a whole chicken into reasonably small pieces for serving isn't exactly carving. It's more like breaking off parts that break anyway, and slicing the rest.

DO THIS FIRST:

1. Have two clean kitchen towels ready to use like pot holders. Through the towels the chicken won't feel or act slippery.

2. Let the chicken cool a little. It will cooperate better once it's settled down from roasting.

DO THIS SECOND:

1. The drumsticks are facing up. You are looking down. Use the towels to protect your hands. Grab a thigh with one hand; with the other hold on right in the chicken's crotch.

2. Bend back the whole section—thigh and drumstick together. If it won't rip completely off the carcass, it's because a tendon on the carcass end of the thigh is holding firm. Give yourself a little help by cutting through any skin, and the tendon, with a paring knife.

3. You now hold in your hand the thigh-drumstick piece. Personally, I stop there, because we're a dark-meat loving family. Anyone at my table can eat this entire section.

4. If you want to divide the thigh and drumstick, look for the little indentation where the two meet. Find it with the forefinger of your non-knife hand. On a human, this area would be a knee. Either break the two pieces apart here (a towel holding each part), or slice them apart with a paring knife. You'll know you've found the soft spot because the knife will go through, just as if you'd found the cartilage under your own knee. If your knife hits bone, keep inching along the indentation until it suddenly goes through.

5. Now do the same thing on the chicken's other side.

DO THIS THIRD:

1. The peak of the breast bone is facing up. Hold on to the white meat with a towel in your non-knife hand. With the other hand, make a cut into the breast right down the middle. You're in the right place if your knife is over the bone (actually it's cartilage).

2. Take an entire half-breast off the carcass—skin, meat and all. You can pull it off with your hands (and towel) or give it a little help by pushing the meat away from the rib-cage bones with a knife.

3. Set the freed breast on a cutting board. Cut it like a loaf of bread, and put the nice slices on a serving platter.

4. Do the other side.

WRAPPING IT UP:

1. Arrange the legs on the platter with the breast meat and take it to the table.

PRIME RIB OF BEEF

LET'S TALK

• If the bones on your roast were cradled, remove them and slice the meat like it was nothing more than a loaf of bread.

• To carve brisket or flank steak: Notice a grain going lengthwise down the meat. Cut perpendicular to this grain. This is know as cutting against the grain, or to put it more simply, cutting across the grain. If you cut with the grain, the slices will shred.

In the old days, upper-class men were expected to know how to carve a roast of beef. In contemporary times, carving fell to the head of the household—in most cases a man again, but of a generation not so skilled at the table. Perhaps that began the fall of carving.

For anyone who doesn't know where to stick the fork or stick the knife, a large piece of meat such as a prime rib of beef can seem to breathe menacingly from its place setting. If you've cooked a prime rib with the bones attached, your job is to cut horizontal slices that run perpendicular to the bones. If you have purchased the same cut, but had the butcher remove the bones and tie them back on in a maneuver called "cradling," so you get the benefit of the bones' flavor without having to do much carving (see page 259), your job is that much easier.

DO THIS FIRST:

1. Put the meat on a cutting board with a trench that catches juices. (See Sauce from the Pan Juices from Roasting, page 70.)

2. Stand the meat on its large end, with the ribs in a stacked position. (Remember, this is a standing rib.)

3. Have ready a long slicing knife and a long-pronged fork.

WRAPPING IT UP:

1. Use just the tips of the tines of the fork to hold the meat. Use a gentle sawing action with the knife and don't change the angle of the knife once you've begun to slice.

2. Bracing the meat with the fork on the bone side, take a slice off the top, running the knife horizontally through the meat. You'll hit bone on the other side. Stop slicing. Reposition the knife, pointing down, right beside the bone and, following the outline of the bone, free the slice.

5

BREAKFAST

THE EASIEST
COMPANY MEAL
OF ALL

MORNING FARE

If you're new at entertaining and want to start easy, morning is the time of day for feeding 5 or 50 without cooking very much at all. Serving in the morning (or late morning) gives you the night before to make everything—even the mistakes—ahead of time.

The most primitive form of a company breakfast is fruit, cheese, bakery breads and pastries, coffee, and juice. Actually, there's more shopping than cooking. And it is a schmoozer's dream menu. You put everything on platters, take it to the people, and let the food run out while you have a good time.

On the following pages you'll find some ideas for no-cook breakfasts along with easy recipes for hot breakfast food that always pleases crowds.

REBECCA SAUCE FOR DIPPING FRUIT

TECHNIQUE—Combining ingredients
BEST EQUIPMENT—Medium bowl
BEST TOOL—Whisk

This is a dip for whole strawberries, pieces of pineapple—just about any fruit—and was named for the daughter of the Louisville chef who invented it. Rebecca Sauce improves after a day or two. The rum becomes more pronounced, which is a good reason to make this a day ahead. It should take about 5 minutes.

Makes about 2¼ cups

> 2 cups sour cream
> ½ cup brown sugar
> 1 tablespoon vanilla
> 1 tablespoon dark rum or bourbon

DO THIS FIRST:

1. Get out a medium mixing bowl. Empty the sour cream into the bowl.

DO THIS SECOND:

1. Measure the brown sugar and add it to the sour cream.

2. Whisk the sour cream and brown sugar until the mixture is blended and fairly smooth. It won't be completely smooth at this point.

3. Measure the vanilla; pour it into the sour cream.

4. Measure the rum; pour it in.

WRAPPING IT UP:

1. Whisk and whisk until the sauce is very smooth. Cover with plastic wrap. Keep the Rebecca Sauce in the refrigerator until you're ready to serve it.

- Cheese slicers come in two dominant designs. One looks like a sling shot, but the "sling" is absolutely taut. The other style looks like a spatula but with a sharp-edged slat on the bottom that drags across the cheese for super-thin slices.

FORMULA ONE:
For 8 people. Put out a plate holding three kinds of cheese, ½ pound of each.

FORMULA TWO:
For any number of people. Figure 3 ounces of cheese per person, regardless of how many guests. If you're having 10, you'll need 30 ounces. Round it off to 2 pounds; it's better to err on the side of too much than to get caught with too little.

BREAKFAST CHEESE PLATTER

BEST EQUIPMENT — Wooden cutting board, at least 12 inches wide
BEST TOOL — Cheese slicer, plus a couple of small knives

Cheese makes breakfast, or any meal for that matter, elegant without cooking. You unwrap the cheeses and set them on a wooden cutting board. Add a cheese slicer and cheese lovers will help themselves.

Some of the cheeses most suitable for breakfast are universal favorites. Firmer cheeses pair well with fruit, such as slices of apples or pears, or a cluster of grapes (which require no cutting).

Soft cheeses, such as Brie, are good spread on crackers. An unspeakably delicious combo is Brie smeared on a slice of sweet apple. Cream cheese with chives is a classic pairing with smoked salmon.

Here is a list of cheese you can find in the cheese specialty case at most any supermarket. Start with one or two of them. If you want three cheeses, make the third choice from the blue category.

Firm
Gouda or Edam — two Dutch favorites, for slicing
Swiss Emmenthaler or Jarlsberg, or American Swiss (unsliced) — good slicing-at-the-table cheese
Double Gloucester, or other Cheddar — from England or America.

Medium-Soft
Havarti — good Danish cheese
Butterkäse — a German favorite
Gjetost — Scandinavian

Blue

Roquefort—French
Gorgonzola—Italian
Saga Blue—Danish
Maytag Blue—American
Stilton—English
Cambozola—a mix of Camembert and
 Gorgonzola and shaped like a Brie. Always
 popular.

Soft

Brie or Camembert—Buy about a ⅓-pound
 wedge, and have it at room temperature. Avoid
 Brie or Camembert sold in tin cans.
Mushroom or Herbed Brie—about a ¼-pound
 wedge, at room temperature, for variety
Goat cheese (chèvre—pronounced *shev*)—Buy a
 small 3-ounce log (look for the cute goat face
 on the label) for spreading on crackers or firm
 fruit.

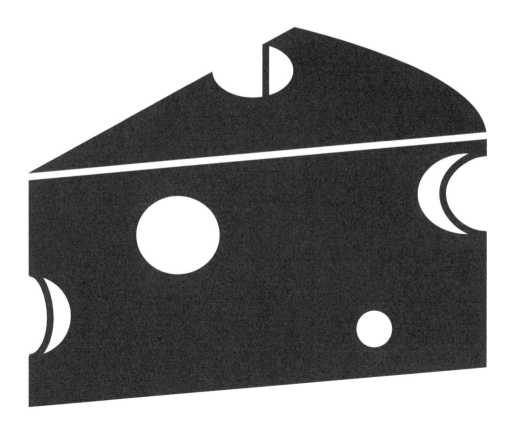

• You'll have enough bread if you allow a 1- to 1½- pound loaf for 5 to 8 people. If it's rolls, figure 1½ rolls per person. Some guests may not eat any, but some might eat three.

• It's always best to buy bread as fresh as humanly possible, even in the morning before your brunch begins. Call a bakery a few days ahead to reserve what you need. You can pick it up as early as 7 am the day of the brunch. Remember, bakers bake all night, so they're there that early.

• If your city is short of specialty bakeries, buy bread as fresh as you can at the grocery store and freeze it double-wrapped in plastic wrap.

• No matter what you do, the staling process will invade the bread over a couple of days. It happens faster in the refrigerator than on the counter or in the freezer.

• You can truly reverse the staling process. Unwrap the frozen bread and refresh it in an oven preheated to 350° to 375°F for 5 minutes. By doing this you will chemically restore the original crispness to the crust.

• When serving bread, you MUST have butter.

BREAD

Store-bought bread is the rage as a specialty item that comes with crustiness and ethnic memories. Even accomplished home bakers who could make their own can't resist it for convenience and quality. Therefore, take a load off. If you'll be serving bread at brunch, feel no shame in getting it at the store. If you'd like to make something easy on your own, see My Mom's Blueberry Muffins, page 100.

How Bread Makes a Good Appearance at Brunch:

In a basket, on a plate or platter, in a piece of crockery lined with a clean kitchen towel, or on a cutting board.

If you're serving a variety of breads, you can pile them into a large basket lined with a nice cloth. Some possible choices are:

• Bagels, pre-sliced—available in delis, supermarkets, and shops devoted expressly to the production of bagels

• Cinnamon rolls—popular in malls, shopping centers. Cinnamon rolls (or buns) can be purchased by the dozen and are always gratefully acknowledged at brunch.

• A good egg bread or French bread, sliced thickly—Some stores have a machine that cuts a whole loaf of bread into perfect slices. You shouldn't be charged for this service, but some businesses may levy a small fee. It's worth it because the slices will be uniform.

SMOKED SALMON PLATTER WITH CAPERS AND RED ONIONS

TECHNIQUE — Chopping
BEST SERVING WARE — Big serving platter

A lot of restaurant critics say all a chef has to do to impress customers, without really cooking, is send out the smoked salmon. Believe it. The theory also works at home. The hidden genius behind setting it out is in buying well.

Serves 10

DO THIS FIRST:

1. Buy about 1 pound of sliced smoked salmon — the good stuff (lox). Refrigerate until you'll serve it.

DO THIS SECOND:

1. When you're ready to serve, take the slices of salmon from the wrapper and arrange them in soft folds on a platter or dinner plate.

2. Rest two forks on the plate, so folks can serve themselves.

WRAPPING IT UP:

1. Decorate the smoked salmon with:

- Thin slices of red onion — Scatter on top.
- Black olives — Put a clump off to one side.
- Capers, drained from a jar — Scatter on top.
- Lemon wedges (thin) — Scatter on top to keep the platter looking fresh. The yellow of the lemon is a nice contrast to the pink of the smoked salmon.

OTHER GOOD THINGS TO HAVE AT BRUNCH:
A plate of tomato slices, but only in season!
A plate of avocado slices

ANOTHER BRUNCH BUFFET FAVORITE:
Granola and milk — Stack a number of dessert-size bowls next to the granola and stand spoons upright in a glass for people to help themselves. Put out on the table:
Stirred-up regular yogurt, plain or flavored
A honey pot
Raisins
Cashews

• A hand-held mixer tends to overbeat eggs, which toughens them. Once you see the eggs get frothy, stop beating. The froth is full of bubbles, which are full of air. The air works against a texture you want to be creamy and soft.

• These won't taste good without some butter.

• You may make these eggs using low-fat (2%) milk or skim milk.

• When the cold eggs hit the hot milk, for a moment nothing will happen. That's because the eggs temporarily cool down the pan. But in a blink of an eye, you'll see the miracle of coagulation. The curds will form quickly and the mixture will become more and more yellow.

• It is doubtful that you will need to adjust the temperature of the burner from its starting point of medium-high.

• Eggs must be nature's insulation material because they hold heat so well. That's why you've got to stop cooking them when they're not truly done. If you like scrambled eggs soft, get them out of the pan when they're still juicy. If you like them medium, stop cooking when they're soft. I simply can't discuss scrambled eggs cooked beyond this stage.

• This cooking method works as well for 4 eggs as it does for 8. If making a smaller batch, halve this recipe or divide by 4. Make sure to use a skillet small enough for the smaller amount of milk to cover the bottom.

AMAZING SCRAMBLED EGGS ON THE SPOT

TECHNIQUE — Barely boiling
BEST COOKWARE — Wide non-stick skillet
BEST TOOL — Wooden spatula

This is the most artful deliberate curdling of eggs in all of cooking. What you get is a batch of silken scrambled eggs that at first appear to be made backwards. But the technique works, and is perfect for making soft, creamy scrambled eggs in the midst of distractions.

Serves 4

½ cup milk
½ stick butter (4 tablespoons)
8 eggs
Salt and pepper, to taste

DO THIS FIRST:

1. Get out a wide non-stick skillet and set it on a burner, but don't turn it on yet.

2. Pour the milk into the skillet. Put the butter in the milk.

3. Have ready a serving bowl, or individual plates.

DO THIS SECOND:

1. Crack the eggs into a large mixing bowl, but don't whip them yet. Sprinkle with salt and pepper.

DO THIS THIRD:

1. When you're ready to make the eggs, turn the burner to medium-high. Heat the milk until the butter is completely melted and the milk is hot enough to bubble up. Don't rush it, and don't let the milk come to a big boil.

2. While the milk is heating, beat the eggs. You can use a whisk or a hand-held electric mixer.

WRAPPING IT UP:

1. When the milk is very hot, pour in the beaten eggs. They'll begin to knot up in a matter of seconds.

2. Use a wooden spatula to push, not stir, the mixture across the skillet, until the eggs glisten and are not quite set. You won't have to adjust the heat.

3. Scoop the eggs into the serving bowl or onto the plates and serve immediately. They'll firm up on their way to the table.

For easy omelet varia-
tions, see page 92.

NO-FLIP CHEESE OMELET

TECHNIQUE—Sautéing, baking
BEST COOKWARE—Medium non-stick skillet with
 oven-proof handle (very important!)
BEST EQUIPMENT—Medium mixing bowl, whisk,
 rubber spatula
MUST HAVE—Pot holders, hot pad for the table

You might recognize this type of omelet as a
frittata. Omelets that avoid flipping and folding
by ending up under a broiler are called frittata in
Italy. A good deal of the rest of the universe calls
this same thing an omelet—and that goes for
Spain, Japan, and the entire Middle East. Major-
ity rules. An omelet it is.

The skillet you use will go from burner to
broiler and finally to the table. That's why the
skillet needs an ovenproof handle, and that's
why your table needs a hot pad.

Serves 4

>8 thin slices meltable decent-quality cheese
> (Monterey Jack, Cheddar, Swiss, Gouda,
> Muenster)
>2 tablespoons butter
>8 eggs
>3 tablespoons milk
>Salt and pepper, to taste
>
>*Optional beautifier: 1 tablespoon fresh
> chopped parsley*

DO THIS FIRST:

1. Preheat the broiler. Set the rack about 3
inches below the heat element.

2. Have the cheese in slices on a plate near the
stove.

3. Get out a medium-size non-stick skillet,
about 10 inches wide. Put the butter in the skillet
and have it ready on the stove.

4. Crack the eggs into a mixing bowl. Add the
milk, salt, and pepper. Use a whisk or portable
electric beaters and whip the eggs just until you
see froth, then stop.

DO THIS SECOND:

1. Turn the burner under the butter to medium-high. When the butter is hot and foamy, pour in the eggs.

2. The eggs should cool the pan upon impact. If they look like they're cooking furiously, especially along the edges, immediately turn the heat down to medium.

3. In about 10 seconds, you'll notice the edges have cooked. Lift up the cooked parts with a rubber spatula, push gently a little bit toward the center, and let some of the as-yet-uncooked egg flow outward.

4. Keep lifting and letting the egg run outward all around the pan until the eggs are barely set and still very juicy in the center. At this stage, underdone is better than overdone.

DO THIS THIRD:

1. Lay the cheese like spokes all around the omelet.

2. Immediately rush the skillet under the broiler. Don't go anywhere! Stand there and keep watch for 30 seconds. The omelet will puff and the cheese will melt. For additional browning, give it 10 seconds more.

WRAPPING IT UP:

1. Take the skillet out of the oven. Use pot holders! Sprinkle the omelet with parsley.

2. Bring the skillet to the table, set it on a hot pad, and dish out wedges of omelet to all takers.

VARIATION #1: NO-FLIP SPICY OMELET

1. Chop 1 medium onion. Mince 1 small fresh jalapeño. Sauté both in 2 tablespoons of butter over medium-high heat for 5 minutes.

2. Pour in the beaten eggs and make the No-Flip Omelet as on page 90, with or without the cheese. *Note:* If you don't want to mince a jalapeño, you can get plenty of spice from ⅛ teaspoon cayenne, ½ teaspoon chile powder, ⅛ teaspoon cumin, or by spooning your favorite spicy salsa all over the cheese just before the omelet goes under the broiler.

VARIATION #2: NO-FLIP MUSHROOM OMELET

1. Slice 10 medium white mushrooms. Sauté them in 2 tablespoons butter over medium-high heat for 6 to 8 minutes. Give a few stirs. This is enough time to pull out the mushrooms' liquid, then boil it off.

2. If the mushrooms are cooked but there are still watery juices in the pan, pour them off but leave the mushrooms in the pan.

3. Mix the eggs as in the No-Flip Cheese Omelet. With the heat still medium-high, pour the eggs over the mushrooms. Swirl the eggs so they cover the pan and the mushrooms evenly. Continue making the omelet as in Do This Second, page 91; you may use the cheese or leave it off.

VARIATION 3: NO-FLIP STRAWBERRY-SOUR CREAM OMELET

1. Mix 1½ cups sliced strawberries with 2 tablespoons sugar. Then mix ¾ cup sour cream with 2 tablespoons brown sugar, to replace the cheese.

2. Just before the broiling step in the No-Flip Omelet, spread the strawberries over the omelet. Spread the sour cream over the strawberries. Broil about 2 minutes.

RICH BAKED EGGS

TECHNIQUE—Baking
BEST BAKEWARE—Small oval dishes

One of the easiest ways to cook eggs is to bake them. It's like hardly cooking at all. For company, baked eggs have many advantages. The eggs bake in the oven without any moving, flipping, or folding from you. And, you can easily increase the recipe. This recipe serves 2. For 4 people, use 8 eggs in 4 baking cups; for 6 people, use 12 eggs in 6 baking cups, and so on.

Serves 2

> 2 tablespoons butter
> 2 tablespoons cream
> 4 eggs
> Salt and pepper

> *Mo' hotta: Red Devil or Tabasco sauce*

DO THIS FIRST:
1. Preheat the oven to 325°F, with an oven rack on a lower notch. Get out two small cups or shallow dishes that are ovenproof.

2. Put 1 tablespoon of butter into each cup. Set the cups in a microwave on High for 30 seconds to melt the butter, or melt it in the oven as it heats, but be careful that it doesn't burn.

DO THIS SECOND:
1. Pour the cream into the melted butter. Crack 2 eggs into each cup. Bake 20 minutes. (Set a timer.)

2. When the bell rings, open the oven and take a look. The yolks should be set softly; the butter and cream will be swirling over the tops of the eggs. If you want firmer yolks, bake 5 minutes more.

WRAPPING IT UP:
1. Set each hot cup on a plate (use pot holders). Holding on to the plates (which are not hot) take the eggs to the table.
2. Serve with more salt and pepper and hot sauce, such as Tabasco or Red Devil.

- You may use white bread, soft whole wheat, French or Italian sourdough, or baguette (using enough slices to fill out each layer).

- Use your judgment about whether or not to cut off the crusts. If they're soft, leave them on. If they're chewy, as on some baguettes, trim them away.

- If you are lucky enough to find a tub of whole milk large-curd cottage cheese in what has become a confusing line-up of low-fat, 1% fat, or fat-free cottage cheese, your strata will have the best consistency. Small curd cottage cheese won't ruin things, but fat-free cottage cheese knots up during baking.

- Strata first made its appearance a few decades ago as a way to use leftover bread and cheese. If this were sweet, it would be very much like bread pudding.

- Stale bread is the standard here, but fresh bread works fine, too.

- To make fresh bread quickly "stale," set out the slices on the countertop for about 1 hour.

- Stop beating the eggs and milk when you see foam. That foam will bake into tough air pockets. Mixing the eggs only enough to blend them helps them bake up rich and smooth.

STRATA WITH COTTAGE CHEESE

TECHNIQUE—Baking
BEST BAKEWARE—8- or 9-inch square glass baking dish, or oval ceramic baking dish that holds 6 to 8 cups
BEST EQUIPMENT—Medium bowls, measuring cups
NICE TO HAVE—Portable electric mixer, or whisk

Strata could make a host out of Bart Simpson. Strata is a boon to brunch because, by definition, it is a make-ahead. If you pull this together the evening before, all you'll have to do the next morning is uncover it, stash it in the oven, and make the coffee. You don't have to serve your strata piping hot. It is ready when the guests are ready. It will stay warm up to 2 hours.

Serves 4 to 6

7 tablespoons (⅞ stick) butter
16-ounce tub large-curd cottage cheese
2 tablespoons fresh chopped parsley
2 green onions
1 tablespoon mustard
6 slices bread
6 eggs
1½ cups milk
Salt and pepper, to taste

DO THIS FIRST:

1. Get out an 8- or 9-inch square baking dish (a glass one is good). Smear a film of butter (about 1 tablespoon) all over the bottom, sides, and corners.

2. Empty the cottage cheese into a medium mixing bowl. Chop the parsley as finely as you can and stir it into the cottage cheese.

3. Slice off the hairy ends of the green onions, then slice the white parts and some of the green as thinly as you can. Add them to the cottage cheese.

4. Put the remaining butter and the mustard into a little bowl. Microwave on High for about 15 seconds, uncovered, just to soften the butter. Mash the butter and mustard with a fork until they're smooth.

DO THIS SECOND:

1. Spread half of the mustard-butter on 3 slices of bread. Arrange the bread buttered-side up in the bottom of the baking dish. You'll have to cut one of the slices into pieces so all the bread will fit in a single layer. Don't worry about this patchwork look.

2. Spoon half the cottage cheese over the bread.

3. Spread the rest of the butter on the remaining 3 slices of bread. Arrange these slices on top of the cottage cheese, buttered side down. Again, cut one of the slices so all the bread fits nicely.

4. Spoon the rest of the cottage cheese over the bread and spread it evenly.

DO THIS THIRD:

1. Crack the eggs into a medium-size bowl. Add the milk, salt, and pepper. Use a whisk or portable electric mixer to beat the eggs until they're completely blended but not frothy.

2. Slowly pour the eggs all over the bread. If the mixture backs up and looks like it will overflow, wait until some of the egg is soaked in before pouring in the rest.

3. Cover the strata with heavy-duty foil. Put it in the refrigerator until the next morning.

WRAPPING IT UP:

1. The next morning, preheat the oven to 350°F.

2. Bake the strata, cover off, for 1 hour. It will puff, turn golden brown and set in the center. While the strata bakes, get out a wire cooling rack.

3. Cool the strata on the rack for 5 minutes before attempting to cut it.

• The 5 minutes cooling-off time gives the custard a chance to collect itself and finish setting before anything as invasive as a big knife gashes the consistency.

• You can serve strata at the table and cut portions directly from its baking dish. This makes the appearance of the baking dish all the more important.

• The best utensil for withdrawing that first, finicky piece is a small spatula usually used for picking up wedges of pizza.

- A dark, grainy German-style mustard always pairs up well with ham and cheese. If you have ballpark or Dijon mustard on hand, use that.

- The bread selection starts with white bread, but crustless rye bread does well in furthering the German twist. If all you have is baguette, whole wheat, sour-dough, or honey bread, all will work well.

- When shopping for the ham, look in the cold meat case for an item labeled "center-cut" slice. It most likely will be shrink-wrapped. Depending on how thick it is cut, a slice can weigh from 1 to 5 pounds.

- Besides Cheddar or Swiss, other cheeses that bake well in strata are Colby, Longhorn, and Monterey Jack.

- When you shred the cheese, you'll have about 6 cups.

- Eggs beaten with milk technically is custard. Once baked, you'll notice the texture is similar to that of quiche.

HAM AND CHEESE STRATA

TECHNIQUE — Baking
BEST BAKEWARE — 9×13-inch oblong glass baking dish, or a good-looking oval that holds 14 cups
BEST EQUIPMENT — Medium bowls, measuring cups, box grater
NICE TO HAVE — Portable electric mixer, or whisk

The combination of ham, cheese, and eggs is reminiscent of quiche, but because strata doesn't have a crust it's much easier, with an appearance just as wondrous.

Serves 8

> 8 tablespoons (1 stick) butter
> 2 pounds baked ham
> 1½ pounds cheese (Cheddar or Swiss)
> 3 tablespoons mustard
> 8 slices bread
> 8 eggs
> 2½ cups milk
> Salt and pepper, to taste

DO THIS FIRST:

1. Get out a rectangular baking dish (a glass one is good). Smear a film of butter (about 1½ tablespoons) all over the bottom, sides, and corners.

2. Cut the ham into cubes about the size of gaming dice. Leave the cubes on the cutting board.

3. Tear off a length of waxed paper. Shred the cheese on the medium holes of a box grater onto the waxed paper, and leave it there.

DO THIS SECOND:

1. Put the remaining butter and the mustard into a little bowl. Microwave on High for about 15 seconds, uncovered, just to soften the butter. Mash the butter and mustard with a fork until they're smooth.

2. Spread half the mustard-butter on 4 slices of the bread using a table knife. Arrange the bread in the bottom of the baking dish, buttered side up. You'll have to cut one of the slices into pieces so all the bread will fit in a single layer. Don't worry about this patchwork look.

3. Sprinkle half the ham over the bread. Sprinkle half the cheese over the ham.

4. Spread the rest of the butter on the remaining 4 slices of bread. Arrange these slices on top of the cheese, buttered side down. Again, cut one of the slices so all the bread fits nicely.

5. Sprinkle the rest of the ham over the bread, then the rest of the cheese.

DO THIS THIRD:
1. Crack the eggs into a mixing bowl. Add the milk. Add the salt and pepper. Use a whisk or portable electric mixer to beat the eggs until they're completely blended.

2. Slowly pour the eggs all over the layers. If the mixture backs up and looks like it will overflow, wait until some of the egg soaks in before pouring in the rest.

3. Cover the strata with heavy-duty foil. Put it in the refrigerator until the next morning.

WRAPPING IT UP:
1. The next morning, preheat the oven to 350°F.

2. Bake the strata, cover off, for 45 to 50 minutes, until puffed, deeply golden, and set.

3. While the strata bakes, get out a wire cooling rack. When it's done, cool the strata on the rack for 5 minutes before attempting to cut it.

BREAKFAST BURRITO BUFFET

TECHNIQUE—Sautéing, boiling
BEST COOKWARE—10½-inch skillet, small pot
BEST TOOLS—Mixing bowl, box grater, chef's knife and cutting board
GREAT TO HAVE—7 various bowls for the buffet fixings

If you devote unswerving focus to the preparation, and set out your burrito buffet with its self-explanatory sequencing, it will run its course thereafter with little input from you. A lot of the chopping can be done the night before. This is a great opportunity to serve margaritas (See Drinks by the Pitcher, page 296).

Serves 6

> 1 pound Monterey Jack cheese
> Your favorite salsa, red
> Your favorite salsa, green
> Sliced jalapeños
> Sprigs of cilantro
> 1 dozen flour tortillas
> 15-ounce can refried beans
> 1 recipe Amazing Scrambled Eggs (page 88)

DO THIS FIRST:

1. Shred the cheese. Put it in a medium bowl with serving tongs.

2. Pour the salsas into separate bowls. Add small serving spoons.

3. Put the jalapeño slices in a small bowl with a small spoon.

4. Pick off sprigs of cilantro and wash them. Tamp them dry with paper towels. Put them in a small bowl.

5. Take all the bowls to your buffet area. These will be preceded by the eggs, refried beans, and tortillas, so leave room.

DO THIS SECOND:

1. Preheat the oven to about 150°F—not much hotter.

2. Take the tortillas out of their plastic wrapping and divide the stack in half. Wrap each stack in foil. Put them in the warm oven until you're ready for them. (Keep one stack warm in the oven until the first stack is used.)

3. Have ready a "tortilla warmer" basket, or a plate lined with a cloth towel you can fold over the tortillas so they'll stay warm on the buffet.

DO THIS THIRD:

1. Open the can of refried beans and empty it into a small pot. Add 1 or 2 tablespoons of water and stir until the water is absorbed.

2. Bring the beans to a boil over medium heat. For the 3 or 4 minutes this will take, you'll have to keep an eye on the beans and stir them so they don't stick or burn.

3. Put the beans in a bowl with a cover. Take the tortillas and the beans (with a serving spoon) to the buffet. The tortillas are first in line; the beans are second.

WRAPPING IT UP:

1. Before making the Amazing Scrambled Eggs, get out their serving bowl and a big serving spoon.

2. Make the Amazing Scrambled Eggs. When they're done, transfer them to the serving bowl. Add the serving spoon and set the eggs down on the buffet after the refried beans.

3. Come and get it.

LET'S TALK

• The tortillas are warmed in the oven instead of the microwave. This is one instance when a microwave is more trouble and requires your presence. The oven is passive and will keep the tortillas warm until you need them.

BREAKFAST BURRITO
BUFFET LINE-UP OF
BOWLS, IN ORDER:
1. Tortillas
2. Refried beans
3. Amazing Scrambled Eggs
4. Cheese
5. Jalapeños
6. Salsa
7. Salsa
8. Cilantro

• Paper muffin cups are available at just about any grocery store. They'll be near the baking products, and they come in all sorts of colors and themes.

• A little money, like under $1, spent on baking cups spares you the greasing of the 12 muffin wells, and also makes the baked muffins easy to hold when you're driving to work.

• Baking powder makes the muffins rise. You'll get a nice dome on these, but don't expect them to look like Baked Alps.

• Overmixing muffin batter makes the muffins tough.

• If you add the egg first to the hot melted butter, it might start to cook.

• As you stir in the blueberries—fresh or frozen—the batter might get a blue tinge. Don't worry. The muffins miraculously bake up white.

• If your blueberries are frozen use them straight from the freezer—no thawing necessary.

MY MOM'S BLUEBERRY MUFFINS

Some 12 years ago I wrote a story in the Louisville *Courier-Journal* about my mother's blueberry coffee cake, the batter for which can also be poured into muffin tins. A response disproportionate to the relative importance of a simple recipe came for years.

Muffins have two mixed components that join up at the end of the instructions. It's so easy I've never understood why it was necessary to invent muffin mix. You've got your own muffin mix right here under the heading Dry Mixture.

Makes 12

Topping
½ stick **butter (4 tablespoons)**
⅓ cup **flour**
½ cup **sugar**
½ teaspoon cinnamon

Dry mixture
2 cups flour
3 teaspoons baking powder
½ teaspoon salt
⅔ cup sugar

Wet mixture
½ stick butter (4 tablespoons)
⅔ cup milk
1 egg

2 cups fresh or frozen blueberries

DO THIS FIRST:

1. Unwrap the butter for the Topping and leave it on the counter to soften.

2. Line a 12-well muffin tin with paper baking cups. Preheat the oven to 400°F.

3. Get out three mixing bowls.

DO THIS SECOND:
1. To make the topping, put the butter, flour, sugar, and cinnamon in a big bowl. Rub them between your fingers and palms until you've made "crumbs," about the size of peas. This may take 2 to 3 minutes.

DO THIS THIRD:
1. Measure all the ingredients for the Dry Mixture directly into a big bowl.

DO THIS FOURTH:
1. Melt the ½ stick butter for the Wet Mixture (about 45 seconds on High, uncovered, in a microwave). Add the milk, then the egg. Stir a little, just to break up the egg.

2. Combine the wet and dry mixtures. Just stir gently with a fork.

3. Stir in the blueberries.

DO THIS FIFTH:
1. Pour the batter into the muffin cups.

2. Cover each with 2 tablespoons of topping. Bake 30 to 35 minutes.

3. While the muffins bake, line a bowl or bread basket with a cloth napkin or decent-looking (clean) towel.

WRAPPING IT UP:
1. When the muffins are done, take the muffin tin out of the oven. The topping should be browned and crunchy and the tops mounded. Use pot holders! Let the muffins cool in the tin for at least 5 minutes.

2. Upturn the tin. The muffins will fall out.

6

PARTY SNACKS AND APPETIZERS

STUFFED ARTICHOKES

TECHNIQUE—Boiling/baking
BEST COOKWARE—Dutch oven, oblong baking dish
BEST EQUIPMENT—Mixing bowl, chef's knife and
  cutting board
BEST TOOLS—Kitchen scissors, tongs

Rather than being a walk-around-with-a-drink-in-your-hand appetizer, this is a sit-down way to start eating. The made-ahead artichokes will wait grandly on their individual plates, at room temperature, until everyone is ready to come to the table. This is the sort of recipe which proves that if you exert yourself a little beforehand, you'll have it easy later.

Serves 6

> 6 fresh artichokes
> 2 teaspoons minced garlic
> 4 green onions
> 2 cups bread crumbs
> ½ cup grated Parmesan cheese
> ¼ teaspoon dried thyme
> ⅛ teaspoon (just a pinch) cayenne pepper
> 3 tablespoons olive oil
> Salt and pepper, to taste
> 2 additional tablespoons olive oil

DO THIS FIRST:

1. Using a huge chef's knife, whack off the top third of each artichoke.

2. Slice the bottom stem off each artichoke so they stand flat.

3. Remove and throw away every leaf on the two layers at the base. If any other leaves look stringy, get rid of them, too.

4. With scissors or a knife, cut off the thorny ends of all the remaining leaves.

DO THIS SECOND:

1. Put about 2 inches of water in a big pot, such as a Dutch oven. If you have a round cake cooling rack, put it in the bottom of the pot. If not, it's okay.

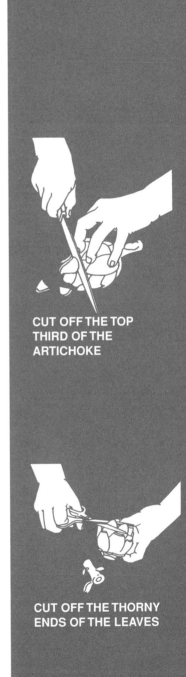

CUT OFF THE TOP
THIRD OF THE
ARTICHOKE

CUT OFF THE THORNY
ENDS OF THE LEAVES

2. Add a few shakes of salt to the water. Cover the pot, turn the heat to high, and bring the water to a boil.

3. Put the artichokes into the pot, stem end down. Cover, turn the heat to medium-high and cook the artichokes for 30 minutes.

4. Take the artichokes out of the pot with tongs. Let them drain upside down on a wire rack.

DO THIS THIRD:

1. While the artichokes are cooling, make the stuffing. Mince the garlic as finely as you can. Push it off the cutting board into a big mixing bowl.

2. Cut off the hairy roots of the green onions. Slice both the white and green parts fairly thin, stopping where the leaves get flabby. Add to the garlic.

3. Measure the remaining ingredients, except the 2 tablespoons of olive oil, and add them to the bowl. (If you have Italian-seasoned bread crumbs, leave out the thyme.) Stir and mash with a wooden spoon until the crumbs clump together.

DO THIS FOURTH:

1. Get out an oblong baking dish and have it convenient to your work area. Preheat the oven to 375°F, with an oven rack in the middle.

2. In the center of the artichoke is a hairy thistle. Pull it out with your fingers. You'll notice a handy little cup forming inside the artichokes. To make sure you've got all the hairs (why do you think they're called "chokes"?) you'll have to use a spoon to scrape the bottom of the cup clean.

3. Spread out the leaves just a little. With the artichokes sitting on a plate, start spooning stuffing into the centers, then tuck more stuffing into the leaves. Don't pack it in too tightly. It's supposed to be somewhat fluffy. And it's okay if some of the stuffing falls out of the leaves as you go. The plate will catch the excess, and you can use it in the next artichoke.

4. As each artichoke is stuffed, set it in the baking dish.

WRAPPING IT UP:

1. If you have a little more stuffing left, sprinkle it on top of the artichokes. Now drizzle the 2 additional tablespoons of olive oil over the centers of the artichokes.

2. Pour ½ cup water into the baking dish (without splashing the artichokes). Bake the artichokes, uncovered, for 15 minutes. They'll get browned on top.

3. Remove the artichokes from the oven and let them cool in the pan. You can serve them warm. Or you can treat them as a make-ahead.

MAKE-AHEAD OPTION:

1. Refrigerate the cooled artichokes in their baking dish, covered tightly with plastic wrap, until you're ready to serve.

CUT-UP VEGETABLES

I never saw a raw piece of broccoli special enough for a party until the late '60s. I don't know who started it, but I know why. Raw broccoli has fewer offending calories than a potato chip. Of course, the great equalizer is the dip that comes up with each mouthful of broccoli. Those florets can suck up sour cream better than a flimsy chip, so you might as well go ahead and eat the chip.

Raw vegetables are here to stay. If you want to get away with cutting but not cooking, let me suggest the following:

Celery—the best of all scoopers; clean, trim, and cut into whatever lengths you like

Carrots—peel please, then cut lengthwise into sticks

Jicama—peel first, then slice into ¼-inch-thick rounds

Broccoli and cauliflower—leave enough stem on the floret to act as a natural "handle"

White mushrooms (not too big)—wipe them clean with a dry paper towel; present them whole

Red onion slivers—peel and quarter a small red onion, then separate the layers

Endive—pricey but good scoopers; separate the leaves, then fan them out

Snow peas—Chinese style, good for thicker dunks because less of it will adhere

Small radishes or long skinny radishes—clean them and present

Daikon—peel, then cut into thin slices

"CALIFORNIA" ONION DIP WITHOUT USING A MIX

TECHNIQUE—Sautéing/"sweating"
BEST COOKWARE—A 12-inch-wide heavy skillet
HANDIEST APPLIANCE—Food processor, blender,
  immersible blender, or portable electric mixer

It's hard to wean the pantry of convenience products. Dried soup mix shows up on brisket as often as it truly becomes soup—or dip. You won't find packaged seasonings in this dip. Real onions on low heat work just fine.

Makes 3½ cups

    8-ounce package cream cheese
    2 very large onions (white or yellow)
    2 tablespoons vegetable oil
    2 cups sour cream
    1½ tablespoons Worcestershire sauce
    Few drops Tabasco
    1 tablespoon dried parsley flakes

DO THIS FIRST:
  1. Take the cream cheese out of the refrigerator to soften.

  2. Peel and slice the onions and caramelize them in the oil, as explained on page 52. Let them cool.

WRAPPING IT UP:
  1. Chop the cooled onions.

  2. In a blender, food processor, or portable electric mixer, blend the onions with the remaining ingredients until smooth. This is *the* dip for chips. You could also serve it with vegetable dippers (see page 106).

LET'S TALK

• Onions cooked for a long time release sugar, and the onions "caramelize."

• If you are using a portable electric mixer, put all the ingredients in a bowl for mixing.

• If you use yogurt instead of sour cream, the dip will be runny.

• If you want to use fresh parsley, use 2 tablespoons finely minced.

• This is the way to thicken yogurt for any purpose—another dip, a sauce, or topping.

• If you have an odoriferous refrigerator, cover the draining yogurt with plastic wrap.

• Shredded cucumber keeps tzadziki crunchy. If you prefer, make the dip smooth. Process the peeled and seeded cucumber and ½ cup of the yogurt in a food processor or blender until smooth. Then add the other ingredients, including the rest of the yogurt.

• If you're going to go the machine route, might as well add the garlic, too.

• Mint is often used in tzadziki. If you can get fresh mint, chop a few leaves very finely and sprinkle them on top.

• If the yogurt is not very acidic, which is fairly common in U.S. yogurt, add ½ teaspoon of lemon juice.

CUCUMBER DIP (Tzadziki)

TECHNIQUE—Grating/mincing
BEST TOOLS—Cutting board and chef's knife
NICE TO HAVE—Food processor

Tzadziki in Greece is extremely thick because the yogurt there is very thick, particularly in Rhodes. Thirty miles across the water in Turkey, yogurt is so thin it dribbles. Our American yogurt can be thick as sour cream, but it takes overnight.

Serve your tzadziki with pita bread cut into wedges, as you'd cut a pizza.

Makes 3½ cups

4 cups plain yogurt
1 medium cucumber
1 tablespoon finely minced garlic
½ teaspoon dried dill
1 tablespoon lemon juice
Salt and pepper, to taste

DO THIS FIRST:

1. The day before serving, get out your biggest wire mesh strainer. If you don't have a big one, get out a colander.

2. Stack 2 sheets of paper towels, then lay them inside the strainer. Set the strainer across the rim of a bowl. If you're using a colander, put the colander in a wide bowl.

3. Empty the yogurt into the strainer. Put the whole arrangement in the refrigerator and let the yogurt drip all night.

DO THIS SECOND:

1. Next day, peel the cucumber with a vegetable peeler. Cut it in half lengthwise. Run a spoon down the centers to scoop out the seeds.

2. Grate the cucumber on the medium holes (shredding holes) of a box grater. Put it in a medium-size serving bowl.

3. Mince the garlic as finely as you can. Add it to the cucumber.

WRAPPING IT UP:

1. Throw away the thin liquid that drained out of the yogurt. Upturn the strainer over the cucumbers and let the thickened yogurt fall out. Peel off the paper towels and throw them away.

2. Measure and add the dill, lemon juice, salt, and pepper. Stir it up and take a taste. The dip should be sharp from garlic, yet cool from cucumber, and should have enough salt to bring all this out.

CHILE CON QUESO

TECHNIQUE — Sautéing
BEST COOKWARE — Wide non-stick skillet
BEST TOOLS — Chef's knife and cutting board
GREAT FOR SERVING — Crock pot

This may shock you, but real chile con queso isn't yellow. It's white, it's stringy, and the chiles are green. If you've been given the gift of a crock pot, now's the time to find it. Set it on low to keep the chile con queso warm for the whole party.

Serves 8

> 2 onions
> 2 teaspoons minced garlic (or scoop it from a jar)
> 1 fresh jalapeño chile
> 1½ pounds Monterey Jack cheese
> 3-ounce package cream cheese
> 3 7-ounce cans whole green chiles
> 4 tablespoons butter (½ stick)
> Salt and black pepper

DO THIS FIRST:

1. Peel the onions. Halve them through the poles, then chop the halves.

2. Mince the garlic, and add it to the onions.

3. Cut the stem off the jalapeño, then halve the jalapeño lengthwise. Flick out the seeds and throw them away. Mince the chile extremely small.

4. Cut the Monterey Jack and cream cheese into cubes about the size of gaming dice. Save the cheese on a plate.

5. Open the cans of chiles. Chop the chiles a little. The pieces don't have to be perfect or all the same size. Have all the ingredients near the stove.

DO THIS SECOND:

1. Get out a wide skillet. Put the butter in the skillet and set it over medium-high heat. When the butter is foamy, add the onions and garlic. Sauté until the onions are fairly limp and have barely turned gold, about 4 minutes.

2. Add the chiles and jalapeño. If the onions look like they're browning too fast, turn the heat down to medium. Keep sautéing about 3 minutes more.

3. Turn the heat to low. Add the cheeses a little at a time. Use a wooden spatula to stir them in, and don't stop stirring until all the cheese has melted.

WRAPPING IT UP:

1. Sprinkle the dip with salt and pepper.

2. Serve immediately with tortilla chips or other dippers.

• If the screen in your sieve isn't fine and you're afraid the cheese will fall through, line it with 2 wet paper towels before putting the cheese in.

• If you don't have a sieve, but you do have a colander, line it with 3 wet paper towels to cover the holes while letting liquid drain away.

• Okay, I confess. I've made this without the draining step. The spread is definitely looser, but not an embarrassment. If yours comes out more like dip than spread, serve it with chips.

• Ricotta cheese is made from the liquid waste that comes off other cheese as it's being made. Rather than let this "juice" (actually whey) go to waste, manufacturers re-cook it, acidify it, and turn it into ricotta, which literally means *to cook again*. Because this whey is skimmed from another cheese, it confuses us into thinking that all ricotta cheese is made with skim milk. Actually, ricotta cheese may come from the whey of cheese made from whole, low fat, *or* skim milk, and the milk may be from cows, sheep, or goats.

• A pinch of cayenne is what will stay on the tip of a pointy knife.

• Getting the spread cold will firm it up.

• To make this spread into a dip, thin it with 2 tablespoons of sour cream. It's powerful on bland dippers, such as celery, jicama, mushrooms, or cauliflower.

RICOTTA CRACKER SPREAD

BEST EQUIPMENT — Mixing bowl
BEST TOOL — A fine-mesh sieve
MUST HAVE — Cutting board and chef's knife
BEST UTENSILS — Wooden spoon and rubber spatula

It's amazing how this spread changes over a couple of days in the refrigerator. A pronounced garlic foreground becomes the background as the dip mellows and develops a milder flavor. Take note, this spread comes with almost no fat.

Makes about 2 cups

> 15-ounce container ricotta cheese
> 2 green onions
> 1 teaspoon minced garlic
> ½ teaspoon salt
> Generous black pepper
> Pinch of cayenne pepper
> 1 tablespoon lemon juice

DO THIS FIRST:

1. The day before serving, put the ricotta in the finest-mesh sieve you have. Balance the sieve over a bowl. Cover the whole apparatus with plastic wrap and put it in the refrigerator overnight. Extra liquid will drain out and leave the cheese nice and thick.

DO THIS SECOND:

1. Decide on a nice serving bowl slightly larger than the tub the ricotta came in.

2. Dump the ricotta from the sieve into a mixing bowl.

DO THIS THIRD:

1. Slice the green onions, then mince them as fine as you can. Add them to the bowl.

2. Mince the garlic really fine, and add it to the bowl.

3. Stir well with a wooden spoon, until all the ingredients are smoothly blended.

4. Add the salt, pepper, cayenne, and lemon juice. Keep mixing until the cheese is smooth and looks like it will spread on a cracker.

WRAPPING IT UP:

1. Use a rubber spatula to scrape the cheese out of the bowl into a serving bowl. Cover with plastic wrap and put it in the refrigerator for about 4 hours.

DEVILED EGGS

TECHNIQUE — Boiling
BEST COOKWARE — Medium-size pot
BEST EQUIPMENT — Smooth knife, a spoon

Here is the all-time disappearing act. There are never enough deviled eggs, no matter what mean things people say about eggs. With a little handwork, you're a star at your own party. When these eggs are being filled they're a little like cookie dough. Their numbers start shrinking while still in the presence of the person making them.

Makes 12

6 eggs
1 tablespoon lemon juice
½ teaspoon dry mustard
2 tablespoons mayonnaise (or more)
2 tablespoons melted butter
½ teaspoon salt
⅛ teaspoon cayenne

It's better with garnish: About 2 tablespoons minced fresh parsley

DO THIS FIRST:

1. Hard-cook the eggs: Place the eggs in a pot just large enough to hold them in a single layer. Add cold water to cover the eggs by 1 inch.

2. Cover; bring to a boil over high heat.

3. When it reaches a boil, turn off the heat. Let the eggs stand in the hot water, lid on, 15 to 17 minutes. Have a colander ready in your clean sink.

4. Pour the eggs into the colander; run cold water over them until they are cool to the touch.

5. To peel, roll each egg on a countertop until the surface is completely crackled. Remove the shells.

DO THIS SECOND:

1. Slice the eggs in half lengthwise. Flick out the yolks into a bowl. Set the whites on a platter.

2. Mash the yolks with the lemon juice. Add the remaining ingredients and stir and mash with a fork until smooth. Add more mayonnaise if you like the filling mushier.

WRAPPING IT UP:

1. Spoon the yolk filling into the whites, mounding it high.

2. Cover the platter with plastic wrap and put it in the refrigerator until you are ready to serve.

3. Just before serving, sprinkle all over with parsley.

- Use regular or light beer.

- Don't waste expensive beer for this boiling situation. If it's strong, it will only get stronger as it cooks. Use your money to buy a micro-brewed beer to drink when you eat the shrimp.

- The longer beer cooks, the stronger it gets.

- Depending on the BTUs of your stove, the liquid may or may not return to a full boil—although this is desirable.

- Shrimp cooked with the shells on won't curl as much as peeled shrimp.

SOUSED SHRIMP COCKTAIL

TECHNIQUE—Boiling
BEST COOKWARE—Big pot with a lid, such as a Dutch oven
BEST EQUIPMENT—Colander, big bowl

There's just a hint of beer flavor in these shrimp. They boil with shells on to keep them from curling and to keep as much flavor as possible on them while they chill.

Serves 8
   3 cans beer
   1 onion
   6 cloves garlic
   1 lemon
   3 bay leaves
   1 tablespoon pickling spice
   2 pounds shrimp (leave the shells on)

DO THIS FIRST:

1. Open the beer, pour it in a large pot, such as a Dutch oven, and let it stand while you get the rest of the ingredients together. Have the pot near your cutting board.

DO THIS SECOND:

1. Peel the onion, cut it in half through the poles, then cut the halves into slices about ½ inch thick. Put the slices in the big pot.

2. Smash the garlic cloves on the countertop using the bottom of a jar, or whack them with the side of the blade of a big knife. Peel off the papery skin, then add the crushed cloves—you don't have to chop them—to the pot.

3. Slice the lemon into about 6 rounds. Add the slices to the pot.

4. Add the bay leaves. Measure and add the pickling spice. It's okay if the beer is still foamy.

DO THIS THIRD:

1. Take the pot to the stove. Cover the pot, turn the heat to high, and bring the liquid to a boil. You'll see steam escaping from the lid when boiling is going on inside the pot.

2. Meanwhile, put the shrimp in a colander. Rinse under running water until the water is clear.

3. When the liquid boils, uncover the pot and add the shrimp. Keeping the heat high, cook about 4 minutes. Give it a few stirs. The shrimp will turn pink.

4. Return the colander to the sink, but set it inside a big bowl to catch the cooking liquid.

DO THIS FOURTH:

1. Turn off the heat. Take the pot over to the sink and pour the shrimp into the colander. Let the cooking liquid seep down into the bowl. Put the liquid on the countertop to cool.

2. When the cooking liquid is cool, put the shrimp back in it.

WRAPPING IT UP:

1. Cover the bowl of shrimp with plastic wrap. Refrigerate. The Soused Shrimp will take on more flavor overnight. (You can keep them up to three days.)

2. To serve, pour off some of the liquid. Either peel the shrimp and return them to the liquid or let your guests peel their own. Serve cold.

• The smaller the mush-rooms, the better. They're slippery little devils, and they're just easier to eat — and stab with a toothpick — if they're small. If you can't find small ones packaged for you, you'll have to dig into the bulk mushrooms and find them yourself.

• When you add the mushrooms to the boiling water, they'll bob instead of sinking.

• Instead of lemon juice, any vinegar will work very nicely. Try apple cider vine-gar, or white wine vinegar. The color of red wine vine-gar isn't very complimentary to the grayish mushrooms.

MARINATED MUSHROOMS

TECHNIQUE — Boiling
BEST COOKWARE — Dutch oven
BEST EQUIPMENT — Cutting board and chef's knife, colander
BEST SERVING WARE — Crockery bowl, medium-size souffle dish, shallow bowl with flared sides

This recipe goes together quickly and easily. You have only two ingredients to chop. The dressing is so good that you can serve the mushrooms alongside a salad and let people spoon some of the mushrooms' dressing over their greens.

Makes 3 to 4 cups

1 to 1½ pounds small white mushrooms
1 tablespoon plus ½ teaspoon salt
2 teaspoons finely minced garlic (or scoop it from a jar)
¼ cup fresh chopped parsley
¼ cup lemon juice or vinegar
½ cup olive oil

DO THIS FIRST:

1. Fill a big pot or Dutch oven two-thirds full of water. Put it on the stove over high heat, covered, and bring it to a boil.

2. Have a colander ready in your clean sink.

DO THIS SECOND:

1. Meanwhile, rinse the mushrooms. If the stems have blackened ends, use a paring knife to cut them off.

2. When the water boils, add 1 tablespoon of salt. Then add all the mushrooms. Cook over high heat for 3 minutes, uncovered.

3. Take the pot over to the sink. Use potholders! Pour the mushrooms into the colander.

DO THIS THIRD:

1. Get out a mixing bowl. Mince the garlic as finely as you can and put it in the bowl.

2. Chop the parsley as finely as you can and add it to the garlic.

3. Measure the lemon juice, oil, and remaining salt directly into the bowl.

WRAPPING IT UP:

1. Add the mushrooms. Stir with a big spoon.

2. Serve in a shallow bowl with toothpicks or forks.

MAKE-AHEAD OPTIONS:

1. You can make these mushrooms 2 hours before you'll serve them without refrigerating. Stir them now and then, though.

2. If it's going to be more than 2 hours, cover the bowl with plastic wrap and set it in the refrigerator. Take it out about 15 minutes before serving to give the olive oil time to turn back into a liquid.

THINGS ON TOOTHPICKS

The toothpick is an entertaining marvel that obviates the need for forks and the washing that those forks would require later. What goes, and what does not go, on a toothpick depends on what stays on a toothpick. The texture of asparagus makes it too slippery for toothpicks. But most food, if cut small enough, will adhere. You can set out toothpicks in their own container, or stick a toothpick into each cube of cheese or each piece of melon.

You can serve an entire fruit salad without plates or bowls if you have toothpicks nearby. Because of the small mouthfuls, guests will eat less of food on toothpicks than if the same food were served on plates.

Caterer's trick: Next to the toothpicks set out a cup or little bowl with one discarded toothpick. This cues your guests that this is where used toothpicks go, not on the floor.

THINGS YOU SERVE ON OR WITH TOOTHPICKS:

Cubes of cheese
Pitted olives
Peeled shrimp
Small scallops
Marinated pearl onions
Marinated mushrooms
Cherry tomatoes, if
   they're small
Pieces of smoked fish
Cubes of meat
Dried fruit
Fresh fruit

I have a friend who can walk into a house and find the cheese and crackers. The best cracker for cheese is so respectfully uninteresting that it allows you to taste the cheese instead of any herb, garlic, spice, seed, salt, or grain in the cracker. The most inconspicuous crackers are plain and thin, such as Carr's water crackers, matzo, or lavosh.

OLIVES, NUTS, AND CHEESE

Even if guests catch you by surprise, you'll be prepared if you have a back-up supply of olives, nuts, and cheese.

Olives can be as ordinary as plain green or plain black. Or you can have pimiento-stuffed, or exotic small black Nicoise or Kalamata olives, or garlic-flavored green olives from California. Put another small dish near the dish of olives. Eat an olive yourself, then deliberately leave the pit in the second dish. Guests will have no question about what to do with their pits.

Nuts come from all over the world and can be as plain or as exotic as olives. Whole almonds, skins on, are a delicacy. So are fresh pecans from Texas, intact walnut halves, and roasted but unsalted pistachios that haven't been dyed red. If the nuts have shells, leave a side dish for the debris. Rather than think of shelling nuts as an annoyance, people like fidgeting with them. They'll crack and peel and pop nuts in their mouths as long as the supply lasts. For a rare treat, shelled macadamias or whole cashews are rich and filling. Not a single nut mentioned is worth serving if it isn't fresh.

Firm **cheeses** last a number of months in the refrigerator if they're wrapped well. High-quality Swiss (from Switzerland) and various hard mountain cheeses last the longest and are the handiest in a pinch. The same is true for Italian or Argentinian Parmesans, and the one or two good American Parmesans. Present hard cheeses on a wooden cutting board, or a nice plate, with a scraping spatula so people can peel off thin slices. Softer cheeses—Brie, Camembert, the blues, and goat cheeses—perish more quickly and are less likely to bail you out just when you need something if you've kept them too long.

7

SALAD

For meal-size salads see Greek Salad (page 210) and Seven-Layer Salad (page 207)

SALAD KNOWLEDGE

HOW MUCH WILL YOU NEED?

Figure on a good handful of greens per person (after it's washed and torn).

Butter, Boston, or Bibb
1 large, loose head serves 4 or 5
Romaine
1 large head serves 6 to 8
Iceberg
1 large, dense head serves 8 to 10

DRESSING YOUR SALAD

Every salad has its own schedule for when it's time to get dressed. Some salads are pre-mixed, such as slaws and other salads that are more marinated than coated with dressing. Salads with fresh greens you went to the trouble to wash and spin-dry would go limp and die with such treatment. For these, save the dressing for when the salad is served. If you're quick, you can toss the salad with the dressing before serving it, but that means your idea of how much dressing is right comes to the table whether people want dressing or not, or wish you'd been more generous with it (that would be me). It's often better to let guests dress their own. If you've got greens on a buffet, you can leave a little pitcher of dressing next to it so people can pour on as much or as little they prefer—or none.

HOMEMADE CROUTONS

TECHNIQUE: Sautéing
BEST EQUIPMENT: Cutting board and chef's knife

Croutons seem special, probably because they've got a French name. Just keep in mind that they started their existence long ago as left-over bread, so you don't have to make this into a big deal. Croutons don't have to be perfect and they don't have to be so hard that they're annoying to chew.

Makes about 3 cups

> 4 or 5 slices of bread
> 2 tablespoons butter

DO THIS FIRST:

1. Cut the crusts off most any type of bread — white, sourdough, whole wheat, even rye bread. Cut the bread into cubes about the size of gaming dice.

DO THIS SECOND:

1. Melt the butter in a skillet over medium heat. Sauté the bread in the hot butter. Keep tossing the cubes around the pan until they are coated with butter, the skillet goes dry, and the bread gets toasted. This can take 5 or 6 minutes.

2. You can use the croutons now. They'll firm up a little as they cool.

LET'S TALK

• For crisper croutons, spread the sautéed croutons on a big piece of aluminum foil. Bake them about 15 minutes in a preheated 300°F oven. Truthfully, they're more buttery without this added step.

• You can multiply this recipe to fit the number of slices of bread you have.

• Store extra croutons in an airtight container in the refrigerator.

• You can cover the salad with plastic wrap and keep it in the refrigerator until ready to serve. It won't last too long because salt eventually breaks down the tomatoes and makes them mushy.

• If you chill the salad, the oil will solidify slightly. Take it out of the refrigerator about 15 minutes before serving, to allow time for the oil to come to room temperature.

• If the cherry tomatoes at your store are bigger than ¾ inch in diameter, cut them in half. They'll hold more marinade, and be easier to eat.

• If the tomatoes are small enough to remain whole, they'll last overnight in the refrigerator. If cut in half, they'll last about 2 hours before they start to get mushy.

• You can recognize basil in the produce department by its Kelly-green leaves that are rather large and floppy, and a very sweet, strong scent.

• When you roll the basil into a log, roll it lengthwise.

• The vinegar can be plain, cider, sherry, red wine, or balsamic.

CHERRY TOMATO SALAD

BEST EQUIPMENT—Cutting board and chef's knife
BEST SERVING WARE—Medium-size glass bowl

Not even a tomato to cut! This can be a salad, or a salad-appetizer served with toothpicks.

Serves 6

> 2 baskets (pint-size) cherry tomatoes
> 1 small red onion
> 1 tablespoon minced garlic
> 6 leaves fresh basil
> ½ teaspoon salt, to start with
> Lots of black pepper
> 2 tablespoons vinegar
> ⅓ cup olive oil

DO THIS FIRST:

1. Decide on a great-looking serving bowl. Glass would be perfect for this.

2. Take the caps off all the tomatoes. Put the tomatoes back into the pint baskets, then rinse them well under running water.

3. Empty the baskets onto paper towels and get the tomatoes as dry as is reasonable.

DO THIS SECOND:

1. Put the tomatoes in a mixing bowl.

2. Peel the onion. Halve it, then cut it into pieces about the size of gaming dice. They don't have to be perfect. Add to the tomatoes.

3. Mince the garlic very fine, or scoop it from a jar. Add it to the tomatoes.

4. Roll up the basil leaves into a tight log and cut the log into thin slices to make tiny basil threads. Add to the tomatoes. *Clean up all the debris from the cutting board, countertop, and knife.*

WRAPPING IT UP:

1. Sprinkle the tomatoes with the salt, pepper, vinegar, and oil.

2. Turn them over a few times with a large spoon. Transfer the salad to the serving bowl.

SIMPLE SALAD WITH WALNUTS

BEST EQUIPMENT—Salad spinner, jar with a lid

This salad got its name because it's simple to make and a simple pleasure to serve and eat. If you use Sugared Nuts instead of plain nuts, just about everyone at the table will want the recipe. I'm not kidding.

Serves 6 to 8

> 1 head Romaine (about 1 pound)
> ¾ cup Sugared Nuts (page 51) or plain walnut halves
>
> *Vinaigrette*
> ¼ cup red wine vinegar
> 1 teaspoon salt
> Ground black pepper, to taste
> 1 cup olive oil or vegetable oil

DO THIS FIRST:

1. Get out a big bowl and your salad spinner.

2. Wash the lettuce leaf by leaf.

3. Tear the leaves into 1-inch pieces. Dry all the leaves in a salad spinner or by rolling them in a cloth kitchen towel.

4. Put the lettuce into the bowl. Sprinkle with nuts.

DO THIS SECOND:

1. Measure all the vinaigrette ingredients except the oil into a jar or a bowl.

2. Cover the jar and shake, or whisk if using a bowl. You don't have to shake hard.

3. Pour in the oil. Shake or whisk again. Taste to see if the vinaigrette needs more salt or pepper.

WRAPPING IT UP:

1. Take the bowl and vinaigrette to the table.

MAKE-AHEAD OPTION:

1. Cover the salad with plastic wrap and chill well.

2. Make the dressing and chill.

• A simple salad with walnuts becomes a spectacular simple salad if the vinaigrette uses half vegetable and half walnut oil.

• Extras can make a Simple Salad not as simple, but still uncomplicated. Try adding:

1 small red onion, peeled and cut in very thin slices

About 6 strips of cooked bacon, crumbled or chopped

2 to 3 green onions, white and green parts, sliced

¼ cup whole leaves of flat Italian parsley

Slices of radish

• You can make this salad with a mixture of lettuces—Romaine, Butter (Bibb or Boston), Leaf, and/or Red Leaf.

• You can make the vinaigrette with lemon juice instead of vinegar.

CAESAR SALAD

BEST EQUIPMENT—Salad spinner
BEST TOOLS—Cutting board and chef's knife,

Ah, the great Caesar, ruler of all the salad empire. From its seat of power—that would be Tijuana, Mexico, where a man named Caesar Cardini invented Caesar salad at his restaurant—the Caesar has inspired a devoted following. Many are your friends, who upon coming to your house will always appreciate that you made this for them. You can mix some of the dressing into the salad for your guests, but it's never enough. Have extra dressing in a pitcher on the table.

Serves 8

> 2 teaspoons minced garlic
> 1 tablespoon anchovy paste
> 1 egg
> ¼ cup lemon juice
> Dash of Tabasco
> 1 tablespoon Worcestershire sauce
> ⅔ cup olive oil
> ⅔ cup vegetable oil
> ½ cup freshly grated Parmesan cheese
> 1 head Romaine lettuce, limp outer leaves
>   removed

DO THIS FIRST:

1. Peel and mince the garlic. Put it in a medium-size mixing bowl.

2. Add the anchovy paste and mash it into the garlic.

3. Crack the egg into the bowl.

4. Pour the lemon juice, Tabasco, and Worcestershire into the bowl. Use a whisk or fork to scramble all the ingredients until they're blended and there is no trace of clear egg white floating around in the bowl.

DO THIS SECOND:

1. Measure the oils and combine them in a measuring cup (with a pour spout). Pour one-third of the oil into the egg mixture. Whisk hard to get these two components blended.

2. Add another portion of oil. Again, whisk hard.

3. Add the rest of the oil and whisk hard. If all has gone well, the dressing should be smooth.

4. Stir in the Parmesan. You will have about 2 cups of dressing. Keep it in the refrigerator until you're ready to serve the salad.

DO THIS THIRD:

1. Wash the inner leaves of the Romaine, leaf by leaf under running water.

2. Tear the leaves into bite-size squares. As you go, put the torn lettuce in a salad spinner. Spin it dry.

3. Place the lettuce in a large bowl.

WRAPPING IT UP:

1. When it's time to serve, take the dressing out of the refrigerator and give it a couple of stirs.

2. Spoon enough dressing onto the Romaine to coat the leaves. The leftover dressing ought to come to the table for those friends who like a heavier touch of Caesar.

LET'S TALK

• About using raw eggs, here's some comfort. The University of California extension says raw eggs are safe if the shells are clean and unbroken. The acid contributed by the lemon juice in this dressing, plus cold temperature, are safeguards against the growth of bacteria. Even so, use the dressing quickly and keep it cold until you serve it.

• One tablespoon of anchovy paste equals about 2 anchovy filets. If you're using these, mash them on your cutting board. Press hard on the tines of a fork and pull the fork back and forth over the anchovies.

• A combination of olive oil and vegetable oil makes a lighter base for what will become a heavy, thick dressing once the Parmesan goes in.

• Croutons (page 123) were part of the original Caesar. If you've got 2 cups, add them to the Romaine.

BLUE CHEESE COLE SLAW

• Blue cheese is streaked with blue veins that carry the *Penicillium roquefortii* mold. You'll have a pretty good example of blue cheese if you use Saga Blue, Danish Blue, English Stilton, or Italian Gorgonzola. Roquefort is a blue cheese specific to the caves of Roquefort, France. The most prestigious American blue cheese is Maytag.

• Some blue cheeses are crumbly; some are creamy. Either consistency can be mashed into this dressing.

• The vinegar can be plain white, cider vinegar, or, if you're in an adventurous mood, Japanese rice vinegar, which has a lighter bite. Red wine vinegar will turn the slaw an unappetizing gray.

• The background of the dressing will be creamy and smooth around small lumps of blue cheese. These lumps are desirable. Leave them alone.

• If one small head of cabbage weighing about 2 pounds is shredded, it will fill an 8-cup bowl. However, once doused with dressing, the cabbage compacts to about one-fourth the undressed volume.

• A head of cabbage approaching three pounds will present some problems. The raw, sliced volume is enormous, and you'll need a bowl that holds 12 cups-plus. Also, the yield from the dressing recipe won't coat so much cabbage generously.

TECHNIQUE—Cutting/mixing
BEST EQUIPMENT—Chef's knife and cutting board
GOOD TO HAVE—Very large mixing bowl
BEST TOOLS—Measuring cups and spoons

As with many slaw recipes, you'll notice increased deliciousness after this spends at least a night in the refrigerator. It will continue to improve for two to three days after that. This is the only reason you need to categorize this recipe as a make-ahead.

Serves 12

> 1 small onion
> 1 cup crumbled blue cheese (3 to 4 ounces)
> 1 cup mayonnaise
> ½ cup vinegar
> 2 tablespoons honey
> 1 teaspoon salt
> ½ teaspoon white pepper
> 1 head green cabbage (small to medium)

DO THIS FIRST:

1. Get out a medium size bowl, a fork, and a large spoon, such as a soup spoon.

2. Peel the onion and cut it in half through the poles. Chop it, then mince it as finely as you can, until it packs nicely into a ½-cup measuring cup. Put the onion into the bowl.

3. Crumble the blue cheese with your fingers. Measure it in a 1-cup measuring cup, then add it to the onion.

DO THIS SECOND:

1. Measure the mayonnaise and add it to the bowl. Measure and add the vinegar, honey, salt, and pepper.

2. Mix with the fork until the dressing is creamy, although it will—and should—have lumps. If the lumps are big, use the back of the spoon to mash larger lumps of cheese into submission.

DO THIS THIRD:

1. Get out a very large mixing bowl.

2. Cut the head of cabbage into quarters. At the point of each wedge, decide where the core ends and the leaves begin. At this juncture, cut off the cores and throw them away.

3. Hold a wedge in place on the cutting board so a flat side is down. Now cut across the wedge to make ⅛-inch-wide strips, or just make the slices as thin as you can. Place all the shredded cabbage in the mixing bowl.

WRAPPING IT UP:

1. Pour the blue cheese dressing over the cabbage. Mix it with your hands or with two big spoons until the dressing and the cabbage are mixed.

2. Leave the slaw on the counter while you clean up. In about 20 minutes, it will have compressed by one-third of its original volume.

3. Cover the cole slaw with plastic wrap and put it in the refrigerator. In 30 minutes or so, give the slaw a good mixing. If chilled overnight, it will continue to compress to about one-fourth its original volume.

• As you begin to cut the cabbage, floppy leaves on the outside will fall off on their own. Throw them away.

• The finer you slice the cabbage, the easier a time you'll have mixing the slaw. Thinly sliced cabbage will also compress more quickly.

• Slaw is easier to eat if its cabbage is cut thin.

• You can't really overdo the initial mixing of the cabbage with the dressing. The more you mix, the faster the cabbage will compact. You may also realize that your hands are the best mixing machine for this amount of cabbage.

• After a few hours, or the next day, you'll probably want to transfer the slaw to a smaller bowl.

• Cabbage is an all-year item, but it's sweet and crunchy in early spring and late fall. The best cabbage for slaw is common green cabbage. If you see a flat, enormous cabbage named Holland or Dutch cabbage, give it a try in slaw; it's got less bite. Savoy cabbage, the celadon-colored cabbage with crinkly leaves, makes an impressive slaw, too.

• Regardless of the type of cabbage, the core is uncooperative in slaw-making. I suspect it is at the origin of the phrase "hard-core." It refuses to wilt when the leaves do. It's also bitter, so get rid of it.

SPINACH SALAD WITH HAM, EGGS, AND MUSTARD DRESSING

BEST EQUIPMENT—Salad spinner, cutting board, chef's knife

HANDIEST TOOLS—Egg slicer, glass jar (or plastic container) with a lid

Only the chore of washing and drying spinach is between you and this great salad. Friends who ate this salad gave me the most astonishing compliment: "This tastes like a salad in a restaurant!" Such are the comparisons of approval. It's good with spicy soups, such as Texas Crowd Chili (page 200), or soup with smokiness, such as Beer-Cheese Soup (page 150).

Serves 6

> 1 bunch fresh spinach (1 pound)
> ¼ cup vinegar (red wine vinegar would be best)
> 1 tablespoon Dijon mustard
> ½ teaspoon salt
> Black pepper, to taste
> ½ cup good olive oil
> 4-ounce piece smoked ham
> 4 hard-cooked eggs, peeled
> 1 small red onion

DO THIS FIRST:

1. Fill one side of your double sink with cold water, or use a big bowl in your single sink. Soak the spinach about 15 minutes. The leaves will float and sand will sink to the bottom.

DO THIS SECOND:

1. Meanwhile, make the dressing. Measure the vinegar, mustard, salt, and pepper into a jar. Cover and shake until smooth and creamy.

2. Add the olive oil. Cover and shake again until extremely well blended. Taste. It might need salt, pepper, or more mustard, all of which are entirely up to you.

DO THIS THIRD:

1. Lift the spinach out of the water into a bowl, or into the other side of the sink. Drain the water, then wash the spinach leaf by leaf under running water. As you go, tear off ungainly stems. Tear big leaves into medium pieces.

2. Spin the leaves dry in a salad spinner, in batches. Transfer each batch from the spinner directly to a salad bowl. Give the spinach a good fluff with your hands.

DO THIS FOURTH:

1. Cut the ham into slivers about 2 inches long. Sprinkle them over the spinach.

2. Slice the eggs in an egg slicer. Sprinkle over the spinach.

3. Peel the onion. Slice it into really thin rings. Sprinkle over the spinach.

WRAPPING IT UP:

1. Bring the salad to the table. In front of your awed guests, douse it with dressing, and lift and toss to coat the salad well before serving.

- The ham can be purchased a little piece at a time from a deli counter in your supermarket, or shrink-wrapped in the meat case. A domestic Black Forest-type ham is particularly wonderful. If you can't find smoky ham, baked ham will be fine.

- Or, forget the ham and instead fry 4 slices of bacon because, as the world knows, bacon and spinach were made for each other. Crumble the bacon over the salad.

- If you don't have one of those egg slicers constructed like a press with taut wires, chop the eggs in fairly large, irregular pieces and sprinkle them on the salad.

TABOULI

BEST EQUIPMENT—Chef's knife and cutting board, serrated knife
BEST COOKWARE—Tea kettle

Your trade-off for not having to actually cook anything in this recipe is mincing and dicing in what I estimate will be a 30-minute relationship with a good knife and a cutting board. The cutting need not be perfect. But remember, the smaller the pieces of parsley and mint, the more surface areas will be available to contribute flavor to the dish. Then, all that's left is mixing and tasting. It should taste refreshing and lemony.

Tabouli traditionally is served on leaves of Romaine lettuce. This is completely up to you. I like it as a side dish and find if I put it in a pretty bowl, I don't need too much garnish.

Serves 6

2 cups boiling water
1 cup bulghur (cracked wheat)
2 large tomatoes
3 entire green onions
1½ tablespoons minced garlic
⅓ cup chopped fresh parsley
¼ cup chopped fresh mint
½ cup lemon juice
1 teaspoon salt
¼ teaspoon black pepper, or more to taste

DO THIS FIRST:

1. Pour 2 cups water into a tea kettle. Bring it to a boil over high heat.

2. Put the raw bulghur in a largish bowl. Pour the boiling water over the bulghur. Let sit 1 hour. While the bulghur plumps, prepare the remaining ingredients.

DO THIS SECOND:

1. To seed the tomatoes, halve them at the equator with a serrated knife, then squeeze the halves, flicking out the seeds into the garbage. Dice the tomatoes and put them in a big mixing bowl.

2. Cut off the hairy roots of the green onions. Stack the onions on your cutting board and slice them thinly all the way down—from white end to green end. Add them to the bowl.

3. Mince the garlic and add it. (*Wash your cutting board and knife.*) Chop the parsley and mint and add them to the bowl.

WRAPPING IT UP:

1. Drain the bulghur by squeezing it in small amounts between your palms. Literally wring it out as dry as you can. Add it to the tomatoes.

2. Add the lemon juice, salt, and pepper. Mix and chill until very cold.

• Italian flat-leaf parsley asserts bigger parsley flavor. If you cannot find flat-leaf parsley, curly parsley will be okay.

• It's okay if the minced parsley is a little stemmy. Cut away woody, long stems, but for the most part, don't spend a lot of time removing sprigs from stems. The stems add flavor, but they must be cut very small.

• Mint is easy to grow. Through no care on your part, it takes over your yard. If you grow exotic mint, bill your dish as Spearmint Tabouli! Peppermint Tabouli!

• Taste the tabouli after you add the salt. It may need more. Because of the blandness of the bulghur, and the salt-needy tomatoes, tabouli benefits from salt. How much is up to you.

• Tomatoes are a must
for this salad, but the other
ingredients are less important. If you've got everything
but the bell pepper, you can
still make this salad. The
same is true if you're out of
cucumber, or out of green
onions.

• Green onions come in
varying sizes. If they're
skinny, use 4. If they're mon-
sters, use 2.

• This salad makes a
good leftover.

SIMPLE ISRAELI DICED SALAD

BEST EQUIPMENT—Chef's knife and cutting board

When kibbutzniks eat salad, a phenomenon of sorts occurs. The tomatoes, bell pepper, onion . . . whatever . . . must be diced. When all cut, the salad resembles a fresh salsa.

Serves 6

2 medium tomatoes
1 cucumber
3 green onions
1 bell pepper
1 teaspoon minced garlic
2 tablespoons lemon juice
2 tablespoons olive oil
1 teaspoon salt
¼ teaspoon black pepper

DO THIS FIRST:

1. Halve the tomatoes across the equator. Squeeze each half over the garbage can and flick out the seeds. Dice the tomatoes and put them in a big mixing bowl.

2. Wash the cucumber. Slice it in half length-wise. Scoop out the seeds with a small spoon by running it down the seed bed. Throw the seeds away, then dice the cucumber. Add it to the bowl.

3. Cut off the hairy roots from the green onions. Stack the onions on your cutting board and slice them all the way down until most of the green ends are sliced, too. Put them in the bowl.

4. Slice the bell pepper just to the side of the core. Cut two side pieces from the core, then the remaining piece. Discard the core and seeds. Cut the pepper into thin strips, then stack the strips on your cutting board and cut across them to form diced pieces. Add to the bowl.

5. Mince the garlic and add it to the bowl.

DO THIS SECOND:

1. Measure the remaining ingredients into the bowl.

WRAPPING IT UP:

1. Mix with a spoon or your hands. Eat as a salad or side dish, or with pita bread.

• If you don't have a microwave oven, cook the corn like this: Have a colander ready in your clean sink. Measure 3 cups of water into a big pot and set it on the stove. Cover the pot, turn the heat to high, and bring the water to a boil. When the water boils hard, add the corn. Keep the heat high and boil the kernels 45 seconds if fresh, 1½ minutes if frozen. (The water may not return to a boil). Take the pot over to the sink and pour everything into the colander. Use potholders! Let the corn drain.

• The vinegar can be plain, apple cider, or white wine vinegar. Red vinegar will dull the color of this bright salad.

• Olive oil will taste good with all these spices and herbs, but a neutral vegetable oil is fine, too.

• Even if you're using fresh corn, cook it slightly. A few bites of fresh raw sweet summer corn is mighty tasty, but too much wreaks havoc on our digestive tracts.

• Jars of pimientos are usually tucked into a grocery store near the olives.

• Celery seeds and dry mustard are both available in the spices department.

• A little minced garlic wouldn't hurt this salad. Give it 1 teaspoon.

• While we're on the subject of extras, mince half a fresh, seeded jalapeño pepper and add it, too. Whoo-ee!

CORN SALAD

TECHNIQUE — Boiling
BEST TOOL — Small sharp paring knife
BEST EQUIPMENT — Big mixing bowl

Surely there's more to do with fresh corn than steam, boil, or grill the cobs. When corn is selling for something like seven ears for $1, you can afford to take the kernels off the cob and make a bright yellow salad. This salad is piquant, so it straddles that enigmatic fence between salad and relish. You can make it many days ahead, and serve it cold or at room temperature. Did someone say picnic?

Serves 6

> 5 or 6 ears fresh corn, or 3 cups frozen corn kernels
> 1 small red onion
> 4-ounce jar chopped pimientos
> 1 tablespoon brown sugar
> ½ teaspoon celery seeds
> ¼ teaspoon dry (powdered) mustard
> ½ teaspoon salt
> Generous ground black pepper
> 3 tablespoons vinegar
> 2 tablespoons olive oil

DO THIS FIRST:

1. Get out a big mixing bowl. Cut the kernels off the cobs. Put them in the bowl.

2. Add ½ cup water to the corn. Cover with plastic wrap and microwave on High for 45 seconds if the corn is fresh, 1½ minutes if it's frozen.

3. Put a colander in your clean sink. When the microwave buzzer goes off, pour the corn into the colander. Give it a few shakes to get rid of the excess water.

DO THIS SECOND:

1. Put the drained corn back into the mixing bowl. Mince the onion. You should have about ½ cup. Add it to the bowl. Drain the pimientos and add them to the bowl.

WRAPPING IT UP:

1. Add the rest of the ingredients. Mix with a spoon. Cover and put in the refrigerator. It will keep for 1 week.

HOW TO CUT CORN OFF THE COB: Tear off the green husks and silky threads. Hold a cob upright inside a big bowl. Poise a paring knife on top of the cob. Find the "sweet" spot between the kernels and the cob, and glide the knife down the cob to free the kernels. They will fall into the bowl.

NEW POTATO SALAD

TECHNIQUE — Boiling
BEST COOKWARE — Medium pot
BEST EQUIPMENT — Chef's knife, cutting board, colander

Little red potatoes we often call new potatoes are tender and sweet. Because of their high starch content they slice nicely after cooking. You can mix the mayonnaise while the potatoes cool, which enters this recipe in the quick-and-easy category.

Serves 6 to 8

> 2 pounds small new potatoes
> 1 teaspoon minced garlic
> ½ cup mayonnaise
> ½ teaspoon Dijon mustard, from a jar
> 1 tablespoon lemon juice
> 1 tablespoon dried dill weed
> ½ teaspoon salt, to start
> Ground black pepper

DO THIS FIRST:

1. Wash the potatoes in cold water. You don't have to peel them. Put them in a medium saucepan. Add enough water to cover the potatoes by 1 inch.

2. Put the pot over high heat, covered. When you see steam escaping from under the lid, turn the heat down to medium and cook the potatoes, cover on, about 12 to 15 minutes. A knife should be able to glide into the flesh. Meanwhile, put a colander in the sink.

3. Take the pot to the sink and pour the potatoes into the colander. Cool them until you can touch them.

DO THIS SECOND:

1. While the potatoes cool, get out a big mixing bowl. Mince the garlic and put it in the bowl.

2. Measure and add the rest of the ingredients.

3. Now cut the potatoes into ¼-inch-thick slices. Add them to the bowl.

WRAPPING IT UP:

1. Mix the potatoes into the dressing with your hands, unless you can be extra-gentle using a rubber spatula. Try to keep the potato slices intact.

2. Taste. Do you think it has enough salt? Cover with plastic wrap and chill until very cold.

• The green herb can be parsley, dill, basil, fennel, or tarragon.

• New potatoes range in size from as small as marbles to as big as tennis balls. Somewhere in the mid-size is best. You'll get slices from them just right for a mouthful.

• This recipe needs mayonnaise, not salad "dressing" (such as Miracle Whip). Everyone knows I love both, so I'm not playing favorites. It's just that salad dressing is a little too sweet for the effect I'm going for here.

• If you don't have a fresh lemon to squeeze, use lemon juice from a bottle.

• The potato slices are delicate and easily wounded. Just this once try mixing with your hands. It's very satisfying. You can literally feel how evenly the potatoes and dressing are mixing. Look, you were going to wash a mixing spoon if you'd used it, so why not just wash your hands?

CHINESE CHICKEN SALAD

TECHNIQUE—Mixing
BEST EQUIPMENT—Big salad bowl
BEST TOOLS—Chef's knife and cutting board
HANDY TO HAVE—Jar with a lid, salad spinner

Just one look at the ingredients and you know you have to go to the store. That is, unless you happen to stock your cupboards with pickled ginger and wonton wrappers. I am married to a Chinese chef and my cupboards don't have some of these ingredients either. When we make Chinese chicken salad at home, we don't mess around. We go to the store for the ingredients so we can make this the right way. We're especially intent on buying wonton wrappers so we can have our fill of homemade crispy noodles. What appears to be a long list of ingredients is nothing more than a tablespoon of this...a tablespoon of that. I think if you make this salad once you'll fall in love with it. It's a lunch in itself.

Serves 8

Dressing
2-ounce chunk fresh ginger
⅓ cup vinegar
⅓ cup sugar
1 tablespoon sesame oil
1 tablespoon soy sauce
1 tablespoon hoisin sauce or plum sauce
2 tablespoons water
2 tablespoons crushed peanuts (or walnuts or almonds)
Few sprinkles white pepper

Salad
1 head iceberg lettuce
2 cups chicken chunks—from stir-fried, baked, roasted, boiled, or broiled chicken
Crispy fried wonton strips (recipe follows) or canned crispy fried noodles
Fruits, such as raisins, pineapple chunks, mandarin orange sections, slices of pear or Asian pear

---

LET'S TALK

• Instead of heating the ginger in the sugar and vinegar, you can use 4 tablespoons of white pickled ginger, found in Asian stores. White pickled ginger is the secret ingredient, the one you don't see in make-believe recipes for Chinese chicken salad.

• Sesame oil, hoisin sauce, plum sauce, and soy sauce are easily located in any supermarket.

• Iceberg lettuce is revered in Hong Kong. It's used to line steamer baskets and clay pots. The firmest leaves are saved to become the lettuce cups to hold a famous appetizer of chopped squab.

• Fresh assorted lettuces, such as romaine, butter, or curly give this salad a modern touch. But do include some iceberg for crunch and a touch of sweetness.

• Another way to measure the chicken is to figure on 2 ounces per person.

• Chunks of turkey make a wonderful topping. I have seen for myself a turkey in China.

DO THIS FIRST:

1. Peel the ginger, then mince it as finely as you can. You should have about ¼ cup—it doesn't have to be exact.

2. Put the vinegar and sugar in a small pot. Bring it to a boil, uncovered, and boil 1 minute. Add the ginger and boil 1 minute more. Take off the heat.

3. Pour the mixture into a mixing bowl. Add the rest of the dressing ingredients. You'll have about ¾ cup.

DO THIS SECOND:

1. Wash the lettuce, tear it into bite-size squares, and spin it dry in a salad spinner.

WRAPPING IT UP:

1. Toss the lettuce thoroughly with the dressing in a bowl. Mound the lettuce on individual salad plates or in a big salad bowl. Top with handfuls of chicken, wonton strips, and fruit.

2. People can't get enough of fried wontons. Put extras in a bowl on the table.

• Wonton skins (or wrap-
pers) are 2-inch squares of
super-thin dough. They usually come in 1-pound stacks
of countless wraps—some
packages have 100, some
75—depending on the artful-
ness of the wonton maker
and how thin the company
made the wontons.

• Look for wonton wrap-
pers in the produce section
near the bean sprouts and
tofu. If you buy too much, or
want to start a stockpile, you
can freeze them.

• If you don't have a
deep-frying (or candy) thermometer, the visual clue the
oil gives when it's very hot is
that it ripples. You could
also flick a drop of water off
a finger; if it sizzles and
pops, the oil is ready.

• The wonton strips will
stay crispy for 3 days if you
store them in a plastic tub
with an airtight lid, at room
temperature.

CRISPY FRIED WONTON STRIPS

TECHNIQUE—Frying
BEST COOKWARE—Wok or wide pot
BEST TOOL—Slotted spoon or tongs

Canned crispy noodles are a barely acceptable artifice. Real fried wontons are ¼-inch wide and 2 inches long, a fine fried mouthful.

Makes about 6 cups

10 wonton skins
Vegetable oil

DO THIS FIRST:

1. Cut the stack of wonton skins into strips ¼ inch wide.

2. Pour 2 to 3 inches of vegetable oil into a wok or medium-size pot. Turn the heat to medium-high and heat the oil until it's very hot (375°F on a candy thermometer).

3. Have ready nearby a cookie sheet lined with paper towels, for draining the cooked strips.

DO THIS SECOND:

1. Add the wonton strips to the oil in batches. Leave room for them to bob around. The strips will curl. After a minute or less, they'll be golden.

WRAPPING IT UP:

1. As the wonton strips become done, take them out of the oil with a slotted spoon or tongs, and drain the batches on the paper towels. You might have to turn the heat down to medium if the oil is frying the wontons too fast.

8

SOUP

For Chicken Soup
and Matzo Balls, see
Passover menu, page
285.

CARROT SOUP

TECHNIQUE—Sautéing/boiling
BEST EQUIPMENT—Dutch oven
BEST TOOL—Vegetable peeler
MUST HAVE—Blender

The price of a bag of carrots is the economic base for this elegant soup. Provided you leave it in the blender long enough, it is very smooth and creamy, which company loves.

Serves 6

> 2 tablespoons butter
> 1 pound carrots
> 2 tablespoons brown sugar
> 2 tablespoons frozen orange juice
>   concentrate
> 3 cups canned chicken stock
> ¼ cup cream or whole milk
> 1 teaspoon salt, to start
> White pepper, to taste

It's better with garnish: Fresh minced chives, or a sprinkling of dried chives

DO THIS FIRST:

1. Get out a big soup pot, such as a Dutch oven. Drop the butter into the pot, and have it ready and waiting on your stove.

2. Peel all the carrots. Slice them into rounds about ¼ inch thick. They don't have to be perfect because they'll eventually be pureed. Leave them on the cutting board, but take them over to the stove.

DO THIS SECOND:

1. Measure the brown sugar into a small bowl and have it convenient to the stove.

2. Measure the orange juice concentrate into another small bowl and have it convenient to the stove, too.

DO THIS THIRD:

1. Turn the heat under the Dutch oven to high. Wait for the butter to melt and bubble.

2. Add the carrots, turn the heat down to medium, and cook and stir until the carrots are about halfway softened. This should take 8 to 10 minutes. Don't rush it. It's okay to overcook these carrots, but it's not okay to burn them.

3. Stir in the sugar and orange juice concentrate. Right away pour in the chicken stock, turn the heat to high, and bring the pot to a boil as fast as your stove can do it, uncovered.

4. When it boils, turn off the heat. Cool the soup before attempting to puree.

DO THIS FOURTH:

1. Get out a blender. Bring the soup pot and a ladle to the blender. Have ready a work bowl on the other side of the blender.

2. Ladle batches of soup into the blender. Blend on the highest speed until very smooth and velvety. Empty each batch into the work bowl.

WRAPPING IT UP:

1. When the soup is pureed, pour it back into the pot. Add the cream.

2. Taste the soup. Now add the salt and a pinch or so of white pepper. Taste again. If you like what happened but believe more salt will improve the soup, add a pinch at a time until the soup tastes great.

3. Use low heat to make the soup hot enough to serve. Sprinkle with chives.

MAKE-AHEAD OPTION:

1. Store the soup in a tightly covered container in the refrigerator overnight. Reheat it in the same storage container, covered loosely, in the microwave. Or reheat it in a pot on the stove over low heat, covered, until warmed through, which should take about 10 minutes. You'll have to stir it a few times.

• For the smoothest soup, leave the blender on for each batch at least 1 full minute. The chances of overblending are not as great as stopping short of beautifully smooth.

POTATO SOUP

- This soup is also good served cold.

- Yes, I left the word *leek* out of the title of this recipe. I sneaked them in instead. In truth, if you make this soup, you will have made Potato-Leek Soup—a classic.

- Leeks look like fattened scallions. They've got a long white part which was under-ground, and even longer floppy, dark green leaves which grew above ground.

- Unlike scallions, which offer edible white and green parts, leeks pretty much come to the end of their use-fulness at the green part. The big leaves are tough and don't have the kind of flavor associated with the white parts.

- The whites of leeks are sweet. They have an un-mistakable onion flavor but remain mild and durable through long cooking.

- The white part of leeks is notorious for harboring sand between the layers. If the layers are tight, cut the leek in half lengthwise, and twist the pieces under run-ning water to force the sand out.

TECHNIQUE — Sautéing/boiling
BEST COOKWARE — Dutch oven or other large pot,
BEST TOOLS — Cutting board, chef's knife, potato peeler
MUST HAVE — Blender

This rich, lavish soup is basically just potatoes, leeks, and liquid, with little of that liquid coming from cream or milk. Credit the potatoes, the cheapest route to the kind of satisfaction that comes only from the feeling that you've eaten something terribly bad for you.

Serves 8

2 tablespoons butter
4 leeks
4 firm medium-size russet potatoes
4 cans chicken stock (about 4 cups, total)
¼ cup cream or whole milk
1½ teaspoons salt, or to taste
White pepper, to taste

It's better with garnish: Fresh minced chives, or a sprinkling of dried chives

DO THIS FIRST:

1. Get out a big soup pot, such as a Dutch oven. Drop the butter into the pot, and have it ready and waiting on your stove.

2. Cut off the hairy roots of the leeks. Now cut off all the green leaves. Make your cut right where the leeks turn from green to white, and throw the leaves away.

3. Hold the resulting white parts upright under running water to flush out any sand.

4. Cut the leeks crosswise in slices as thin as you can get them. Pile the slices on a dinner plate as you go.

DO THIS SECOND:

1. Turn the burner under the pot with the butter to high.

2. When the butter foams, slide the leeks off the plate into the pot. Stir them up very well, with the heat still high, for a full minute.

3. Now, turn the heat down to medium-low. Keep stirring until the leeks have calmed down because of the lower heat. Let them cook gently, uncovered, for about 20 minutes. Stir once in a while, to redistribute them in the pot.

DO THIS THIRD:

1. Meanwhile, fill a large bowl with cold water. Peel the potatoes, dropping them into the water as you go.

2. Cut the potatoes into cubes about the size of gaming dice (½ inch), storing the cubes in the water until you've finished all the cutting.

DO THIS FOURTH:

1. Lift the potato cubes out of the water and into the hot leeks.

2. Open the cans of chicken stock and pour them in. Make sure you've got enough liquid to cover the potatoes.

3. Turn the heat to high and bring the soup to a boil, uncovered. When you see a big-bubble boil, cover the pot.

4. Turn the heat down to medium-low and let the soup simmer, covered, for 40 minutes. *(This is plenty of time to clean up, get out a blender and a big bowl, preferably with a pour-spout, and mince the chives.)*

WRAPPING IT UP:

1. When the soup is finished cooking, the potatoes will be so soft you can pierce them easily with a fork. Take off the lid and let the soup cool.

2. In batches, blend the soup until perfectly smooth. Pour each batch into the waiting bowl. When all the soup is blended smooth as cream, pour it back into the pot.

3. Swirl in the cream, salt, and pepper. Reheat just to warm through. Serve sprinkled with chives.

• If you don't have enough chicken stock to cover the potatoes by 1 inch, add water until you do.

• If you want to use a food processor instead of a blender, go ahead, but it'll leak (no pun intended).

• Cream puts this soup over the top. It's just ¼ cup divided over 8 servings. Half-and-half or milk do a good job of finishing, too.

• Chives are delicate green shoots also in the onion family. You can find them fresh in the "herb" section of the produce department in just about any big grocery store. Sometimes they're so tender that the best way to mince them is with scissors.

• If you've refrigerated leftover soup, the next day the soup will be very thick. It can be thinned to its original consistency as you reheat it. Add a few tablespoons of cream, milk, chicken stock, or water, until it's thin enough to be pourable.

• If you have leftovers and it's a hot day, serve the soup cold. You may call your cold Potato-Leek Soup by its proper name—Vichyssoise.

• *Bisque* often refers to seafood soups made of strained materials, flavors extracted from shells, and a final meeting with cream. Now bisque is tossed around as a word that implies an intensely flavored soup base with a creamy ending, but not necessarily one of the "cream-of" soups.

• Using a clove-studded onion is easier than chopping an onion and sautéing it.

• Keeping the onion whole as a holder for the cloves eliminates straining.

• If your pot is too wide, the tomato soup won't be deep enough to cover the onion.

TOMATO BISQUE

TECHNIQUE — Boiling
BEST COOKWARE — Medium pot that holds 10 or 12 cups

Such a glamorous title for an amazingly simple soup. Tomato sauce or tomato puree from a can gets finessed with sneaky extras to make it impossible for anyone to doubt its purity.

Serves 6

> 1 medium onion
> Spice jar of whole cloves
> 28-ounce can tomato sauce or tomato puree
> 1 teaspoon salt
> Ground black pepper, to taste
> 2 cups cream or half-and-half

DO THIS FIRST:

1. Peel the onion but leave it whole. Stick about 20 cloves all over it, and put it in a medium-size pot.

2. Open the can of tomato sauce and pour it in. Fill the can with water and pour it into the pot. Add the salt and pepper. Stir it smooth.

DO THIS SECOND:

1. Turn the heat to medium and slowly bring the pot to a simmer. This may take as long as 10 minutes.

2. Turn the heat down to low and simmer, uncovered, for 20 minutes. Keep an eye on it and stir a few times so it doesn't burn. The level of liquid will drop and the flavor will intensify. *This is your time to clean up and get out soup bowls and spoons.*

WRAPPING IT UP:

1. Remove the onion with tongs and throw it away.

2. Pour the cream into the soup, stirring to swirl it in.

3. Let the soup get hot again, then ladle it into bowls and serve it.

COLD CUCUMBER-BUTTERMILK SOUP

TECHNIQUE — Blending
BEST EQUIPMENT — Chef's knife and cutting board
GOOD TO HAVE — Blender

Cold soup isn't for everyone. At least that's what they say. On a hot day serve this in small bowls at the beginning of a meal. The soup is so cool and refreshing that it convinces a lot of people, although probably not all, that cold soup isn't such a bad idea.

Serves 6

2 cucumbers
2 medium cloves garlic
4 cups buttermilk
½ teaspoon salt, to start
Few shakes white pepper
2 teaspoons fresh chopped dill

DO THIS FIRST:

1. Get out a big mixing bowl. Get out your blender.

2. Peel the cucumbers with a vegetable peeler. Cut them in half lengthwise and scoop out the seeds with a small spoon. Throw the seeds away.

3. Now cut the cucumbers into chunks and have them ready near the blender.

4. Peel the garlic cloves.

DO THIS SECOND:

1. Blend the cucumbers, garlic, and buttermilk until smooth. After blending, pour the mixture into the mixing bowl.

2. Add the salt, pepper, and dill. Taste. Does the soup have enough salt?

WRAPPING IT UP:

1. Cover the bowl with plastic wrap, or store the soup in a big plastic storage container (6-cup) with a lid. Chill until extremely cold. Like most soups, this will increase in flavor overnight.

2. You can serve this with a few mint sprigs on top for garnish.

LET'S TALK

• You can make this entirely with buttermilk, or use half buttermilk and half plain yogurt.

• If you don't have a blender, you could use a food processor or an immersible portable blender. If you have none of these, grate the cucumber on the medium holes of a box grater, mince the garlic and dill, and combine all the ingredients in one bowl.

BEER-CHEESE SOUP

TECHNIQUE — Sautéing, boiling
BEST COOKWARE — Dutch oven or other large pot
BEST EQUIPMENT — Cutting board and chef's knife,
   wooden spatula for stirring
BEST TOOL — Box grater

This is reminiscent of a famous cheese soup served in Austin's Driskill Hotel. I added the beer, which is sure to embarrass the Texans who didn't think of adding it themselves. The process has a number of steps, but none of them is complicated.

Serves 10

> 1 bottle decent ale, or a can of any
>   nationally-branded beer
> 1 pound cheddar cheese
> ½ medium onion
> 1 rib celery
> 1 large carrot
> ¼ cup flour
> ⅛ teaspoon dry mustard
> Salt and white pepper, to taste
> 3 cups canned chicken stock
> 2 cups half-and-half or milk
> ½ stick butter (4 tablespoons)
> 1 teaspoon (or more) Worcestershire sauce

It's better with garnish: Flecks of paprika

DO THIS FIRST:

1. Open the beer and let it flatten near the stove.

2. Shred the cheese on a box grater onto a big piece of waxed paper.

3. Peel the onion and mince it as small as you can. Scoop it into a neat pile on one side of a large dinner plate.

4. Mince the celery very small. Set it next to the pile of onion.

5. Mince the carrot. Pile it on the plate, too.

DO THIS SECOND:

1. Measure the flour in a ¼-cup dry measuring cup, and have it convenient to the stove.

LET'S TALK

• Keep the cheese in the refrigerator until you need it. It grates better when it's cold.

• The smaller you can get the minced pieces of onion, carrot, and celery, the more pleasant they will be in a soup that's supposed to be smooth. When you're cutting, ask yourself just how big a piece of, say, carrot you want to bite into when the soup is finished. If the pieces on your cutting board look bigger than the pieces in your answer, keep cutting until they're small.

• The smaller you can get the minced vegetables, the more quickly they'll soften during sautéing. In other words, you can speed up the cooking by taking a little more time with the prep.

• The cheese may be mild, sharp, or smoky cheddar. A beautiful soup emerges when you use white cheddar.

• To save time, you could chop the carrot and celery together, as if they were one ingredient.

• The longer you simmer the soup at the stage the beer is added, the stronger the beer taste will be when the soup is finished.

2. Measure the dry mustard, salt, and pepper together into a small cup, such as a coffee cup. Have the cup convenient to the stove.

3. Measure the chicken stock, ideally into a large measuring cup with a pour-spout. Measure the half-and-half into a separate measuring cup. Have both convenient to the stove.

DO THIS THIRD:

1. Melt the butter in a Dutch oven over high heat. When the butter is foamy, slide the onion, carrot, and celery off the plate into the pot.

2. Wait for the vegetables to get sizzling hot, then turn the burner down to medium or medium-high. Sauté the vegetables, uncovered, until they're soft and tender, about 5 minutes. The heat is right if you can hear the vegetables cooking without burning. *(Neaten your work area and wash the dirty utensils and measuring cups.)*

DO THIS FOURTH:

1. Sprinkle the flour on the vegetables. Stir, which will turn the vegetables into an unsightly mash. Keep stirring for a full minute.

2. Reach for the chicken stock and pour it in— slowly. Keep stirring while you add the beer.

3. Add the Worcestershire and the mustard-salt-pepper mixture, giving a few good stirs. Crank the heat to high and bring the soup to a boil. When it boils, turn the heat back down to medium, or medium-low, and simmer the soup 3 minutes, uncovered.

WRAPPING IT UP:

1. Add the half-and-half and cheese, with the heat at medium-low. Stir until very smooth, which will happen as soon as all the lumps of cheese melt.

2. Let the soup heat through, but don't let it boil. You have to be observant.

3. Ladle the soup into bowls or a soup tureen. Fleck with paprika.

- A soup tureen is a covered bowl, sometimes decorative, made especially for serving soup. It may or may not come with a ladle.

- A great garnish is plain popped popcorn.

- You'll notice a greater, yet more subtle, beer background the second day, if you've refrigerated any leftovers.

CLAM CHOWDER
(New England-style)

TECHNIQUE—Sautéing, boiling
BEST COOKWARE—Big soup pot, such as a Dutch
  oven
BEST EQUIPMENT—Chef's knife, cutting board,
  wooden spatula
HANDIEST TOOL—Can opener

New England clam chowda' is an uncomplicated soup with no cream—it's just lightly thickened by potatoes. Unlike some of the pasty
versions we've all gotten at the company cafe-
teria, real clam chowder shouldn't have enough
surface tension to float the clams. No one expects
you to open and clean your own clams and
strain the juice for sand. You'll get a fine pot of
chowder with bottled clam juice and canned
clams.

Serves 10

> 1 large onion
> 2 russet potatoes
> 6 slices bacon
> 2 cups milk
> 3 8-ounce bottles clam juice
> 5 6½-ounce cans chopped clams (save the
>   juice)
> ¼ cup flour
> 3 tablespoons butter

> *It's not clam chowder unless it's served with:*
> *soda crackers (a.k.a. oyster crackers)*

DO THIS FIRST:

1. Peel the onion, halve it through the poles,
then cut the halves into little cubes the size of
gaming dice. Keep the pieces on a dinner plate
handy to the stove.

2. Peel the potatoes with a potato peeler, then
cut them into ½-inch cubes. Put the potatoes into
a bowl and keep it handy to the stove.

DO THIS SECOND:

1. Cut the bacon into 1-inch pieces and put them in a big pot, such as a Dutch oven. Set the pot on medium heat and cook the bacon until it's crisp. This will take about 12 minutes. Give a couple of stirs.

2. Measure the milk and have it convenient to the stove.

3. Pour the bottled clam juice into a 4-cup measuring cup. Open the cans of clams. Drain the juice into the bottled juice. You should end up with about 4 cups. It doesn't have to measure exactly.

DO THIS THIRD:

1. When the bacon is browned, pour some of the rendered grease now in the pot into an old tin can (use one from the clams). Leave about 2 tablespoons of bacon fat in the pot.

2. Put the pot back on the burner. Turn the heat up to medium-high. Add the onion and sauté until it's soft, about 2 minutes.

3. Without changing the heat, sprinkle the flour all over the onion and bacon. Stir with a wooden spatula for 1 full minute. If the mixture turns into a ghastly paste you're doing fine.

DO THIS FOURTH:

1. Pour in the clam juice, which will sizzle, about a cup at a time. Keep stirring so you don't tempt lumps, and don't stop until the mixture smooths out.

2. Add the potatoes. Wait for the soup to boil, then turn the heat down to low. Cover the pot and simmer for 15 minutes. *Clean up the potato-peel and onion mess, wash the cutting board and knife, and put the soda crackers on the table.*

WRAPPING IT UP:

1. Add the milk, clams, and butter. Turn the heat up to medium and let the soup get very hot without letting it actually boil. Then serve it right away.

LET'S TALK

• If necessary to make the clam juice smooth when it's added to the floury onions, switch to a whisk.

• You know the finished soup is nearly at a boil when you notice little bubbles forming around the edges. This is your cue to serve it.

WINTER SQUASH SOUP

TECHNIQUE — Roasting/boiling
BEST COOKWARE — Dutch oven or tall stock (soup) pot
BEST EQUIPMENT — Chef's knife and cutting board,
  blender

Maybe the name of this recipe should be Any Winter Squash Soup. Whatever winter squash you see at the store is suitable. I've used pumpkin, golden acorn squash, regular acorn squash, butternut squash, and jack-be-littles. You could microwave the squash to pre-cook it for its appearance in the soup, but it won't caramelize as well as it will if you roast it in the oven.

Serves 8 to 10

  5 pounds winter squash
  2 leeks
  2 stalks celery
  6 cups chicken stock
  Salt and pepper, to taste
  ¼ cup maple syrup
  1 cup cream or half-and-half
  Few grates whole fresh nutmeg

DO THIS FIRST:

1. Preheat the oven to 350°F with an oven rack in the middle. Get out a cookie sheet. If you don't have a cookie sheet, use a big piece of aluminum foil.

2. With your biggest knife, halve the squash lengthwise. Open it up and scrape out the seeds with a soup spoon.

3. Lay the halves flat side down on the cookie sheet or foil. Bake 1 hour. A knife point should be able to easily pierce the outer skin, which may wrinkle. Let the squash cool before attempting to get any of the pulp out of the skin.

DO THIS SECOND:

1. Cut off the hairy roots of the leeks. Cut off all the green leaves at the juncture where the white begins. Throw the leaves away.

2. Hold the white parts upright under running water to wash out sand. Cut the leeks in rough chunks.

DO THIS THIRD:

1. Put the leeks, celery, and chicken stock into a large soup pot, such as a Dutch oven. Put it on a burner, turn the heat to high, and bring it to a boil, uncovered.

2. When it boils, turn the heat to low. Cover and simmer a good 15 minutes.

3. When the squash is cool, scoop the flesh into the simmering soup. Add salt and pepper. Stir very well to break up the squash and blend it into the soup.

4. Simmer 15 minutes, uncovered. Take the pot off the heat and cool the soup.

DO THIS FOURTH:

1. Get out a blender. Bring the soup pot and a ladle over to the blender. Set a large work bowl (with a spout, if you have one) on the other side of the blender.

2. Ladle the contents of the pot into the blender—in batches, or you'll have an explosion. Blend a good 2 minutes per batch for the smoothest soup possible. Pour each batch into the work bowl.

WRAPPING IT UP:

1. Rinse the pot and pour in the pureed soup. Stir in the maple syrup and cream with a big spoon. It will streak at first, then the color will even out. Turn off the heat and cover the pot until 10 minutes before you want to serve. It will stay warm up to 2 hours.

2. Reheat the soup before serving, uncovered, on medium heat—no hotter! If a skin has formed on top, lift it out with a spoon.

3. Sprinkle with nutmeg—just a dusting. Ladle it into soup bowls and take the bowls to the table. Or bring the pot to the people and let them ladle it out themselves.

• When reheating the made-ahead version (see page 156), you don't have to stand there and babysit it. Over medium heat, nothing terrible will happen to your soup. I will say this, however. The thicker the pot, the more protection you have against scorching. If you've got an electric stove and a thin pot, leave the burner on low. The reheating will take longer but the lower heat will pose far less of a hazard to this Big-Effort soup.

• If you take the pot to the people, remember to use a hot pad underneath.

MAKE-AHEAD OPTION:

1. After pureeing, pour the soup into a storage container. Cover it and put it in the refrigerator. It will last a week.

2. Give yourself a good 20 minutes to set the stored soup up for serving.

3. Pour the puree into a pot. Stir in the maple syrup and cream.

4. Set the pot on a burner and turn it to medium heat. Check now and then to see how the soup is heating up, and give it a couple of stirs. You don't have to bring it to a boil, just get it good and hot.

5. Sprinkle with nutmeg.

9

BIG MEAT

AND OTHER

MAIN DISHES

- Chicken wings are about $1.50 a pound and come 10 to 12 in a standard grocery-store package. If you are tempted to cut off the tips, think of them as handles for your guests.

- Tongs handle the wings better than spoons or spatulas. If possible, hold the wings by the tips.

- Removing the cover halfway through the baking gives the wings a nice gloss.

- If you serve the wings hot from the oven, have ready a trivet or cooling rack to set the hot baking dish on.

- You'll need about 3 to 3½ ounces of ginger to give you ⅓ cup.

- A large amount of fresh ginger, like fresh garlic, is somewhat spicy; you'll notice a kick in this sauce.

- If you can't find fresh ginger, use ⅓ cup fresh minced garlic. Sneaking in garlic powder instead will not give you a great sauce, just one that tastes like garlic powder. However, sneaking in 1 teaspoon of dried ginger powder instead of using fresh ginger won't give you a bad sauce, just one that will make your guests wonder where the bite is coming from.

BIG POT OF GINGER CHICKEN WINGS

TECHNIQUE—Baking
BEST COOKWARE—A very large baking dish, such as a lasagne pan
BEST EQUIPMENT—Tongs (squeeze or scissors style)
MUST HAVE—Aluminum foil, pot holders

For a party where your guests can eat with their hands, there's nothing more fun than gnawing on the most economical appendage a chicken can offer. These unflappable wings can bake in the same piece of cookware they're served in. Allow 3 wings per person.

Serves 12

> 3 dozen chicken wings
> 1 cup sherry
> ¼ cup soy sauce
> ¼ cup lemon juice
> ⅛ teaspoon white pepper
> ⅓ cup peeled and finely minced
>   fresh ginger

DO THIS FIRST:

1. Preheat the oven to 350°F, with a rack in the lower third. Decide on a big, good-looking baking dish, one you can bake in and serve from. A graniteware turkey roaster or a Dutch oven that holds about 8 quarts and has an ovenproof handle are great.

2. Wash the wings in a colander. Dry each one well with paper towels.

3. Arrange the wings in the baking dish, tips down. Overlapping the wings might be necessary.

DO THIS SECOND:

1. Measure the sherry, soy sauce, lemon juice, and white pepper directly into a medium-size pot.

2. Use a vegetable peeler to take the skin off the piece of ginger. Cut the ginger in fine slices, then mince. Add to the pot.

3. Turn the heat to medium-high and bring it to a boil. Boil 1 minute. Pour the sauce over the wings.

WRAPPING IT UP:

1. Bake, covered with a lid or aluminum foil, for 45 minutes.

2. Take the baking dish from the oven and spoon sauce over the wings. Return the dish to the oven, uncovered, for 30 minutes more. Keep spooning sauce over the wings every 5 minutes or so.

3. Serve the wings in the baking dish or transfer them with a slotted spoon to a good-looking serving platter or bowl.

MAKE-AHEAD OPTION:

1. Make the sauce and pour it over the wings in a bowl. Cover and refrigerate overnight. Next day, pour the wings and sauce into the baking dish and bake.

THICK WHITE BEAN SOUP WITH CHICKEN THIGHS

TECHNIQUE — Sautéing/boiling
BEST COOKWARE — Big pot, such as a Dutch oven
BEST TOOLS — Tongs, cutting board and chef's knife
BEST GADGET — Can opener

This is a cross between a stew and a soup.

Serves 6 to 8

> 1 big onion
> 4 ribs celery
> 2 tablespoons minced garlic (about 8 peeled cloves)
> 6 chicken thighs
> 2 14½-ounce cans chicken stock (about 4 cups)
> 14-ounce can chopped tomatoes
> ¼ cup olive oil
> 1 tablespoon Herbes de Provence
> 1 teaspoon salt (to start)
> ¼ teaspoon white pepper
> 3 15-ounce cans small white beans (such as Great Northern beans)

DO THIS FIRST:

1. Peel the onion, cut it in half through the poles, and chop it into pieces the size of gaming dice. You should have about 2 cups, but it doesn't matter if the amount is exact. Pile the onion onto a dinner plate.

2. Wash the celery and cut off the white ends. Make lengthwise cuts down the stalks, then slice across the cuts to make chopped celery. You should have about 2 cups, again not an exact amount. Pile the celery next to the onion.

3. Mince the garlic as finely as you can, or scoop it out of a jar. Mound the garlic with the onion, and have the plate convenient to the stove.

DO THIS SECOND:

1. Take the skin off the thighs and throw it away.

2. Open the cans of stock and tomatoes, leaving the juice in the tomatoes. Have the cans convenient to the stove.

DO THIS THIRD:

1. Get out a big pot and set it on a burner. Measure the olive oil and pour it into the pot. Turn the heat to high. When the oil is hot (it will ripple) push the onion, celery, and garlic off the plate into the pot.

2. Sauté for 5 minutes with the heat high. Keep the vegetables moving by stirring with a wooden spatula. These vegetables need only to soften, not brown.

DO THIS FOURTH:

1. Pour in the chicken stock and tomatoes. Add the thighs, herbs, salt, and pepper. With the heat still high, wait for the soup to boil.

2. When it boils, lower the heat to medium-low, so the soup simmers.

3. Cover the pot and simmer for 30 minutes. You don't have to babysit it, but you will have to uncover it and stir once or twice so it doesn't burn. *(You have ample time to clean up the entire mess and get out a plate for cooling the thighs.)*

DO THIS FIFTH:

1. Take the thighs out of the soup and put them on a plate (use tongs). When they're cool enough to touch, take the meat off the bones. Throw the bones away and add the meat back to the soup.

2. Open the cans of beans. Pour all the beans into a colander set in your sink. Rinse the beans under cold water, then add them to the soup.

WRAPPING IT UP:

1. Simmer 30 minutes more, uncovered, keeping the heat medium-low. Excess liquid will boil off to make the soup pleasantly thick.

2. Serve the soup hot from a big bowl, or ladle it into individual bowls.

MAKE-AHEAD OPTION:

1. You can freeze the completed soup in covered plastic containers for up to 3 months, or refrigerate it for two or three days. As with most soups, it's better the second or third day, which gives you a good reason to make this ahead.

2. If you freeze it, defrost it on the "defrost" setting of a microwave, or allow the containers of soup to defrost in the refrigerator. It doesn't matter if ice crystals are present when you transfer the soup to a pot. They'll melt once the soup is over heat.

3. To reheat, pour the soup back into the pot you used to make it. Heat over low heat, stirring every 5 minutes or so. It will take 20 to 30 minutes to get it hot through and through.

FROM SCRATCH THICK WHITE BEAN SOUP WITH CHICKEN THIGHS

LET'S TALK

• Using dried rather than canned beans brings about subtle differences in consistency. The canned-bean version is more like a thick soup. The dried-bean version is more like thin stew.

The beauty of this method is that the dish bakes sight unseen in the oven for about 1½ hours. You have to stir it only 3 times.

> All the ingredients on page 160 except the canned beans
> 1 pound small dried white beans

DO THIS FIRST:
1. Buy a 1-pound package of small white beans, such as navy beans. Set a colander in your sink and pour in the beans. Look for dark or broken beans and rocks (yes, rocks) and get rid of them. This is called "sorting." Now rinse the beans under cold water.

2. Transfer the beans into a big bowl. Fill the bowl with water—a good 5 or 6 cups—and soak the beans 6 hours or overnight.

DO THIS SECOND:
1. When you're ready to cook, pour the soaked beans into the colander to drain off the soaking water. You'll notice that the beans are somewhat bloated and have definitely softened. They'll measure about 5 cups.

2. Follow the recipe on page 160, but when you add the chicken stock and tomatoes also add the soaked beans (no soaking liquid).

3. Turn the oven to 325°F. When the soup boils, cover it and set the pot in the oven. Bake 1½ hours, making sure you stir every 30 minutes (set a timer). This replaces the simmering step.

WRAPPING IT UP:
1. Continue with the recipe from Do This Fifth, skipping the canned beans steps.

• If you'd rather use breasts only, buy them boneless but skin-on. When you come home, cut each one, crosswise, into two pieces.

• The seeds inside a jalapeño (or any chile, for that matter) harbor most of the hots, but it's a seedy hot and can often be bitter. They'll come out almost in one motion if you slip a paring knife under the seed bed.

• In determining how small to mince fresh jalapeño, ask yourself just how big a piece you'd want to encounter inside your own mouth, and keep mincing.

• The coconut milk is not the kind added to mixed drinks. Instead, check the "Asian" aisle in a supermarket for a can labeled unsweetened juice of coconut.

• A great taste-substitution for the curry powder is 2 tablespoons Thai or Vietnamese sweet red chili sauce.

• What may seem like a great deal of brown sugar is there to offset the heat from the jalapeño. It will also contribute huge powers of caramelization to the chicken as it grills.

GRILLED COCONUT CHICKEN

TECHNIQUE — Grilling (covered)
BEST COOKWARE — Kettle-type grill with a fitted cover; outdoor gas grill
BEST EQUIPMENT — Big bowl, big spoon, cutting board and chef's knife
HANDIEST TOOLS — Paper towels, tongs

Sweetness and hotness in combination is a hallmark of Asian cooking. This chicken goes together quickly in one big bowl and sits while you light the grill and get other things going for the meal. By the time it's cooked, the marinade will have become a caramelly brown.

Serves 6

2 whole cut-up chickens
1 fresh jalapeño pepper
14-ounce can coconut milk
2 tablespoons curry powder
⅔ cup brown sugar
⅓ cup chopped fresh cilantro
1 tablespoon chopped fresh mint
½ teaspoon salt

DO THIS FIRST:

1. Get out a big mixing bowl. Rinse the chicken under warm water. Dry each piece with paper towels. As you go, put the chicken in the mixing bowl.

2. Cut the stem off the jalapeño. Cut it in half lengthwise so you can see the seeds. Flick them out and throw them away. Mince the jalapeño as small as you can. Add it to the chicken.

3. Add the rest of the ingredients. Mix with your hands or a mighty big spoon.

4. Cover the bowl with plastic wrap and put it in the refrigerator overnight, or marinate it at room temperature 2 hours. Take it out of the refrigerator 1 hour before grilling.

DO THIS SECOND:

1. If you have a gas grill, follow the directions that came with it. For a basic kettle-type charcoal grill, heat a cone-shaped pile of charcoal briquets on the lower grate of your grill until ash white.

2. Push equal piles of coals to opposite sides of the grill. Between the piles put an aluminum pan to catch drips.

3. Top with the grilling rack. Cover the grill, vents wide open, and let it heat up about 5 minutes.

DO THIS THIRD:

1. Put the chicken on the grill skin side down. Keep the sauce handy.

2. Cover the grill, keeping top and bottom vents open. Grill 40 minutes.

3. Take off the cover. Turn the chicken over with tongs. Spoon sauce on the chicken. Close the cover and grill 30 minutes more.

WRAPPING IT UP:

1. While the chicken is grilling, decide on a serving platter.

2. After grilling, take the chicken off the grill and place it directly on the serving platter. Serve hot or at room temperature.

• The type of grill set-up here is known as indirect grilling. That's because you have turned your grill into an oven. With the vents open it's roughly between 300° and 400°F inside the grill—a nice range for baking. But you get the benefits of grilling, including cooking outdoors and the smokiness that becomes part of the taste of this chicken.

• If your grill doesn't have a cover, you can still make this chicken. Cook it directly over hot charcoal, skin side down first. Spoon sauce over it more often so the chicken won't be dry, and douse flare-ups with water from a spray bottle.

• If you don't have a grill, or it's winter and you'd rather not go outside, you can bake the marinated chicken skin side up in a baking dish at 350°F for 1 to 1¼ hours. Spoon sauce over it a couple of times during baking.

165

• The best beer for this marinade is stout, which is dark and sometimes even chocolatey because of the long roasting of its malt. Microbreweries near your town may have just the beer. Of course, the basic brands of beer are fine, too.

• The marinade goes into a glass baking dish instead of an aluminum one because the acid in the marinade will "pit" aluminum, and in turn, aluminum will donate an unwanted off-taste to the food. Sometimes generic recipe writing will call anything that's not aluminum a "non-reactive" pan. I think the word "glass" uses fewer letters and communicates better.

• You can use pottery, crockery, enamel-covered steel, or stainless steel.

• The marinade will smooth out if you just mix it with a fork. The reason I don't call for a "non-reactive" bowl for the marinade is that no one makes aluminum bowls anymore.

• If you marinate the meat ahead, cover it and put it in the refrigerator, but not longer than one day. It will get mushy. As you walk past the refrigerator on random sojourns into the kitchen, stop to turn the meat over and give it a good swish.

FLANK STEAK MARINATED IN BEER

TECHNIQUE — Grilling
BEST COOKWARE — Rectangular glass baking dish
BEST TOOLS — Cutting board, chef's knife, tongs

Quick, get me some flour tortillas. There's nothing like this marinated beef rolled up fajita-style.

Serves 8

Marinade:
1 can beer
¼ cup brown sugar
3 tablespoons apple cider vinegar
1 teaspoon minced garlic
½ teaspoon salt
¼ teaspoon white pepper

Steak:
2 pounds flank steak
¼ cup vegetable oil

DO THIS FIRST:
1. Mix all the marinade ingredients in a bowl.

DO THIS SECOND:
1. Put the meat into a rectangular glass baking dish.

2. Pour the marinade over it.

3. Marinate at room temperature for 1 hour, uncovered. If convenient, turn the meat over once or twice and swish it around.

4. Fire up the grill about 30 minutes before you'll cook. Have the coals in the center of the bottom rack. Make a salad or side dish and finish setting the table.

DO THIS THIRD:
1. Pull the meat out of the dish with tongs. Hold it over the dish and let any free-flowing marinade drip off.

2. Put the meat on a big plate. Use your hands to rub the vegetable oil all over it.

WRAPPING IT UP:

1. Put the meat in the middle of the hot grill rack, over the coals. Grill about 7 minutes per side, for rare.

2. Meanwhile, back in the house, put the marinade in a small pot. Set it on a burner over medium heat until it simmers. Keep it simmering until nearly half of it cooks away. You now have "sauce."

3. Pull the steak off the grill with tongs and put it on a serving plate. Slice the meat thin. Serve with the sauce.

• The oil keeps the meat moist and prevents it from sticking to the grill.

• Boiling the marinade drives off water. Rather than think you are losing quantities of sauce, consider instead that you are concentrating flavor.

• Use T-bone, Porter-house, club, rib, or sirloin steaks. If you share, you can serve six people with four steaks.

• Ginger is one of the legendary spices Columbus hoped to find before he got lost in the Western Hemisphere. You can find it in the "weird food section" of the produce department of most major supermarkets.

• These steaks will be great even without the ginger and using plain, everyday black pepper.

GRILLED PEPPERCORN STEAK

TECHNIQUE—Grilling
BEST EQUIPMENT—An extra pepper mill
BEST TOOLS—Squeeze tongs, cutting board, and chef's knife

If you've never used fresh ginger before, you're in for a surprise. Besides its obvious gingery taste, it's got a bit of a kick to it, not unlike the kick you get from garlic. This makes sense when you remember that ginger, particularly when dried and sold in powdered form, is categorized as a spice.

Serves 4 to 6

4 1½-inch-thick steaks
About a 2-inch piece of fresh ginger
Mixed peppercorns (Szechuan, white, black, or other variety)
Salt

DO THIS FIRST:

1. Go outside and fire up your grill, with the charcoal in the middle of the bottom rack. (*This will give you 30 to 40 minutes to fix the steaks and set the table.*)

2. Take the steaks out of the refrigerator and put them on a big plate.

DO THIS SECOND:

1. Take the skin off the ginger with a potato peeler or paring knife. Slice the ginger into thin slivers, then mince it as finely as you can.

2. Use your hands to rub the ginger into both sides of the steaks.

DO THIS THIRD:

1. Put a variety of peppercorns into a pepper-mill. Grind pepper heavily over both sides of the steaks. If any pepper falls off, press it back onto the meat with your fingers. (*You still have time on your hands. Make a salad or side dish and clean up. Don't rush the coals; they'll be hot for a long time.*)

WRAPPING IT UP:

1. Moments before you put the steaks on the grill, sprinkle them with salt.

2. Grill the steaks about 6 minutes per side, for rare.

COUNTRY HAM
(Start 3 days before serving)

TECHNIQUE — Baking
BEST COOKWARE — The biggest disposable aluminum roasting pan you can find
BEST EQUIPMENT — A big plastic bucket (5-gallon)
HANDIEST TOOL — Heavy-duty aluminum foil

Just because a recipe is easy doesn't always mean it's quick. The time involved in preparing a country ham for baking will have no effect on your daily existence. You put in your 10 minutes once a day for three days. This is not a big deal for what you are about to experience.

Country ham and Coke have gone together ever since country cooks discovered Coke's desalinating qualities. By that we mean that a heavily salted country ham is a well preserved ham, and attempts must be made to withdraw some of the salt so the ham bakes with balanced flavor. You have the choice to bake it in Coke, bourbon, or a little of both.

Serves about 30

> 12- to 14-pound country ham
> 3 liters Coke Classic (not diet)
> 10 32-ounce bottles cider vinegar
> 2 fifths bourbon (or 1 fifth bourbon and one additional liter Coke)
> 3 pounds dark brown sugar
> Sprigs of fresh parsley and fresh mint

DO THIS FIRST:

1. Buy your country ham from a butcher who can slice off the hock for you.

2. When you get the ham home, put it in the sink. It will (and should) have some mold on it. Scrub it off with a stiff, wet brush. Rinse the ham well under running water.

DO THIS SECOND:

1. Set the ham in a large plastic pail and soak it for 3 days. For each day use 1 liter of Coke and 3 bottles of vinegar, and fill up the pail with water until the ham is submerged.

2. Cover the pail with a lid of tight-fitting foil. Change the soaking solution every 24 hours. Discard the soaking liquids after using.

DO THIS THIRD:

1. To bake the ham, line a large disposable aluminum roasting pan with 2 thicknesses of heavy-duty aluminum foil. (This is a messy critter!)

2. Lift the ham from its last soaking, scrub it once more, rinse, and place it in the pan with the black skin facing up.

3. Pour the bourbon, or bourbon and Coke, plus the remaining bottle of vinegar over and around the ham. Add water so the liquid comes halfway up the ham.

4. Pat the top with 2 pounds of brown sugar.

DO THIS FOURTH:

1. Make a roomy tent of heavy-duty foil over the ham by double-folding the edges of two sheets together. Crimp tightly to make a good seal around the rim of the roasting pan.

2. Place the pan in the oven on a rack on the lowest notch. Set the temperature at 250°F. Bake 4 to 6 hours. When done, the bone should jiggle freely.

3. While the ham is baking, get out a cooling rack and a big fork. Place a sheet of aluminum foil under the rack.

4. When the ham is done, take the roasting pan out of the oven and set it on a table or counter. Now lift the ham, using potholders and a long fork, to the cooling rack. Throw the cooking liquid away and turn the oven off.

WRAPPING IT UP:

1. When the ham is cool, heat the oven to 500°F. Carefully slice off the black rind, leaving a ½-inch-thick layer of fat.

2. Draw a paring knife through the fat, but without going all the way down to flesh, to score a diamond pattern in the fat.

3. Press the remaining pound of brown sugar on the ham, pressing it firmly into the diamond pattern.

4. Bake 15 to 20 minutes, until the sugar melts and forms a crust on the ham. Cool completely. This will take 2 to 3 hours.

TO CARVE:

1. Put the cooled ham on a cutting board. Get out a large pretty platter.

2. It's easier to just leave the bone in. As you make slices, sweep the knife along the ham in the same direction as the bone. This is called slicing "with the bone" (see Carving, page 77).

3. It is traditional to slice country ham paper-thin. Place the slices on a serving platter. Garnish with parsley and fresh mint.

YUCATAN-FLAVOR ROAST PORK

TECHNIQUE—Roasting
BEST COOKWARE—Oblong baking dish with low sides
BEST EQUIPMENT—Measuring cup, instant-read meat thermometer, brush

Here is an easy pork roast on the verge of exotic. It is no more difficult than roasting a chicken. While the pork roasts, you have time to talk on the phone and cook a vegetable.

Serves 8

> 1 tablespoon chile powder
> ½ cup orange juice
> 1 teaspoon minced garlic
> ½ teaspoon salt
> ½ teaspoon black pepper
> 3½-pound boneless pork roast

DO THIS FIRST:

1. Get out an oblong baking dish or roasting pan. Line the bottom and sides with foil, dull side up.

2. Preheat the oven to 350°F, with an oven rack in the middle.

DO THIS SECOND:

1. Measure all the ingredients except the pork into a bowl. Mix. Brush the resulting marinade all over the pork.

2. Lift the pork into the baking dish.

WRAPPING IT UP:

1. Roast the pork for about 70 minutes (20 minutes per pound), brushing on more marinade every 20 minutes or so. Take a thermometer reading at 50 minutes.

2. When the pork is between 140 and 150°F on the thermometer, it's finished cooking. Take the pan out of the oven. Using tongs or two big spatulas, lift the pork out of the pan and put it on a cutting board. Let it cool 10 minutes. Don't worry, it will still be hot.

3. Slice it thin. Serve hot or cold.

• You could add chopped tomatoes; herbs such as fish-loving dill, parsley, or thyme; or vegetables such as mushrooms to the baking dish.

• If all you see displayed in the fish case are floppy, thin filets, tell the fish retailer to cut a large filet for you.

• Until the management of fish departments realize that there is a demand for big pieces of fish, you might have to call and request what you want. Requesting a 4-pound chunk of fish off the whole is no different from asking the butcher for a 4-pound pork loin before it's cut into chops.

• When you buy your fish, mention that it will be roasted, and that you'll need a large piece. Don't get confused with the terminology. The main difference between roasted fish and baked fish, to me, is innuendo.

• A 4-pound filet is the first choice for this recipe. Next best is a chunk of fish from the middle or tail end. This will probably include bones. Bones speed up the roasting a little because they act as little lightning rods. Bones also help the fish stay juicy because they help hold it together. A great option for this recipe is half of a 6- to 9-pound salmon, to make a 3- to 4-pound roast. Ask for the tail end.

BIG PIECE OF ROASTED FISH

TECHNIQUE — Roasting
BEST COOKWARE — Glass 8-inch square baking dish
BEST EQUIPMENT — Tongs, cutting board, chef's knife

A big piece of fish, such as a large filet of halibut or a salmon "roast," is becoming quite the chic alternative to a big beefy centerpiece. And well it should. The wow factor of a big salmon chunk coming to the table seems undeserved when you realize how easy the recipe is.

Roasting won't work on lousy fish. That is not to say that your fish may not be frozen. But nothing beats the flavor, mouth feel, tenderness, and succulence of fresh fish. As the saying goes, after a fish is caught, it doesn't get any better.

Serves 6 to 8

> 4-pound filet of salmon, halibut, or sea bass
> 4 tablespoons butter
> 1 lemon
> Salt and pepper
>
> *It's better with garnish: Fresh minced dill and lemon wedges (not slices!)*

DO THIS FIRST:

1. Preheat the oven to 450°F, with the oven rack on the lowest notch. Get out a pretty platter (oval is always nice for fish).

DO THIS SECOND:

1. Smear a thin film of butter in an oblong baking dish with low sides, preferably glass or crockery. Set the piece of fish in the middle.

2. Cut the remaining butter into little bits and dot it all over the fish. Halve the lemon and squeeze juice all over the fish. Sprinkle with salt and pepper.

DO THIS THIRD:

1. Measure the fish at the thickest part.

2. Bake 10 minutes for each inch of thickness, adjusting for fractions of an inch. Don't turn the fish. While it bakes, clean up the kitchen and cut a second lemon into wedges.

WRAPPING IT UP:

1. Transfer the baked fish to the platter. Garnish with lemon and tufts of dill.

FISH SCHOOL

When buying fish, you've got to have a conversation with the person behind the display case. A real fish market is always the best place to buy fish. However, for many of us fish is now part of the meat case at a supermarket, and chances are a cross-trained butcher is manning the department.

In many cases, the fish you buy will already have been frozen, as have just about all the shrimp in this country, much of the orange roughy, and a good deal of fattier fish, such as swordfish, salmon, and halibut.

WHOLE FISH

Sometimes it's easiest to buy a whole fish. Do not conjure up Moby Dick. A whole fish can be a lot smaller than a basic T-bone. A whole trout can be as small as 6 ounces and is great eating.

If you buy a whole fish but want the head off, the butcher will be happy to remove it. But be warned that the fish will be weighed first to determine its price. You'll end up paying for the head regardless of whether you take it home or the butcher throws it away.

Inexpensive salmon from Alaska, such as Alaskan pink or chum salmon, can be bought frozen whole, head on or off. Simply thaw and roast it whole.

• A 3- to 4-pound filet could be as thick as 2 to 2½ inches. That means your chunk of fish will need 20 to 25 minutes of roasting. Try to get over feeling that's a long time to cook fish. It really can take that long and still come out moist.

• Roasting (or baking) is good for heftier pieces of fish because they cook evenly and give off juices that act to protect the fish from harsh temperatures.

• At the end of roasting, your big filet will probably be in more liquid than when it started out. Unlike the pan juices from meat and poultry, these should be discarded.

• Lemon slices are easy to cut and pretty to look at, but they're absolutely useless if you want squeezed lemon juice. Make wedges by cutting the lemon in half through the poles, then cutting half-moons.

FISH "CHUNKS" THAT ROAST NICELY
- Tail end of salmon
- Tail end of halibut
- Sea bass
- Striped bass
- Halibut

FISH TO ROAST THAT ARE WHOLE, BUT SMALL
- Trout—usually 8 to 10 ounces each. Figure one per person.
- Red snapper—1 whole, 6 to 7 pounds, serves 8. Or buy them 1 to 1½ pounds each; figure one for every two people.
- Redfish—about 3 pounds each. Figure one for every three people.
- Rockfish (sometimes called Pacific red snapper)—from 1½ to 4 pounds each.

- A typical 26-ounce jar of sauce is about right for 8 ounces of pasta. That's half of a one-pound package. I've tried to make the sauce stretch over 12 ounces of pasta, but all I got in return was complaints that the spaghetti was too dry.

- Olive oil gives the jarred sauce some backbone.

- The vinegar counteracts sauce that's too sweet or too salty.

- Even if the prepared sauce came with mushrooms, adding more enhances the flavor. There's a good reason for this. Mushrooms have naturally occurring glutamic acid, which you know as MSG. If the sauce didn't already have mushrooms, the fresh ones add all-around depth.

- The mushrooms will become watery as they cook, and make the sauce watery. Continued simmering will take care of the excess liquid, leaving the sauce with better flavor and a thicker consistency.

- Sometimes prepared sauces are spicy. If yours isn't, and you'd like it to be, add ⅛ teaspoon red pepper flakes, or just add more black pepper.

- Of course other pasta strands work well: linguine, vermicelli, spaghettini, or fettuccine. Also those pasta tubes and shapes that capture sauce and make the dish seem juicy: rigatoni, penne, big elbow macaroni, and medium shells.

PASTA WITH IMPROVED TOMATO SAUCE FROM A JAR

TECHNIQUE — Sautéing/boiling
BEST COOKWARE — Big pot, medium pot
BEST EQUIPMENT — Colander, cutting board, chef's knife

It's no secret that we all do it, but when we do, we wish it could stay a secret. What is this "it" we all do? Use spaghetti sauce from a jar.

I think we regard it as spaghetti sauce because it isn't sophisticated enough to be called pasta sauce. How we use it reveals how well we cook. People not yet in the groove of cooking pour it right from the jar. People who know a little more about cooking won't, and not because they can't keep their hands off it. The truth is not one of them is good enough to use straight. Some are sweet. Some are salty. Some are bland. Some are soupy. The ones with mushrooms don't have enough mushrooms.

Think of the sauce in the jar is a starting point. Here's how to fix it.

Serves 6

Sauce
½ medium onion
2 teaspoons garlic
10 fresh white mushrooms
2 tablespoons olive oil
26-ounce jar prepared spaghetti sauce (herb, mushroom, or "classic")
1 tablespoon red wine vinegar
½ teaspoon ground oregano
½ teaspoon dried basil
Black pepper (add only after tasting)

Spaghetti
1 tablespoon salt
8 ounces spaghetti

DO THIS FIRST:

1. Get out a nice pasta-serving bowl or platter.

2. Chop the onion and set it in a pile on a dinner plate. Mince the garlic and set it on the plate. Have the plate convenient to the stove.

3. Wash the mushrooms if they're dirty. Slice the stems off flush with the caps. Cut up the stems, then cut the caps into slices about ¼ inch thick. Have the mushrooms ready in a bowl near the stove.

DO THIS SECOND:

1. Measure the olive oil into a medium pot (it should hold 8 cups). Turn the heat to high.

2. When the oil ripples, push the onion and garlic off the plate into the pot. Turn the heat down to medium. Sauté 5 minutes, keeping the heat medium.

3. Pour in the spaghetti sauce, mushrooms, and the rest of the ingredients. Give the sauce a couple of good stirs. Simmer the sauce (the burner is still on medium) for 15 minutes. Stir a few times so it doesn't stick.

DO THIS THIRD:

1. Meanwhile, fill a big pot two-thirds full of water. Bring it to a boil, covered, on high heat. Have a colander ready in your clean sink. *(Clean up all the cutting-board debris, get out serving plates, and set the table. This is also a good time to make a salad.)*

2. When the water boils so hard that steam escapes and the lid rattles, remove the cover and add the salt, then the spaghetti (only ½ pound!) a little at a time, so the water keeps boiling.

3. Stir then boil, uncovered, 5 to 8 minutes, or according to the directions on the package, until the pasta is firm to the bite—not mushy, yet cooked.

WRAPPING IT UP:

1. Pick out a strand of spaghetti, run it under cold water, and take a bite. Is it done? That is, soft on the outside but with a filament of resistance in the center? If not, keep boiling and checking.

2. If yes, take the pot to the sink and pour the pasta and water into the waiting colander. Keep the empty pot handy.

3. Put the drained spaghetti back in its pot. Pour the Improved Sauce over the spaghetti, stir to combine, then pour it all into the serving dish.

10

VEGETABLES

AND SIDE DISHES

- Mince the onion first so the potatoes will be the last cut.

- Cold butter cuts up better into small pieces.

- This is a peasant dish. The ingredients don't have to be perfectly overlapped. This will cook and look great even if you scatter the potatoes any old way. No one will see through the top layer of cheese.

- Pour the cream over the potatoes slowly, so it can seep in.

- The browner you can get this, the crunchier the top will be, and the more impressive it will look, providing, of course, you stop short of burning it.

- The number of layers can vary with the size of your potatoes and the thinness of your slices. If your potatoes are big, make four layers instead of three.

- The cookie sheet will catch spills and give an extra layer of bottom insulation to retard burning. If you don't have a cookie sheet, or a spare at this point, use aluminum foil, dull side up.

POTATOES AU GRATIN

TECHNIQUE — Baking
BEST COOKWARE — Oval or rectangular baking dish that holds 12 cups
BEST TOOLS — Food processor, cutting board and chef's knife
BEST GADGET — Vegetable peeler

Anything with the word *gratin* in it (pronounced grah-TAN) has a golden brown crust from oven-baking. So what we really have here, translated, is Potatoes with Golden Crust. Parts of the crust might even stick to your baking dish, and so much the better. Potatoes au Gratin is served in the same dish it bakes in, so I hope you have something nice looking to bring to the table.

Serves 6 to 8

> 1 medium onion
> 6 medium baking potatoes (russets)
> ½ pound Swiss or Emmenthaler cheese
> 1 stick (8 tablespoons) butter, cold
> Salt and pepper
> 1½ cups cream

DO THIS FIRST:

1. Preheat the oven to 425°F, with an oven rack in the middle.

2. Peel the onion, halve it, and mince the halves into pieces as small as you can get them.

3. Peel the potatoes. Slice them into thin rounds that are between ⅛ and ¼ inch thick. (If you have a food processor, use the 2mm blade.)

4. Grate the cheese on the medium holes of a box grater onto a piece of waxed paper.

5. Cut the butter into little pieces.

DO THIS SECOND:

1. Get out a nice looking baking dish (an oval is good) that holds 12 cups. Smear the bottom and sides of the dish with a little butter.

2. Overlap one-third of the potatoes on the bottom. Sprinkle with one-third of the onion, then one-third of the cheese. Sprinkle with salt and pepper. Dot with one-third of the butter pieces.

3. Repeat this layering two more times. Each time, sprinkle with salt and pepper.

WRAPPING IT UP:

1. Pour the cream all over the slices. Cover with foil.

2. Set the baking dish on a cookie sheet. Bake immediately for 45 minutes. Remove the foil and bake 15 minutes more. It should be browned and bubbling on the edges.

MAKE-AHEAD OPTION:

1. Assemble the entire recipe the day before, but don't bake it. Keep it in the refrigerator until 1 hour before baking.

CORN PUDDING

TECHNIQUE — Baking

BEST COOKWARE — A glass baking dish that holds
6 cups (an oval is nice); one bigger baking pan,
rectangular, with low sides

BEST EQUIPMENT — Measuring cups, medium bowl

This is where you learn about preventive measures — defensive cooking, I call it. If you want eggs and milk to bake into creaminess instead of into wounded curds, you build a moat around it. Literally. It's called a water bath. Once you do it, you'll find that it's no more difficult than pouring boiling water out of a tea kettle into a baking dish. Even though it's easy, it's pretty high up there on finesse.

Serves 6

> 4 eggs
> 2 tablespoons sugar
> 1 teaspoon salt
> 3 cups corn kernels, frozen or from 6 fresh
>   ears (see page 137)
> 1 cup cream
> ½ cup milk

DO THIS FIRST:

1. Preheat the oven to 350°F, with a rack in the middle. Fill a tea kettle with water, set it on high heat, and bring it to a whistling boil.

2. Smear a thin film of butter on the bottom, sides, and especially the corners of a 6-cup (1½-quart) baking dish.

3. Get out an even larger baking dish, or use a disposable 9×13-inch aluminum baking pan with low sides, and have it ready near the stove.

DO THIS SECOND:
1. Crack the eggs into a big mixing bowl. Add the sugar and salt, then beat the eggs for 1 minute with a portable electric mixer.

2. Stir in the corn, cream, and milk, and pour the mixture into the buttered baking dish.

WRAPPING IT UP:
1. Put the pudding dish in the middle of the bigger pan. Set the arrangement on the oven rack, but don't push it all the way in.

2. Pour hot water from the kettle into the bigger pan; about a 2-inch depth is good. Scoot the pans all the way into the oven. Bake for 60 to 70 minutes, until a table knife stuck into the center of the pudding comes out clean. If pudding sticks to the knife, bake 5 to 10 minutes more, or until the knife comes out clean.

SAUTEED GREENS

• Sometimes a bunch of greens equals a pound. Sometimes a bunch is a short pound, around 12 ounces, which is typical for spinach. Weigh the bunches at the store. Be sure you have 3 pounds.

• Don't be shocked by how much space this amount of greens takes up when it's raw. During cooking the greens shrink to a shadow of their original volume.

• A huge bowl or plastic tub expedites the rinsing of greens. As annoying as it is, don't be tempted to skip the washing or to breeze through it. Greens are cut low to the ground they grow in, so it's no surprise that sand and grit come with them.

• Don't even think about frozen spinach as an option. If you sneak it in and are disappointed that you got green porridge that tastes like tin, you were warned.

• Even pre-washed spinach needs washing.

• Though they're not in an ocean of water at first, the technique used to prepare these greens for sautéing is boiling.

• Use minced garlic from a jar if you don't feel like mincing it fresh.

TECHNIQUE—Boiling/sautéing
BEST COOKWARE—Big pot, such as a Dutch oven
   or wok
BEST EQUIPMENT—Colander

If you can't resist the taste and nourishment of dark leafy greens, you'll forgive them for needing a last-minute sauté. Sautéing does things to greens that boiling and steaming can't. The small amount of oil or butter used in sautéing adds just the right amount of extra flavor and helps send the greens to the table positively glistening.

Serves 6 to 8

   3 pounds greens (spinach, mustard greens, or chard)
   2 tablespoons minced garlic
   3 tablespoons olive oil or butter
   1 teaspoon salt

DO THIS FIRST:

1. Wash the greens leaf by leaf. Break off the tough, thick parts of the stems and throw them away.

2. Mince the garlic. Set a colander in your clean sink.

DO THIS SECOND:

1. Put the greens, still fairly wet from washing, in a big pot.

2. Turn the heat to high. Boil until the greens are three-fourths wilted. It may take 4 minutes or less.

3. Drain the greens in the colander (you don't have to rinse them), and keep the pot handy.

DO THIS THIRD:

1. Decide on a serving dish.

2. Put the olive oil or butter in the pot you used to wilt the greens. Turn the heat to high.

3. When the oil ripples (or the butter foams), add the greens all at once. Stir for 1 minute, until you're confident that they're hot.

WRAPPING IT UP:

1. Add the garlic and salt. Keep stirring until the greens are wilted but not limp, about 2 minutes.

2. Transfer them to the serving dish, and serve right away.

MAKE-AHEAD OPTION:

1. Once you've wilted and drained the greens, you may store them in zip-style plastic storage bags with the air pressed out, for one or two days before finishing the recipe. You can also pre-cook and crumble 8 strips of bacon a day before to sprinkle over the greens when they're served.

• If you've under-wilted the greens during the first cooking stage, you can correct it by sautéing them a little longer in the sauté step. I like to stop just before the greens wilt to limpness.

• The amount of greens sitting in the colander will help you eyeball the size of the serving dish you'll need.

• If you think this recipe needs something more, cook 8 strips of bacon in a small skillet, crumble them, and sprinkle them all over the finished greens.

SPINACH QUICHE

TECHNIQUE—Baking
BEST COOKWARE—9×13-inch glass baking dish
BEST EQUIPMENT—Wok (or a big pot), cutting board,
  chef's knife, mixing bowl
BEST TOOLS—Box grater

True quiche has crust. But a quiche concept can take liberties. The crust here is just a sprinkling of toasted bread crumbs. This is a good make-ahead if you want to serve quiche cold. Depending on the serving portions, quiche can be a nice side dish or the meal itself. It's also great on a brunch buffet.

Serves 8

2 bunches fresh spinach (1½ to 2 pounds)
Butter, for greasing the dish
2 cups bread crumbs
¾ pound Swiss cheese
8 eggs
1½ cups milk
1½ cups cream
½ teaspoon salt
Lots of black pepper

DO THIS FIRST:

1. Fill a sink or big tub deeply with cold water. Cut the stems off each bunch of spinach in one deft knife stroke. Throw the stems away.

2. Drop the leaves into the water. Swish a little, then leave them there while you do other things.

DO THIS SECOND:

1. Preheat the oven to 350°F. Smear a thin film of butter over the bottom and up the sides of a 9×13-inch glass baking dish.

2. Spread the bread crumbs on a cookie sheet. Put them in the preheating oven to crisp. Every 5 minutes or so, move them around with a spatula, until they're toasty, about 15 minutes, total.

3. Sprinkle the toasted crumbs in the buttered baking dish.

DO THIS THIRD:

1. Get out a wok or big pot, such as a Dutch oven. Have it near the spinach. Lift the spinach out of the sink by handfuls and pile it directly into the wok. You don't have to dry it. But do press it in, even if it's a lot.

2. Rinse the sand out of the sink and set a colander in the sink.

3. Put the wok on high heat, uncovered. Stir the spinach until the water clinging to its leaves boils and the spinach cooks down to a mere 2 cups.

4. Pour the spinach into the colander. Leave it there to drain and cool while you grate the cheese.

DO THIS FOURTH:

1. Grate the cheese on the medium holes of a box grater. Sprinkle the cheese in the baking dish on top of the crumbs.

2. Crack the eggs into a big mixing bowl. Stir in the milk, cream, salt, and pepper until it's smooth.

DO THIS FIFTH:

1. Squeeze the bejabbers out of the cooked spinach, now that it's cool. Take little wads, press them between your palms, and wring and wring. Put the wrung-out wads on a cutting board and chop them roughly.

2. Arrange the spinach on top of the cheese.

3. Pour the egg-milk mixture all over the spinach. Let it seep in.

WRAPPING IT UP:

1. Bake for 45 minutes, until puffed and golden. It's done if a knife stuck straight down into the middle of the quiche comes out clean.

2. Cool about 10 minutes. Serve cut into squares as big or as small as you like.

MAKE-AHEAD OPTION:

1. Bake the quiche, cool it uncovered, and serve at room temperature within 3 hours.

HOW TO WASH GREENS

1. If you have a double sink, fill one side with cold water. For a large amount of greens, or if you don't have a double sink, fill a big plastic tub or pail with water.

2. Add the greens, slosh them around, then leave them alone for 15 minutes. The greens will float and the sand will sink. Carefully scoop the greens from the water.

3. Rinse the leaves leaf by leaf under running water.

- Fry the latkes as soon as the batter is made. Even though they're mixed with other ingredients, the potatoes will start to turn brown.

- Latkes can be frozen. To reheat, place them un-thawed, covered really well with foil, in a 250 to 300°F oven for 30 to 45 minutes. When they're hot, uncover them to re-crisp them.

- It's better to make ahead and freeze than to make ahead and refrigerate. In the refrigerator the sog sets in.

- Cut the potatoes and onions into coarse chunks of equal size. This will facilitate even blending.

- Once during a latke frenzy I found myself out of matzo meal. I did have a box of onion-flavored matzo in the house. I whirled the matzo in the food processor until it became matzo meal. I think those were my best latkes ever.

- Corn oil or canola oil is good for frying.

- To make sure the oil is hot, flick a drop of water off your fingertip into the heated oil. If the water crackles, you're there. If not, keep heating the oil and flick another drop of water into the oil 30 seconds later.

POTATO LATKES

TECHNIQUE — Sautéing (frying)
BEST COOKWARE — 10½-inch cast-iron skillet, or other heavy skillet, up to 12 inches wide
BEST EQUIPMENT — Blender

Every year I eagerly await Chanukah and its potato latkes. I don't know how Chanukah could be celebrated any other way. As a child I watched my mother grate the potatoes for latkes. She always reported having grated until her knuckles bled. About 10 years into her latke-making a new blender was enthroned on her countertop. There it has stayed at the ready.

This is a by-the-batch recipe. Make as many batches as you like.

Makes 16

> 2 medium potatoes
> 1 onion
> 1 egg
> 2 teaspoons salt
> ¼ teaspoon baking powder
> ¼ cup matzo meal or flour
> Vegetable oil, for frying

Always have: Sour cream, applesauce

DO THIS FIRST:

1. Peel the potatoes. Place them in a bowl of ice water to keep them from turning dark as you work. Cut the potatoes into small chunks and put them back in the water.

2. Peel the onion and cut it into chunks the size of eggs. (Use one chunk per batch of latkes.)

DO THIS SECOND:

1. Put the egg in a blender, then the piece of onion. Add the rest of the ingredients except the oil and blend to the consistency of coarse applesauce.

2. Leave the batter in the blender container and have it convenient to the stove.

DO THIS THIRD:

1. As soon as the batter is ready, pour ¼ inch of vegetable oil in a heavy skillet that's at least 10½ inches wide. Turn the heat to high. Get out a ¼-cup measuring cup, preferably one with a decent handle. Spread a double thickness of paper towels on a cookie sheet or on the countertop near the stove.

2. When the oil is hot, dip the cup into the batter. Get it low to the skillet and pour in the batter. Fill the skillet with 4 to 5 pancakes.

3. Lower the heat to medium and keep it there for the duration of the frying. (If you don't notice much action, it's okay to crank the heat to medium-high, but no higher.)

WRAPPING IT UP:

1. Fry the pancakes until you see steam vents sink into the top, about 2 or 3 minutes. Before flipping them, take a look at the bottoms to make sure they're truly golden brown.

2. Flip them with a pancake turner and fry the second side until it's golden brown too.

3. Drain the latkes on the paper towels and serve them hot with applesauce and sour cream.

30-MINUTE MAKE-AHEAD OPTION:

1. To keep cooked potato latkes warm until the last one is fried, heat the oven to 200°F.

2. Put one big cake-cooling rack or two small ones on a cookie sheet. Place the cooked latkes on the rack, cover with foil, and keep warm in the oven.

HOMEMADE APPLESAUCE

TECHNIQUE — Boiling
BEST COOKWARE — Big pot, such as a Dutch oven
BEST EQUIPMENT — Blender, immersible blender, or
food processor
BEST TOOLS — Chef's knife, cutting board, potato peeler

It's useless to specify which apple to use for applesauce. If you see apples for 29 cents a pound, those are perfect. Red Delicious are probably the least delicious in the entire apple kingdom. Using them to make applesauce is really doing them an enormous favor. You'll also get great applesauce from Granny Smith, Fuji, Jonathan, Golden Delicious, McIntosh, Rome — or any combination of them. Each apple lends its own sweetness or tartness, and it's all interesting. Don't worry about texture. That's the blender's job.

The spices and juice used here enhance the features of apples that are tart or sweet. I happen to like sweet things. Adding sugar to tart apples won't throw the World Order out of balance.

Makes 4 cups

4 pounds apples
¼ cup apple juice
½ cup sugar or honey
1 teaspoon cinnamon
¼ teaspoon ground cloves
1 tablespoon butter
¼ teaspoon vanilla

DO THIS FIRST:

1. Get out a big pot, such as a Dutch oven, and bring it to your chopping area.

DO THIS SECOND:

1. Peel the apples with a potato peeler. You can do this over the sink.

2. Use a chef's knife to cut the apples. Cut each apple apart off-center, just to the side of the inner core. Lay the piece still holding the core flat on your cutting board. Cut two side pieces from the core. Turn the apple and cut a third piece, leaving the core like a square peg.

3. Chop the apple pieces into rough chunks. They don't have to be perfect. As you go, put the chopped pieces into the pot.

DO THIS THIRD:

1. Take the pot over to the stove and put it on medium heat. Measure and pour in the apple juice, sugar, cinnamon, and cloves. Stir with a big wooden spoon until the apples are nicely coated with spices.

2. Leave the apples to cook uncovered, with the heat still on medium. *(You'll have about 40 to 45 minutes to clean up and do other things while the apples cook.)*

3. After about 10 minutes, you'll notice that the liquid is bubbling. Leave it alone and let the heat do the work, but give a stir now and then. After 40 or 45 minutes, the apples will be soft, cooked down by half their original volume.

WRAPPING IT UP:

1. If you have an immersible blender, bring it over to the stove and operate it directly in the pot, revving until the apples become a puree as smooth or as chunky as you like.

2. If you'll be using a blender, cool the apples. Have ready a 4-cup storage tub. Puree the apples in batches on the blender's highest speed. Empty the blender into the tub as you go.

3. Stir in the butter and vanilla. Applesauce is delicious warm. Or cover it and store it in the refrigerator.

• My secret ingredients are butter and vanilla, and they are entirely optional. Butter gives the applesauce sheen and a kind of flavor undertone. Vanilla heightens the apple flavor and makes the applesauce smell great.

• If you like chunky applesauce, use a potato masher or hand-held electric mixer instead of a blender.

• A blender makes the applesauce the smoothest. The next-best machine is a food processor.

• If the applesauce is too thin, put it into a pot over medium heat and simmer a few minutes to drive off the excess water. This will happen quickly, so keep a good watch.

• A big graniteware pot is a good choice. If it's too big to keep in your kitchen, store the pot in a garage, basement, or closet.

• Spreading the husks in the bottom of the pot imparts a little more corn flavor to all the steam inside the pot.

• If the pot is too big to fit under the faucet of your sink, fill another large container, even your tea kettle, with water and pour it into the pot in batches.

• If you like corn very crunchy and sweet, cook it just 5 minutes. Overcooking corn makes it starchy instead of sweet.

CORN-ON-THE-COB FOR COMPANY

TECHNIQUE — Boiling
BEST COOKWARE — Huge pot
BEST TOOL — Tongs
MUST HAVE — Corn-cob prongs for serving, pot holders

Serves 8 to 10

10 to 12 ears of corn
Butter and salt, for serving

DO THIS FIRST:

1. Take the husks and strings off each cob. Save about 5 husks. Set the cleaned-up cobs on a big plate as you go.

DO THIS SECOND:

1. Spread the 5 husks across the bottom of a huge pot. Put in about 1 inch of water.

2. Cover. Bring the water to a boil over high heat. *(Clean up all the corn debris. Decide on a serving platter and have it near the stove. Make sure the butter and salt are on the table.)*

WRAPPING IT UP:

1. When the lid rattles or steam escapes, the water is boiling. Add the corn. You'll have to layer it. Cover and cook 5 to 7 minutes.

2. Take out the corn with tongs and pile the ears on the serving platter. Take it to the table immediately.

GRILLED CORN-ON-THE-COB FOR COMPANY

TECHNIQUE: Grilling
BEST TOOL: Tongs
MUST HAVE — Corn-cob prongs for serving

This all-time favorite company side dish offers great rewards. All you do is put corn on a grill for a few minutes and you make just about everyone happy. Don't even think about putting corn husks down your garbage disposal. Instead of being an inexpensive seasonal item the corn will cost you a plumber.

Serves 8 to 10

> 10 to 12 ears of corn
> Butter and salt, for serving

DO THIS FIRST:

1. Take the husks off the corn. Chop off the stems. Chop off any tip that isn't full of good-looking kernels.

2. Place the cobs all over the grate of a hot charcoal or gas grill.

3. Cover the grill, or leave the cover off and grill brazier-style.

4. When the first side blackens, after 5 to 8 minutes, turn the corn over and grill the other side. Use tongs.

DO THIS SECOND:

1. In the meantime, make sure everybody has two corn-cob prongs to stick into the ends of their cob. Get the butter and salt on the table.

WRAPPING IT UP:

1. Take the corn to the table in a big bowl or on a large platter, along with your tongs.

- Sometimes the label for this pasta will, indeed, refer to it as melon seed pasta.

- Orzo needs a strainer instead of a colander because the holes of a colander are so big that the orzo would flow right through them and down your drain.

- Sometimes orzo is packaged in 10-ounce bags. That amount will work fine in this recipe and serve 6, no problem.

ORZO

TECHNIQUE—Boiling
BEST COOKWARE—Large pot, such as a Dutch oven
MUST HAVE—8-inch-diameter fine-mesh strainer with long handle, pot holders

Orzo is a pasta shaped like melon seeds. When it's cooked, it's often mistaken for rice. Unlike any other pasta—and unlike rice, for that matter—orzo is so rich, silky, and smooth that it tastes like it's naturally buttered.

Serves 6 to 8

2 tablespoons butter
1 pound orzo

DO THIS FIRST:

1. Get out a medium-size serving bowl. Put the butter in the bowl.

2. Have a big wire-mesh strainer resting in your clean sink.

DO THIS SECOND:

1. Fill a big pot two-thirds with water. Cover, and set it on a burner. Crank the heat to high and bring the pot to a boil.

2. When the water boils so hard that steam escapes and the lid rattles, take off the cover and add the orzo a little at a time, so the water keeps boiling.

3. Stir then boil, cover off, 5 to 8 minutes, or according to the directions on the package, until the orzo is firm to the bite—not mushy, yet cooked.

WRAPPING IT UP:

1. Pour the orzo into the strainer (use pot holders!). Give a couple of good shakes to get as much water out as possible.

2. Transfer the hot orzo to the serving bowl. Take the bowl to the table. Stir it in front of everybody, pulling up the butter so it coats the orzo.

11

MAKE ONE
SERVE MANY

• The shortest path to lasagne is to have the sauce already made. After that, lasagne is a simple assembly.

• The spinach cooks in only the water that's on its leaves after washing. It looks like a lot of spinach, but you won't believe how small it gets.

• Squeeze the spinach like you'd squeeze clay.

• You don't have to rinse lasagne noodles because they cook a second time during baking.

• A cloth kitchen towel is the best thing to use to drain the hot lasagne noodles. If you use paper towels, you'll need just about the whole roll.

• Heavy duty foil makes a good "cover" for your baking dish.

• Okay, you were hoping for this. To make lasagne fast, use bottled spaghetti sauce, pre-grated cheese, and frozen spinach.

• Your assembly will be quicker if you set out an assembly line of ingredients in order: sauce, noodles, spinach, cheese.

• One of the best reasons to make lasagne is for the leftovers. Freeze leftover portions in zip bags, bowls, or any flat container. Reheat covered in a 250°F oven for 45 minutes or until it's bubbly.

LASAGNE

TECHNIQUE—Baking, boiling
BEST COOKWARE—Dutch oven, 9×13-inch baking dish
BEST EQUIPMENT—Various mixing bowls, tongs
BEST TOOL—Aluminum foil

A short glance will tell you this is not a quickie recipe. But it is easy, once you have all the ingredients ready to layer in a pan. The lasagne bakes, you clean up and serve this massive and hearty meal to your awed friends. Before you start, make a batch of Substantial Meat Sauce (page 202).

Serves 8 to 10

> 2 pounds fresh spinach *or* 3 10-ounce boxes, frozen spinach
> 32-ounce container ricotta cheese
> 2 eggs
> ½ teaspoon salt
> Generous black pepper
> 1 pound mozzarella cheese
> 1 cup grated Parmesan cheese
> 1 pound lasagne noodles
> About 4½ cups Substantial Meat Sauce (page 202)

DO THIS FIRST:

1. Fill a big pot, such as a Dutch oven, three fourths full of water. Cover and bring it to a boil on high heat. Spread a kitchen towel out on a table or countertop. Have 3 more handy.

DO THIS SECOND:

1. If using frozen spinach, thaw it and go to Step 4.

2. Rinse the fresh spinach leaf by leaf and cut off the stemmy pieces. Put the wet spinach in a Dutch oven, cover it, and put it on high heat. When you hear the spinach boiling, remove the cover.

3. Stir over high heat until the spinach wilts, 30 seconds or less.

4. Pour the spinach into a colander. With your hands, squeeze it into a tight ball to force out excess water.

5. Put the spinach in a bowl. Mix in the ricotta, eggs, salt, and pepper. Mix with a fork around and around until very smooth.

6. Grate the mozzarella. Set aside 1 cup. Stir the rest and all the Parmesan into the ricotta.

DO THIS THIRD:

1. Drop 6 lasagne noodles into the boiling water and cook them according to package directions. Lift the noodles from the water with tongs. Lay them on the kitchen towel to drain.

2. Keep cooking noodles 6 at a time until they're all cooked. Stack them in layers between the extra towels.

DO THIS FOURTH:

1. Preheat the oven to 375°F, with a rack in the middle.

2. Layer the lasagne in a 9×13-inch baking dish as follows:

1. On the bottom, a little meat sauce
2. One quarter of the lasagne noodles
3. A layer of sauce, to cover the noodles
4. One third of the spinach-cheese mixture
5. Another quarter of the lasagne noodles
6. A layer of sauce
7. Another third of the spinach-cheese mixture
8. Half of the remaining lasagne noodles
9. A layer of sauce
10. The remaining spinach-cheese mixture
11. The rest of the lasagne noodles
12. The rest of the sauce
13. The cup of reserved mozzarella
14. On top, a tight foil cover

WRAPPING IT UP:

1. There! Now bake your lasagne for 45 minutes.

2. Take the baked lasagne to the table or buffet. Cut it into generous squares with a big knife and scoop out the squares with a spatula.

• After making risotto once, you'll always remember the method.

• Sun-dried tomatoes are not always dried in the sun. Some of them get blown dry in hot wind tunnels. Regardless of how they become dehydrated, some can be so dried that they're not even chewable. Buy dried tomatoes that are a little pliant.

• Dried tomatoes are often sold in bulk in the produce section of grocery stores. If you can't find them, don't worry. They're not as vital to risotto as, say, rice.

• Fresh tomatoes won't work well in this dish. They would exude a great deal more liquid and actually tint the risotto orange.

• The rice that cooks into the creamiest risotto is short-grain. The type used in Italy for risotto is Arborio. It's in the rice section of most supermarkets. Arborio is by far the creamiest and worth the extra money. Medium grain, sometimes labeled Calrose for the particular variety that grows in California, is also wonderful.

• The risotto will cook nicely with long-grain rice. It just won't be very creamy.

• Leftover chicken befuddled a friend who asked, "Where do you buy leftover chicken?" Well, to get leftover chicken you've got to make a chicken recipe but not eat it all. What remains is the leftover chicken.

RISOTTO THAT'S AN ENTIRE MEAL

TECHNIQUE—Sautéing, boiling
BEST COOKWARE—A big skillet, 10½- to 12-inch diameter
BEST TOOLS—Ladle, wooden spatula

This creamy rice dish, filled with enough extras to qualify it as a main course, is all you need for a dinner with friends. Serve it with some great Italian bread, a simple salad, goblets of red wine, and light it all with candles.

Serves 6

¼ cup dried tomatoes (whole is nicer than "bits")
1 onion
½ cup frozen peas
1 cup raw rice
4 cups chicken stock (canned is okay)
⅓ cup grated Parmesan cheese
1 tablespoon chopped fresh parsley
2 tablespoons olive oil
1 cup leftover chicken pieces
½ teaspoon salt
Black or white pepper, to taste

DO THIS FIRST:

1. Drop the dried tomatoes into a bowl of hot tap water to rehydrate while you get the rest of the recipe going.

2. Peel and halve the onion. Chop the halves into nice-looking ¼-inch dice. Pile the onion on a dinner plate.

3. Measure the peas. Leave them in their measuring cup and set it on the plate next to the onion.

4. Measure the rice. Leave it in the measuring cup and set it on the dinner plate, too. Have the plate convenient to the stove.

5. Pour the chicken stock into a pot or bowl and set it near the stove with a ladle or 1-cup measuring cup.

6. Measure the Parmesan and leave it in its measuring cup. Chop the parsley. Choose a pretty bowl for serving. Put the Parmesan and parsley near it for quick use. *This is your last chance to clean up before you eat the risotto.*

DO THIS SECOND:

1. Put the olive oil in a large pot or skillet and turn the heat to high.

2. When the oil is very hot (look for ripples) push the onion off the plate into the skillet. Sauté about 2 minutes, until the onion is soft.

3. Now add all the rice. Stir the grains quickly around the skillet until they're toasty, a good 1 minute.

DO THIS THIRD:

1. Immediately ladle ½ cup of chicken stock into the rice. It will sizzle. Let it come to a boil, stirring.

2. When the rice has absorbed the stock but the pan still has a small amount of liquid, add another ½ cup of stock. Let it boil again. Don't add more stock until the rice absorbs this addition.

3. At this point, if the rice is cooking with gentle bubbling, you can reduce the heat to medium.

4. Continue adding stock in ½-cup increments and waiting for the rice to absorb it, until the rice is plump and is no longer firm. You'll have to bite on it. The rice will get creamier and creamier.

5. You'll be at this about 20 to 25 minutes. You may or may not use up all the stock.

WRAPPING IT UP:

1. When you are nearing the end, drain the tomatoes and add them to the rice. Add the peas, chicken, salt, and pepper. Keep stirring while adding more stock, if necessary to keep the mixture creamy, until the "extras" are heated through.

2. Transfer the risotto to the pretty bowl. Sprinkle with Parmesan and parsley. Stir two or three times—that's all—and serve hot.

• Your leftover chicken can be roasted, baked, sauteed, fried, steamed, or boiled.

• If you don't have leftover chicken, buy a small cooked chicken—smoked is good—and rip the meat off the bones. Add the shreds and pieces to the risotto when the leftover chicken would be added.

• The warmer the chicken stock, the less it shocks the rice each time it's added. Put it in a large glass measuring cup and microwave it on High for 3 minutes, covered with plastic wrap, or heat it in another pot on the stove.

TEXAS CROWD CHILI

TECHNIQUE—Sautéing/braising
BEST COOKWARE—Chili pot (what else?) or
 Dutch oven
BEST EQUIPMENT—Chef's knife, cutting board

This chili comes out thick and rich. I learned to use enchilada sauce as a gravy base from Dotty Griffith of the Dallas *Morning News* when we were roommates. This is straightforward and easy, and boy-howdy does it make the house smell good.

Serves 6 to 8

> 3-pound beef chuck roast
> 2½ tablespoons minced garlic
> 6 tablespoons chile powder
> 2 tablespoons ground cumin
> 2 teaspoons salt
> 2 10-ounce cans prepared red enchilada
> sauce
> 3 tablespoons flour
> ½ cup water

> *It's not only better with garnish, it's GREAT:*
> *Shredded Cheddar or Longhorn cheese,*
> *chopped green onions, slices of pickled*
> *jalapeño, minced fresh cilantro*

DO THIS FIRST:
1. With a sharp knife, trim the fat off the beef. Chop the fat so you have about ¼ cup, and put it in a large pot, such as a Dutch oven. Cut the meat into nice ¼-inch cubes. Pile the meat on a dinner plate.

2. Mince the garlic and have it convenient to the stove.

3. Measure the chile powder, cumin, and salt into one small bowl or cup. Set it near the stove.

4. Open the cans of enchilada sauce, and have them ready, too.

DO THIS SECOND:
1. Melt the fat over medium heat until it coats the bottom of the pot. As pieces become

browned—this will take about 5 minutes—pick them out with tongs or a slotted spoon, until they're all removed, and throw them away.

2. Add the meat, with the heat still medium, and stir and cook until the juices given off by the meat evaporate. Be careful not to actually brown the meat.

3. Add the garlic and stir it into the meat.

4. Add the spice mix and the cans of enchilada sauce. Fill *one* can with water and add that. Stir until all the ingredients combine nicely with the meat.

DO THIS THIRD:
1. Bring the pot to a boil. Cover it, reduce the heat to medium-low, and simmer the chili for 1 hour. *(Clean up the mess. Fill a couple of small bowls with garnishes, and put them on the table.)*

2. Take a bite of meat; it should be tender. If not, give it another 15 minutes or so.

3. Use a fork to stir the flour and water in a small bowl, until a smooth paste forms that will thicken the chili. If you see lumps, mash them until they're gone (very important!).

4. Remove the lid. Slowly pour in the flour thickener with one hand while stirring with the other. Continue cooking, uncovered, so the chili bubbles gently, for about 10 minutes. The chili will thicken even more. This is the most important time to stir so the chili won't stick or scorch.

WRAPPING IT UP:
1. Bring the whole dang chili pot to the table and set it on a hot pad. Have the garnishes in bowls on the table, and tell your friends to help themselves.

MAKE-AHEAD OPTION:
1. You can refrigerate the finished chili in a covered container up to 3 days, or freeze it up to 3 months.

• *Chili* is the stew. *Chile* is Spanish for the hot, dried red peppers that when ground up become chile powder.

• This chili is spicy. The faint-hearted should know that cumin is actually spicier than chile powder.

• Having lived in Texas, I don't put beans in chili. I think it's against the law. Beans seem just filler, although there are recipes for chili that manage to include beans without ruining the batch. You'll have to look elsewhere for that kind of recipe.

• This is a Saturday or Sunday morning recipe. Do it when you know you can hang around the house.

• If you cook the sauce early in the day, you'll have time to refrigerate it. Not only does this make long-cooked recipes taste better, it gives any fat a chance to rise, chill, and solidify to make it easy to lift it off by the time you're ready to re-heat it for dinner.

• Ground chuck is fat-tier than ground round or ground sirloin. Don't waste expensive meat in a recipe that cooks it to death. Chuck is fine here. It is the tastiest of the three. The fat (which, of course, contributes to that flavor) will be drained off.

• Cooking the beef on medium heat is the best way to draw out the most fat without browning or searing the meat.

• With so many tomato products in stores these days, it's a shame to pass up a can of imported Italian plum tomatoes, if you see them. Sizes vary, but something in the 28- or 29-ounce size is a good replacement for the tomato sauce.

• Tomato puree is also a great product. A 28- or 29-ounce can will work in place of the tomato sauce, too.

• Instead of spaghetti, you could use vermicelli or thin spaghetti.

SPAGHETTI IN SUBSTANTIAL MEAT SAUCE

TECHNIQUE — Sautéing/boiling
BEST COOKWARE — Dutch oven, medium-size skillet
BEST EQUIPMENT — Chef's knife and cutting board
BEST UTENSIL — Wooden spoon
MUST HAVE — Colander

This is one of my all-time greatest hits of company meals. It's humble, staunchly American rather than truly Italian, but good and hearty. Serve with a green salad and some bread and lots of Chianti Classico.

Serves 8 to 10

Meat sauce
3 large onions
6 cloves garlic
29-ounce can tomato sauce
2 6-ounce cans tomato paste
3 tablespoons olive oil
1½ pounds ground beef
Generous grinds black pepper
1 teaspoon dried oregano
1 teaspoon dried basil
½ teaspoon dried thyme
2 bay leaves (whole, don't crumble)
2 teaspoons salt

Spaghetti
1 pound spaghetti
Lots of grated Parmesan cheese

DO THIS FIRST:
1. Peel and chop the onions and put them in a bowl.

2. Mince the garlic and put it in the bowl with the onions.

3. Open the cans of tomato sauce and tomato paste, and take the bowl and cans to the stove.

DO THIS SECOND:
1. Put the olive oil in a Dutch oven. Turn the heat to high. When the oil is hot, pour the onions and garlic out of the bowl into the oil.

2. Stir well. Lower the heat to medium. Sauté until the onion and garlic are soft, about 8 minutes.

DO THIS THIRD:

1. Meanwhile, put the ground beef in a medium-size skillet. Turn the heat to medium.

2. Use a wooden spoon to break the meat up into small crumbles as it cooks. When you have a minute, set a wire-mesh strainer over a bowl.

3. After about 12 minutes, when you can't see any more pink and the beef has released a lot of fat, pour the beef into the strainer. Let the fat drip out and throw it away.

DO THIS FOURTH:

1. Add the cooked beef to the onions. Add the tomato sauce and paste. Now fill the tomato-paste cans with water, and add the water.

2. Add the remaining sauce ingredients except the salt, rubbing the oregano, basil, and thyme between your palms to crush them and release their flavor as they fall into the sauce.

DO THIS FIFTH:

1. Simmer the sauce, partially covered, over very low heat, for 1½ to 2 hours. Do not leave the house (although it is tempting). Give a stir about every 15 minutes to prevent sticking. The sauce should gently bubble, not spatter.

2. Toward the end of cooking, add the salt. Taste. Does it need even more? This only you can answer.

WRAPPING IT UP:

1. Cook the spaghetti as explained on page 64. Place the drained spaghetti in a serving bowl or on a platter. Spoon the meat sauce in a large area in the middle, but don't mix it in.

2. Bring it to the table and mix it in front of all gathered. Be sure to have plenty of Parmesan cheese on the table.

• **You can make the sauce and keep it in a covered container in the refrigerator up to 3 days, or in the freezer up to 3 months. Reheat it in the microwave on Medium power, covered with plastic wrap. Or reheat it in a pot over medium heat, stirring often so it doesn't stick.**

• Stew meat comes already cut in cubes from the chuck or short plate, good cuts for long cooking in liquid.

• If you want to save money, buy a 2½-pound chuck pot roast and cut it with a long knife into nice even squares yourself. The extra ½ pound is my fudge factor for the fat you'll no doubt cut off and throw away.

• The flour that coats the meat eventually thickens the liquid into a gravy.

• The potatoes contribute thickening, too.

• All you believers in the powers of unpeeled carrots, take note. Peel the carrots or the skins will float around in your stew like papery rings.

• The thickness of the carrot slices is up to you. I like them thin, about ¼ inch thick. My mom likes them in chunks. Two hours of cooking will cook a carrot in any form.

• The meat will sizzle and smoke as you brown it. Keep the heat high and keep going despite a lot of noise and smokeworks. If you wear glasses, you'll probably have to wipe them off after this step.

• The meat is supposed to stick to the pot. Anything that sticks will help to color and flavor your upcoming sauce.

BEEF STEW AND AIRY LIGHT DUMPLINGS

TECHNIQUE—Braising (boiling)
BEST COOKWARE—Dutch oven
BEST EQUIPMENT—Chef's knife and cutting board
BEST UTENSILS—Big spoon to stir; vegetable peeler

My mother fed us stew many times during the year. It is one of my dad's favorites—a meal in a bowl that's very hearty, easy, and cheap. You'll be surprised at its big flavor despite its being short of herbs and spices. It's also warm and cozy and fits the mood for a Sunday night supper. The dumplings blow up like heads of cauliflower.

Serves 8

1 big onion
1 teaspoon minced garlic
4 carrots
2 big potatoes
28-ounce can whole or crushed tomatoes
14-ounce can beef stock
⅓ cup flour
2 teaspoons salt, to start
Lots of black pepper
2 pounds cubes of lean "stew" meat
2 tablespoons vegetable oil
Airy Light Dumpling batter (page 206)

DO THIS FIRST:

1. Peel, halve, and chop the onion. Put it on a big dinner plate.

2. Mince the garlic and put it on the plate with the onion.

3. Peel the carrots. Cut off the tops and ends. Cut the carrots into nice slices and put them in a work bowl.

4. Peel the potatoes. Cut them into ½-inch cubes. Add them to the bowl with the carrots.

5. Open the cans of tomatoes and beef stock. Have all of these ingredients convenient to the stove.

DO THIS SECOND:

1. Measure the flour into another, big, bowl. Mix in the salt and pepper.

2. Add the meat and roll it around in the flour. Shake off excess flour from each piece and set the meat on a big plate, also near the stove. Throw the excess flour away. You'll probably want to wash your hands.

DO THIS THIRD:

1. Put the oil in a big pot, such as a Dutch oven. Turn the heat to high.

2. When the oil is very hot, slide the meat off the plate into the pot.

3. Stir around on high heat until the chunks of meat are fried brown on all sides. This may take 5 minutes. Get the meat as brown as you can without burning it. Don't worry if it sticks a little.

DO THIS FOURTH:

1. When the meat is browned, take it out of the pot (a slotted spoon is good for this) and put it back on its plate for the time being. The meat most certainly isn't fully cooked at this point.

2. Now push the onion and garlic off their plate into the pot, which is still on high heat. Sauté for about 5 minutes. After the first minute, turn the heat down to medium so the onion won't burn.

DO THIS FIFTH:

1. Add all the remaining stew ingredients, including the meat, but not the dumpling batter.

2. Bring the stew to a boil. When it boils, cover the pot. Turn the heat down to low so the stew simmers, covered, for 2 hours. Please don't just walk away. Check often and stir up the bottom so it doesn't scorch.

3. At the end of cooking, taste the stew to make sure it has enough salt and pepper.

- How darkly you brown the meat shows up later in the richness and deep color of the sauce.

- Tomatoes give this stew a beautiful red tinge.

- At first the stew will look thin and watery. After 1 hour you'll notice some thickening. By the end of the cooking time, it will have developed a thick, rich gravy-sauce, and the pieces of meat and potatoes will be a little smaller than when they started out.

- I worry about those of you whose pots are thin on the bottom. This stew will scorch if not well insulated by your cookware or if you don't stir it enough. Scorching doesn't just stay on the bottom where it forms. It sends its powerful bitterness in little black pieces all through the stew and pretty much destroys the taste.

- For a nice addition to the stew, moments before you add the dumpling batter put in 1 cup frozen peas or corn.

- There has to be plenty of gravy in the stew for the dumplings to steam successfully.

- I've told you that you can peek into a pot of rice without ruining it. But in this case if you peek you'll blow it—the dumplings, that is. All that air expansion from the baking powder will shrink if the cover is removed. Instead of clouds, your dumplings will turn into little belly bombs.

- The dumplings should have the texture of biscuits.

WRAPPING IT UP:

1. Drop the dumpling batter in portions the size of tennis balls over the surface of the simmering stew, which is still on low heat.

2. Cover the pot. Simmer 15 to 20 minutes. No peeking!

3. Open the cover. Ah! Serve some stew with a portion of dumpling.

AIRY LIGHT DUMPLINGS

Make the dumpling batter 15 minutes before the stew has cooked its 2 hours. Use the batter within about 5 minutes.

Makes about 8

> 2 cups flour
> 4 teaspoons baking powder
> 1 teaspoon salt
> 4 tablespoons butter (not too soft)
> ¾ cup milk

DO THIS FIRST:

1. Put the flour, baking powder, and salt in a big mixing bowl.

2. Cut the butter into small pieces. Add it to the flour.

3. Rub the mixture through your hands and fingers, as if you were rolling clay into a snake. Rub until you can't see any more loose flour. This will take at least 3 minutes.

DO THIS SECOND:

1. Pour in the milk. Stir with a fork until you have a smooth, very soft dough-like batter.

SEVEN-LAYER SALAD

TECHNIQUE—Boiling
BEST COOKWARE—Medium-size pot
BEST EQUIPMENT—Chef's knife, cutting board, salad
  spinner

This looks very challenging. But once it's finished you've got a complete lunch or cool summer supper. It makes a very impressive showing with its layers of red, green, and white. The best news is it gets better if it has a chance to sit in the refrigerator overnight, which makes any thought of frantic last-minute details go away.

Serves 12

Mayonnaise
2 cups mayonnaise
¼ teaspoon cayenne pepper

Vinaigrette
3 tablespoons red wine vinegar
1 teaspoon minced garlic (or scoop it from
  a jar)
1 teaspoon prepared mustard from a jar
Salt and pepper
½ cup olive oil

Salad
8 eggs
½ pound bacon
1 pound fresh spinach
4 medium tomatoes
1 medium cucumber
1 small red onion
Salt and pepper
3 ribs very green celery
2 cups bread crumbs

DO THIS FIRST

1. For the mayonnaise: Mix the mayonnaise and cayenne in a bowl. Chill.

2. For the vinaigrette: In a jar with a lid, shake the vinegar, garlic, mustard, salt, and pepper. Add the olive oil and shake until blended. Keep at room temperature a couple of hours, or chill it for longer storage.

DO THIS SECOND:

1. Place the eggs in a medium-size pot. Add cold tap water so the eggs are submerged by 1 inch. Cover, set on highest heat, and bring to a boil as fast as you can. When the water boils, turn off the heat and leave the eggs in the pot for 17 minutes. Drain the eggs in a colander, let cold water run over them to cool them down, then leave them in the colander.

2. Place the bacon strips in a medium skillet. Set it over medium heat. Fry the bacon until it's browned on both sides. Drain on paper towels.

3. While the bacon fries, cut the stems off the spinach. Wash the leaves (see How To Wash Greens, page 187). Spin them dry in a salad spinner.

DO THIS THIRD:

1. Halve, seed, and chop the tomatoes into large squares. Place them in a bowl. Pour the vinaigrette over them.

2. Wash the cucumber. Halve it lengthwise, then cut the halves into lengthwise strips. Cut across the strips at ¼-inch intervals. Place the chopped cucumber in a bowl. Peel, halve, and dice the onion. Add it to the cucumber. Sprinkle with salt and pepper.

3. Peel and mash the hard-cooked eggs. Chop the celery and mix it with the eggs.

4. Crumble the bacon.

WRAPPING IT UP:

1. Get out a clear glass bowl with straight or slightly bowled sides. As you make the layers pay attention to the design forming through the sides of the bowl rather than the center.

2. Spread the bread crumbs on the bottom.

3. Top the crumbs with the cucumber and red onion.

4. Next spoon on the eggs and celery.

5. Scoop the tomatoes out of the vinaigrette with a slotted spoon or small strainer. Let them drain a moment, and scatter them over the egg. Save the vinaigrette for future green salads.

6. Next arrange the spinach leaves.

7. Dollop the mayonnaise in a border around the sides of the bowl. Make sure it touches the sides. Don't fill the center with mayonnaise or the salad will sag.

8. Finally, sprinkle the top with bacon. Wrap the bowl well in plastic wrap and refrigerate at least 3 hours, or overnight.

9. Bring the layered salad to the table. Make sure everyone gets a good look at your hard work. Then scoop out servings after a light-handed mixing.

GREEK SALAD

TECHNIQUE — Chopping
BEST EQUIPMENT — Chef's knife, cutting board, and
  salad spinner
MUST HAVE — Big salad bowl

• If you can't bear the thought of iceberg lettuce, substitute 2 heads of Romaine or use 2 pounds fresh, washed spinach dried in a salad spinner.

• Calamata olives are small black olives often sold in the deli section of grocery stores, or in jars with the rest of the olives. Nicoise olives are a great substitute, but they're more expensive.

• Greek feta is a crumbly cheese traditionally made from sheep's milk and heavily salted in a watery brine. You can find Greek feta at specialty cheese stores and delis. Other good feta cheese may be made from cow's milk and could come from many places besides Greece — Denmark, France, Bulgaria, or the U.S.

Known simply as *salata* in Greek, this country salad is pretty much the same all over Greece and its islands. The iceberg lettuce that food snobs look down on in America is preferred by the Greeks. This is probably because iceberg is cool, crunchy, and sweet. Iceberg lettuce is at its best in April and May and again in October and November. This salad is really a lot of chopping, but no cooking.

Serves 6 to 8

1½ heads iceberg lettuce
4 tomatoes
1 medium-size red onion
2 medium-size cucumbers
1½ cups Greek black calamata olives
¾ pound Greek feta cheese

Dressing
6 tablespoons red wine vinegar
⅔ cup olive oil
2 teaspoons dried oregano
½ teaspoon salt
Lots of ground black pepper

American option: 2-ounce can anchovy filets

DO THIS FIRST:

1. Get out a big bowl. Get out your salad spinner.

2. Cut the heads of lettuce in half, going through the stem. Open them up, slice out the cores, and rip the leaves into bite-size squares. Wash the lettuce and spin it dry in a salad spinner. Put it in the bottom of the big bowl.

3. Halve each tomato across its equator. Squeeze the halves gently while flicking the seeds into the garbage. Cut the halves into wedges or big pieces. Spread the tomatoes over the lettuce.

4. Peel the onion. Slice it into thin rings. Scatter the rings over the tomatoes.

5. Wash the cucumbers. Slice them as thin as you can. Scatter the cucumbers over the onion.

DO THIS SECOND:
1. Top the salad with the olives.

2. Cut the cheese into small squares and layer them over the olives. If you're using anchovies, put them on now.

3. Cover the bowl with plastic wrap and chill the salad while you make the dressing.

DO THIS THIRD:
1. Measure the vinegar, oil, oregano, salt, and pepper into a small container with a lid (a glass jar or a plastic storage container). Shake well.

2. Taste. Is there enough salt? Have you put anchovies in the salad? If so, allow for the saltiness of the anchovies before deciding to add more salt to the dressing.

WRAPPING IT UP:
1. Bring the salad to the table. Pour the dressing over it. Toss and serve, or let guests serve themselves.

2. Serve this salad on small plates. It almost never shows up in bowls.

MAKE AHEAD OPTION:
1. Refrigerate the salad in its bowl and the dressing in its container for up to 2 hours.

2. Combine at serving time.

12

DESSERT

WHIPPED CREAM

BEST EQUIPMENT — Portable electric mixer, mixing bowl (non-plastic)

So you think whipped cream comes out of a can like shaving cream? Even when the can holds real cream, it never tastes as fresh or is whipped as fluffy as cream whipped by you. To turn pourable cream into a topping, you've got to whip air into it. Whip it a lot, and it will become butter. Whip it just so it holds a medium-soft tuft, and you've got whipped cream you'd recognize on top of fruit or any cake.

> **1 cup whipping cream**
> **1 tablespoon sugar**
> **1 teaspoon vanilla**

DO THIS FIRST:

1. Pour all the ingredients into a mixing bowl with high sides. Beat with an electric mixer on the highest speed, moving the beaters in a circular motion, until the beaters form a wake.

DO THIS SECOND:

1. Start to pay attention. Stop the beaters. Dip them into the cream, withdraw them, and turn them over. Does the topknot peak and hold itself up? Or does it droop?

2. If it holds, you're done.

3. If it droops, beat a few seconds more and test again, until the peak holds.

• It's easy to stop beating way short of your goal of "fluffy." The butter should be creamy, light, and airy with no lumps at all—almost like the spreadable stuff sold in tubs.

• The flour is stirred into the dough because beating would develop its gluten, which would make your cookies tough.

• Flicking water off your hand is probably my most unscientific cooking technique, but it will give exactly the right amount to bind the dough. Too much water, and you're up against the tough-cookie thing again.

• You are constantly told here to stop when various stages are attained. Don't mess with the dough any more than is absolutely necessary. Your cookies will be tender and soft as your reward.

• You chill the dough before rolling it to firm up the layering of butter-flour-butter that you made without realizing when you mixed the dough.

SUGAR COOKIES

TECHNIQUE—Baking
BEST COOKWARE—Cookie sheets
BEST EQUIPMENT—Mixing bowls, portable electric mixer
BEST TOOLS—Box grater, wooden spoon, spatula
MUST HAVE—Rolling pin, cookie cutters

I've been whipping out batches of sugar cookies like never before. That's because my little boy is old enough to help. He's 4 and a half, plenty old to roll out dough and make cut-outs with cookie cutters.

Makes 2 dozen

1½ sticks butter (12 tablespoons)
¾ cup sugar
2¼ cups all-purpose flour
1 lemon
1 egg
1 teaspoon vanilla
Dash of salt
A flick or two of water

DO THIS FIRST:

1. Preheat the oven to 350°F, with two oven racks in the lower two-thirds of the oven. Put the butter in a big mixing bowl so it can soften while you pull the rest of the ingredients together.

2. Measure the sugar and leave it in the measuring cup. Measure the flour into a small bowl.

3. Grate the yellow skin off the lemon on the fine holes of a box grater. You can do this over a plate or a sheet of waxed paper. Measure 1 teaspoon of the yellow "zest."

4. Get out the egg and the bottle of vanilla.

DO THIS SECOND:

1. Beat the butter on high speed until it's very fluffy. This may take 2 minutes. Now add the sugar and beat until it's very fluffy again, another 2 minutes.

2. Crack the egg into the butter. Add the lemon zest and vanilla. Beat just to blend in the egg—no more. The dough will be loose and yellow.

DO THIS THIRD:

1. Pour in the flour and dash of salt. Put the beaters away. Stir in the flour with a wooden spoon until the dough is mealy but all the flour is absorbed. Stop stirring the moment this happens.

2. Get your hand wet under the faucet and flick whatever water is clinging to it into the dough. This is an amount beyond measurement. Mix again—your hands work well for this step—into a soft, pliant ball of dough, then stop.

3. Wrap the dough loosely in plastic wrap. Press it into a disc after it's wrapped and chill it for 2 hours.

DO THIS FOURTH:

1. Spread about 1 tablespoon of flour into a circle directly on your countertop. Unwrap the dough, set it on the floured circle, and roll it out until it's ⅛ inch thick.

2. Make your cut-outs with cookie cutters, lift them off the counter, and put them on two ungreased cookie sheets.

WRAPPING IT UP:

1. Bake 10 minutes. Lift the cookies off the sheets with a spatula and let them cool on wire racks.

2. Keep baking the cookies in batches until all the dough is used up.

- Cookies made when the dough is too warm stand a good chance of baking up tough from butter not in suspension literally melting and running out of its binding.

- A true cookie sheet has three sides missing. The heat doesn't have to climb over any sidewalls to get to the dough. The second-best option is a baking sheet with a very shallow rim on all four sides.

- If you want to decorate the cookies, add sprinkles and glitter before you bake them.

- This is a standard butter cookie dough. It can all be mixed by hand.

- The rubbing action of your hands on the ingredients will create lumps that get smaller and smaller the more you rub. The best way to get the dough compressed is while you rub, cross the fingers of one hand through the separations between the fingers of your other hand.

- Another way to turn butter and dry ingredients into fine crumbs is to use a pastry blender. This is a series of bowed, parallel blades held together by a handle which you grasp as you lift the blender up and down while dragging it across the ingredients. It's sort of half chopping, half mashing.

- The dough will be pliant—not so soft that it can't be rolled into a rope, and not so stiff that it crumbles.

- It's hard to give a definition of doneness by color, because the cookies should remain pale after baking. On the other hand, if they turn golden brown, they're way overbaked.

- They'll seem flabby when you cut them and lift them from the cookie sheets to the wire racks. This is absolutely correct. They'll firm up when they're completely cooled.

- If they seem firm when you cut them, they're overbaked.

JELLY COOKIES

TECHNIQUE—Baking
BEST COOKWARE—2 cookie sheets
BEST EQUIPMENT—Big bowl, measuring cups and spoons
HANDIEST GADGET—Table knife

It is impossible for me to experience a festive occasion without my mother's jelly cookies. They require no mixer, no pastry blender, no cookie cutters. I like them because they are colorful, easy, and asphyxiated with butter.

Makes about 5 dozen

1½ sticks butter (12 tablespoons)
2 cups all-purpose flour
⅔ cup sugar
½ teaspoon baking powder
1 egg
2 teaspoons vanilla
Dark jam, jelly, or preserves, such as raspberry, blackberry, or strawberry from a 6- or 8-ounce jar

DO THIS FIRST:

1. Take the butter out of the refrigerator so it can soften a little. Preheat the oven to 350°F. Get out 2 cookie sheets. You don't have to grease them. Get out a big bowl and your measuring cups and spoons.

DO THIS SECOND:

1. Measure the flour, sugar, and baking powder into the big bowl. (Make sure you've got baking powder, and not baking soda!)

2. Cut the butter into small pieces and scatter them on top of the flour.

3. Rub the mixture through your palms as if you were making a clay snake until it looks like fine crumbs. This will take at least 2 minutes by hand. (For apparatus that helps, see Let's Talk).

4. Crack the egg into the bowl. Add the vanilla. Mix to a medium-firm dough. If it is too soft to hold a shape, chill it about 15 minutes.

DO THIS THIRD:

1. Divide the dough into 4 parts. Shape each part into a 13-inch-long rope that is ¾ inch thick. Place 2 ropes on each ungreased cookie sheet.

2. Draw the end of the handle of a table knife right down the center of each rope to make a lengthwise trough. Fill the troughs with jelly.

WRAPPING IT UP:

1. Bake the ropes for 15 to 20 minutes. While they bake get out a couple of cake-cooling wire racks.

2. When done, the cookies will have spread and barely turned pale on the edges. Cool no more than 5 minutes before cutting.

3. To cut, slice the ropes diagonally into ¾-inch lengths while still on the cookie sheets. As you go, lift the cookies with a spatula to the wire racks to cool.

VANILLA PUDDING

- The yolks should be in a bowl big enough to allow for whisking in some hot pudding.

- When the hot pudding mixture is poured into the yolks, the technical term for this is "tempering yolks." This means raising the temperature of the yolks, so when you finally put the yolks into the main pudding they won't curdle.

- To separate an egg, tap it gently on a flat surface to crack the shell. Hold the egg upright over a bowl. Lift up on the shell above the crack line and let the white drool out into the bowl. Transfer the yolk back and forth between shell halves until no white is attached to the yolk. Drop the yolk into a second bowl.

- If you are tempted to cheat and just add whole eggs, don't. Egg whites cook earlier than yolks. By the time the yolks have done their job of thickening, the whites will have long turned to scrambled strands. Just separate the eggs first thing, and get it over with.

- One sign that the pudding is getting hot enough to boil up one big bubble is the tiny bubbles that collect around the edge.

- Butter is added to help "set" the pudding.

- The vanilla is added after the cooking stops. Otherwise it would cook out.

TECHNIQUE—Slow stovetop stirring
BEST COOKWARE—Medium-size pot
BEST UTENSILS—Wooden spoon, whisk

Vanilla pudding might sound like kids' food, but with some extras on top it becomes very grown up. Of course, many people turn into kids when dessert is served, and would never turn down a chance to eat vanilla pudding. Given its appeal, vanilla pudding serves not only many tastes but also many levels of maturity.

Serves 6

> 3 egg yolks
> 2 tablespoons unsalted butter
> ½ tablespoon pure vanilla extract
> ½ cup sugar
> ¼ cup flour
> 2 cups whole milk
>
> *For company, it's better with extras:*
> *Chopped macadamia nuts or pecans; a*
> *topping of chocolate sprinkles; crushed*
> *Heath bars*

DO THIS FIRST:

1. Separate 3 eggs and put the yolks in a soup bowl. Have the bowl of yolks convenient to the stove. Store the whites covered in the refrigerator; you can add a few extra whites to an omelet or strata.

2. Cut the right amount of butter and set it on a plate near the stove along with the bottle of vanilla. Get out 6 small dessert bowls or goblets.

DO THIS SECOND:

1. Set a pot on the stove. Have ready a whisk and a wooden spoon.

2. Measure the sugar, flour, and milk into the pot. Whisk hard so the milk isn't lumpy.

3. Turn the heat to medium. Stand there, stirring slowly with a wooden spoon, until the milk boils up one big bubble. This may take 15 minutes (but it's worth it).

DO THIS THIRD:

1. When you see this one big bubble, immediately take the pot off the heat, but leave the heat on medium.

2. Pour a little of your hot pudding (about ½ cup) directly from the pot into the egg yolks.

3. Whisk the yolks until smooth, then pour them into the main pudding mixture.

WRAPPING IT UP:

1. Put the pudding back over medium heat and cook and stir it about 1 minute more. The pudding is supposed to thicken.

2. Finally, take the pot off the heat and stir in the vanilla and butter.

3. Pour the hot pudding into the dessert bowls or goblets, cool, and chill a few hours. (For easier clean-up, immediately fill the pot with hot tap water and let it soak.)

4. When the pudding is cold, serve it topped with nuts, sprinkles, or crushed candy.

• The taste of vanilla will be strongest when the pudding is hot. As the pudding cools, the vanilla flavor tends to fade. Keep this in mind if you question the addition of a half tablespoon of vanilla.

• Pure vanilla extract is just that. Imitation vanilla is made synthetically with vanillin—not vanilla at all but a by-product of the wood-pulp industry. Look for vanilla labeled "pure" from such locations as Madagascar, Tahiti, or Bourbon Islands. To be labeled pure vanilla "extract" it must be at least 35 percent alcohol by volume. The alcohol is vital for extracting and holding the flavor of the vanilla beans in suspension. Vanilla with less than 35 percent alcohol has to be labeled as a "flavor."

- Zest is just the yellow part of the lemon's skin. Calling it lemon peel, or lemon rind, isn't quite accurate enough. That implies that some of the white, pithy part of the peel is being called for, and because it's so bitter, it definitely is not what you want in your cheesecake.

- There are a few gadgets that take only the thin, colored layer off a lemon or orange. They're called zesters. You probably already have a zester. It's the side of a box grater with the smallest holes. Rub a lemon fast up and down these holes. Tiny flecks of yellow will collect inside the grater.

- The cheesecake may crack during baking, or crack as it cools. Sometimes this happens, sometimes it doesn't. You can still serve a cheesecake with a crack in it. I've done it many times. I've never heard a single objection—and I've listened.

- Slow steady heat in the oven is good assurance that the cheesecake won't develop a crack.

YOUR FIRST CHEESECAKE

TECHNIQUE—Baking
BEST EQUIPMENT—Food processor, portable or table-top electric mixer
BEST COOKWARE—8-inch cake pan or 7-inch springform pan
BEST TOOLS—Rubber spatula, wire cooling rack, citrus zester

Cheese, sugar, and eggs beaten and baked give you cheesecake. If this upsets the mystique that cheesecake is something more, well, that's really all a cheesecake is no matter how much spin it's gotten from secret recipes and exorbitant prices for a slice at a restaurant. The crust isn't really pastry like a pie crust, but more of a pan lining, and it doesn't have to be perfect.

Serves 6

Crust
1¾ cups flour
¼ cup powdered sugar
1 egg

Filling
3-ounce package cream cheese
½ cup sugar
8-ounce tub ricotta cheese
Zest of 1 lemon
2 eggs
2 teaspoons vanilla

DO THIS FIRST:
1. Take the cream cheese out of the refrigerator. Unwrap it and let it soften while you make the crust and get the rest of the ingredients together.

DO THIS SECOND:

1. For the crust: Preheat the oven to 375°F. Measure the flour and sugar into a medium-size mixing bowl. Stir to mix the two together.

2. Crack the egg into the flour. Use a fork to stir really fast until the egg is completely absorbed, which will take less than 15 seconds. After the dough forms a ball, continue to stir-mash a few seconds longer, just to be safe that it's all blended.

3. Press the dough onto the bottom and halfway up the sides of an 8-inch round cake pan or a 7-inch springform pan. Bake for 12 minutes, then take the crust out of the oven to cool. Lower the oven temperature to 300°F.

DO THIS THIRD:

1. Beat the cream cheese and sugar until very fluffy, a good 2 minutes. Beat in the ricotta and lemon zest.

2. Beat in the eggs one at a time, then the vanilla. Pour the cheese mixture over the crust.

WRAPPING IT UP:

1. Bake the cheesecake for 1 hour.

2. Cool it on a rack, without trying to get it out of the pan.

3. Serve sliced in wedges taken straight from the pan, or flip the cheesecake out onto a plate (it will be upside down) then flip it onto another plate to serve it right side up.

OCTOBER CIDER CAKE

TECHNIQUE—Beating, baking
BEST COOKWARE—9×13-inch oblong baking dish; glass is good
BEST EQUIPMENT—Portable or table-top electric mixer
BEST UTENSILS—Measuring cups and spoons, large rubber spatula

An excellent, juicy cake that's a little like a spice cake. It may appear to be a long list of ingredients, but the most challenging thing you'll be doing is measuring them. The easiest frosting of all is Cream Cheese Frosting, and it just happens to be the best one for this cake.

Serves 10

1½ sticks soft butter (12 tablespoons)
1½ cups brown sugar (pack it in the measuring cups)
3 eggs
3 cups plus 2 tablespoons flour
1 tablespoon baking powder
½ teaspoon salt
1 teaspoon ground nutmeg
1 teaspoon ground cinnamon
¼ teaspoon ground cloves
1 cup apple cider
1 tablespoon lemon juice
Cream Cheese Frosting (recipe follows)

DO THIS FIRST:

1. Unwrap the butter but don't throw the wrappings away. Preheat the oven to 350°F.

2. Smear the butter clinging to the wrappings on the bottom, corners, and sides of a 9×13-inch oblong baking dish. If the film seems thin, use extra butter from the refrigerator and smear it on the pan with your fingers.

3. Now sprinkle about 2 tablespoons of flour into the baking dish. Tap it, so the flour moves across the butter and coats the dish. Take the dish to the sink, turn it over, and let the excess flour fall out.

DO THIS SECOND:
1. Put the butter in a big mixing bowl. Beat it at high speed until it's fluffy. Give this about 1 to 1½ minutes.

2. Add the brown sugar a little at a time, and keep beating the butter, on high speed, until all the sugar is added and is completely dissolved. This may take 2 minutes.

3. Crack an egg into the bowl. Mix it in on medium speed. The moment the egg is absorbed, stop mixing. It may take 10 seconds or less for the egg to be absorbed.

4. Repeat with the next two eggs, beating each one only until you can't see the yolk anymore.

DO THIS THIRD:
1. Get out another big bowl. Measure the flour by scooping up more than you need into a 1-cup measuring cup and pushing off the excess with a knife. Put the 3 cups of flour in the bowl.

2. Measure the baking powder (not baking soda!), salt, nutmeg, cinnamon, and cloves directly into the flour. Stir it up with a fork.

3. Measure the cider into a spouted measuring cup and have it close.

DO THIS FOURTH:
1. Add one third of the dry (flour) mixture to the butter. Mix it on low speed. When it goes dry, pour in half the cider and mix until smooth.

2. Add another portion of flour, mix it, and thin it out with the rest of the cider.

3. Finally, stop using the mixer and add the rest of the flour, this time stirring it in with a wooden spoon. Stir in the lemon juice.

WRAPPING IT UP:
1. Pour the batter into the baking dish. Scrape out every drop with a rubber spatula. Anything you don't get, lick later.

- The acid in the lemon juice, which is added last, gives an extra shove to the rising power of the baking powder.

- The cake is done if the toothpick is clean. The magic moment is usually a minute or two after you smell the cake. If you pay attention, that "doneness" smell is the best clue that the cake is nearly done.

- If the cake isn't completely cooled, the frosting will melt.

2. Bake for 35 minutes or until a toothpick stuck into the center of the cake comes out clean—and that means no crumbs. *(While the cake bakes, you'll have time to clean up completely and have a cooling rack ready on the countertop or table.)*

3. When the cake is done, take it from the oven (use potholders!) to a cooling rack. Cool the cake completely before spreading frosting on it. To serve, cut the cake into big squares.

CREAM CHEESE FROSTING

TECHNIQUE—Beating
BEST COOKWARE—Big mixing bowl, electric mixer
BEST UTENSIL—Rubber spatula, table knife

Frosts a 9×13-inch cake

> 1 pound cream cheese
> 2 cups powdered sugar
> 2 to 4 tablespoons apple cider or milk
> 1 teaspoon pure vanilla extract

DO THIS FIRST:

1. Unwrap the cream cheese and let it soften while you measure the other ingredients. (Better yet, let it soften overnight, or when you begin making the October Cider Cake.)

2. Get out a mixer (or a mixing bowl and portable electric beaters).

3. Measure the powdered sugar. (It doesn't have to be exactly "level.") Have the cider, vanilla, and your set of measuring spoons handy.

DO THIS SECOND:

1. Put the cream cheese into the mixer bowl. Add the powdered sugar.

2. Turn the mixer on at low speed at first, or the powdered sugar will blow into your face. Increase the speed to high and beat until the sugar disappears and the cream cheese is exceedingly fluffy. This will take at least 2 minutes.

DO THIS THIRD:

1. If the frosting is very thick, add 2 tablespoons of cider (or milk) to start, and beat again about 15 seconds. If it's still not thin enough to spread, add one or two more tablespoons of cider, and beat again briefly.

2. When the frosting is smooth and has the consistency of soft butter, it's ready. Now you can stir in the vanilla.

WRAPPING IT UP:

1. Spread the frosting on the cooled cake with a table knife. Make swirls.

LET'S TALK

• One of the nicest things about Cream Cheese Frosting is that you can replace the entire amount of powdered sugar with ½ cup honey, in which case you'll have Cream Cheese Honey Frosting, which goes very well with cider cake.

• The powdered sugar doesn't have to be exactly level because this mixture is really a balance of thickness and thinness, both of which are correctable by adding more liquid or more powdered sugar after the initial mixing.

• If you use honey, you'll probably need less cider for thinning purposes.

• If you don't have cider, you can use apple juice. Same diff.

• Sifting puts dry ingredients, such as flour, through a screen to crush lumps and to make the flour fine and airy.

• Sifters are very inexpensive and are even sold on the cookware aisle in grocery stores. Some are mechanical, others have a hand-crank that passes a wire over the screen to move the flour through.

• Another viable sifter is your fine-mesh strainer (if it's at least 8 inches in diameter). Put the flour in the strainer and tap the side until all the flour goes through except for the little lumps, which I usually toss.

• Sifting is one of the Immortal Chores of baking. I know it's a chore because people sneakily skip it. I've learned to spend the 3 or 5 minutes it takes to sift because it really makes a difference in how tender the cake is. Who wants dry cake?

• The instructions here to sift apply even to flour labeled "pre-sifted." Ha! Pre-sifted, indeed. I dare you to compare a pile of plain flour (lumpy) and a pile of sifted flour (like talcum).

• You don't have to sift the 1 tablespoon of flour that coats the baking pans.

• The excess flour left in the pans after coating them is thrown away because even though it looks untouched, it is lightly coated with butter. If you sneak this back into your bag of flour, you'll be adding not only minuscule amounts of moisture, but also an unwanted catalyst that makes flour rancid.

BIRTHDAY CAKE

TECHNIQUE—Baking
BEST BAKEWARE—Two round cake pans (metal or stainless steel) 8 inches in diameter and 2 inches high
BEST EQUIPMENT—Electric mixer, 1 wide bowl, 1 mixing bowl
BEST TOOLS—Measuring cups and spoons, rubber "scraper" spatula, cake cooling racks (sometimes called "grids")

This is a rich, big-crumbed, buttery yellow layer cake. It's great with chocolate frosting on top and in between the layers. The only difference between making this recipe and using a cake mix is that you have to measure the dry ingredients. So I don't know what the big deal is about cake mix. There are two other differences I should mention: it's got real butter and amazing taste.

For the pans
About 1 tablespoon butter
About 1 tablespoon flour

For the cake
1½ sticks butter (12 tablespoons)
2½ cups sifted all-purpose flour
3 teaspoons baking powder
1 teaspoon salt
1½ cups sugar
1 cup milk
3 eggs
1 teaspoon vanilla

Chocolate Frosting (page 229)

DO THIS FIRST:

1. Preheat the oven to 375°F. Take the butter out of the refrigerator, unwrap it, and set it on a plate to soften, but save the wrapper.

2. Smear the buttered side of the wrapper on the bottom and sides of two 8-inch round cake pans. Use the extra 1 tablespoon butter, if necessary, to get a thorough coating. You'll probably want to wash your hands now.

3. Put 1 tablespoon of flour into one of the cake pans. Tap or shake it sideways to thinly cover the butter. Don't forget to tilt the pan so the flour gets into the corners and up the sides.

4. Dump the excess flour into the second pan and coat that pan the same way. Throw any excess flour away.

DO THIS SECOND:

1. For the cake, get out your mixer (or a big mixing bowl and your portable electric beaters).

2. Get out your sifter and a very wide bowl.

3. Scoop about 3 cups of flour from your bag of flour (yes, this is more than you'll need) directly into the sifter.

4. Sift the flour so it falls into the wide bowl. Move the emptied sifter to rest in the mixing bowl that came with your mixer (or the big mixing bowl you'll be using for beating the batter.)

DO THIS THIRD:

1. Measure exactly 2½ perfectly level cups of the sifted flour directly into the sifter.

2. Add to the sifter the measured amounts of baking powder, salt, and sugar.

3. Sift again, so all the dry ingredients fall directly into your mixing bowl.

DO THIS FOURTH:

1. Put the soft butter on top of the dry ingredients.

2. Pour in ⅔ cup of milk. Beat on low speed about 1 to 2 minutes. You'll probably have to use a rubber spatula to scrape down batter flung onto the sides of the bowl.

3. Add the eggs, the rest of the milk, and the vanilla. Beat on medium speed for 1 minute, then on high speed for about 1 minute more. Stop when the batter is off-white, smooth, and fluffy.

• Remember you don't have a level cup of flour unless you've used a 1-cup measuring cup to scoop out more flour than you need, then pushed off the excess with a straight edge, such as a knife, to make the amount of flour level with the measuring cup's rim.

• This is a pretty sneaky way to make a cake. One bowl. No butter and sugar creamed first, which is a typical beginning. No dry ingredients added alternately with the milk, the typical ending of traditional cake making. This recipe proves that one bowl is all you need as long as you don't overbeat the batter.

• Overbeating batter develops the flour's gluten. Gluten is what makes bagels, for example, chewy. Chewiness is not a desirable feature in cake.

• The batter is an eggshell color but after baking it's yellow.

• As the layers bake they'll develop a richly golden brown crust. They'll also rise in the center but sink back into the shape of a disc as they cool.

• The layers have to cool completely or the frosting will melt upon contact. Cooled layers are also easier to pick up and handle as they're being frosted.

DO THIS FIFTH:
1. Divide the batter between the two cake pans.

2. Bake 30 to 35 minutes. *You'll have ample time to clean up the whole mess and set out cake cooling racks.*

3. Chances are the layers will need the full 35 minutes, but do check at 30 minutes. There are a lot of "fast" ovens out there that may bake the layers in the shorter time.

4. Is it done? Stick a toothpick dead center into the layers. If it comes out clean, they're done. If it comes out with batter clinging to it, bake another 5 minutes and check again.

5. Take the pans out of the oven (use pot holders!). Cool the layers on cake cooling racks in the pans for 10 to 15 minutes. Turn the layers out onto other racks, if you have them, or onto pieces of waxed paper. Let them cool completely before you frost them.

WRAPPING IT UP:
1. Take a look at the layers. Are they lumpy? Did they rise a little unevenly? If so, use a serrated knife to carefully slice off the uneven bulges. (Of course, eat the scraps.)

2. Set one layer bottom side up on a serving plate. Using a table knife, spread on about ¼ inch of frosting, just to the edge.

3. Top with the second cake layer, bottom down. Frost all over the sides and top. Wipe smears from the plate with a damp paper towel. Refrigerate until serving.

CHOCOLATE FROSTING

TECHNIQUE — Melting
BEST COOKWARE — Big mixing bowl that's
microwavable
BEST TOOLS — Rubber "scraper" spatula, possibly
a whisk

Use this frosting for Big Batch Brownies
(page 230) or on Birthday Cake (page 226).

4 squares unsweetened chocolate
4 tablespoons butter (½ stick)
3 cups powdered sugar
⅛ teaspoon salt
½ cup cream
2 teaspoons vanilla

DO THIS FIRST:

1. Unwrap the chocolate squares. Chop the
chocolate into rough pieces using a chef's knife
and the two-hand hold (see page 10). Put the
chocolate in a big mixing bowl that can go in a
microwave.

2. Add the butter to the chocolate. Microwave,
uncovered, on Medium power for 45 seconds.
Take the bowl out and stir the chocolate and
butter. If it needs to melt more, put it back in
the microwave, again on Medium power, for
20 seconds. Stir until the chocolate melts into
the butter.

DO THIS SECOND:

1. While the chocolate is still a little warm,
measure the remaining ingredients into it.

2. Stir with a rubber spatula or, if your spatula
is flabby instead of stiff, a whisk, until you get a
smooth frosting.

WRAPPING IT UP:

1. If it's too thick, add 1 tablespoon more cream.

2. If it's too thin, give it a chance to stand —
about 15 minutes — so the frosting can thicken
on its own. If it's still too thin, add ¼ cup more
powdered sugar and stir it in with fast strokes.

• If you want to use a
mixer, portable electric beaters are all you need for this
job. Overbeating will blow
powdered sugar on your
face.

• The microwave is the
gentlest place to melt chocolate, but beware! It is still
possible to burn chocolate,
even in this nice environ-
ment. The best safeguard is
to melt the chocolate until
there's still a small solid
lump left in the melted pool.
Then stir, away from heat,
until the little lump melts.

• If the chocolate burns,
you'll have to start over. No
compromises here, and no
saves.

• You can use "whipping"
cream or "heavy" cream. You
could also entirely replace
the cream with half-and-half
or whole milk. The frosting
will have an imperceptibly
looser body.

• How thick the frosting
gets on its own depends on
the kind of day you're having — rainy, damp, dry, or just
plain hot.

• The cooler it is in your
house, the faster your frosting will "set up." If it's hot
and damp, it will take the
sugar more time to absorb
the moisture from the butter,
so give it the time to do this.

BIG-BATCH BROWNIES

TECHNIQUE — Baking
BEST COOKWARE — 9×13-inch baking pan
BEST EQUIPMENT — Portable or table-top electric mixer, big mixing bowl, cutting board and chef's knife
BEST TOOLS — Wooden spoon, rubber spatula, measuring cups and spoons

* A greased pan prevents the brownies from sticking.

* The floury coating keeps the brownies high and dry, should the butter melt into the batter as it bakes.

* Cut the brownies with a smooth, sharp knife. A serrated knife will rough up the edges.

* Use a spatula (pancake turner) to lift the brownies out of the pan.

* One square of baking chocolate usually equals 1 ounce. Some bars of baking chocolate are divided into ½-ounce pieces, so be careful. If you're luckly enough to find bulk chocolate, buy 4 ounces.

* I'm not big on *never* and *always*, but when it comes to melting chocolate, don't ever cover it. Condensation will collect under the cover and fall back into the melting chocolate, which chocolate finds very aggravating and pays you back for by turning to sand.

* The first round of melting the chocolate in the microwave isn't supposed to completely melt it. In fact, no amount of heating is supposed to completely melt the chocolate. Repeat the abbreviated microwaving once, maybe twice more, but stop when a little lump of chocolate remains. This will keep you from overheating — and burning — the chocolate. Just patiently stir the little lump of chocolate into the melted butter-chocolate mass, until it disappears.

Company loves brownies. This recipe makes enough to please at least 10 people while also giving you some leftovers. Of course, that depends on how big you cut them. This is an easy recipe, but it still will test your patience — you'll want to eat them right away. Try to wait until they "set up." They'll be easier to cut and the frosting won't melt on contact.

Makes about 2 dozen

>2 sticks butter (16 tablespoons)
>1 cup plus 2 tablespoons flour
>2 cups sugar
>3 eggs
>1½ teaspoons vanilla
>4 squares unsweetened chocolate
>½ teaspoon salt
>Chocolate Frosting (page 229)

DO THIS FIRST:

1. Unwrap the butter but don't throw the wrappings away. Preheat the oven to 350°F, with a rack in the lower third of the oven.

2. Smear the butter clinging to the wrappings on the bottom, corners, and sides of a 9×13-inch baking dish. If the film appears thin, use extra butter from the refrigerator and smear it on the pan with your fingers.

3. Sprinkle about 2 tablespoons of flour into the baking dish. Tap the dish, so flour moves across the butter and coats it. Take the dish to the sink, turn it over, and let any excess flour fall out.

4. Measure 1 cup more of flour and keep it handy in its measuring cup.

DO THIS SECOND:

1. Put one stick of butter in a big mixing bowl. Beat on high speed until it's very fluffy, about 2 minutes. Add the sugar and beat again until fluffy, another 2 minutes.

2. Crack in an egg. Beat it in on low speed just until it's absorbed by the butter—and stop! Add the next two eggs one at a time, stopping the moment the egg is absorbed.

3. Stir in the vanilla.

DO THIS THIRD:

1. Put the second stick of butter in a microwave-safe bowl or 2-cup measuring cup. Unwrap the chocolate, cut the squares in quarters with a chef's knife, and add them to the butter.

2. Microwave on Medium power for 1 minute, uncovered. Stir with a rubber spatula. If not smooth, microwave on Medium 30 seconds more. Stir until smooth.

DO THIS FOURTH:

1. Add the melted chocolate and butter to the brownie base. Beat on low speed until blended, or stir it in with a wooden spoon.

2. Stir in the flour and salt with a wooden spoon. The moment the batter is smooth—stop!

WRAPPING IT UP:

1. Pour the batter into the baking dish. Bake 45 minutes.

2. Cool in the pan at least 1 hour. Frost and cut into squares.

• When handling chocolate, it's better to err on the side of cool temperatures than hot. You can always continue to gently heat the chocolate into a state of melted submission. But if you burn it, you'll have to start over. That means in this case not only preparing more chocolate but more butter, too.

• On second thought, maybe you should burn the chocolate—once. As a learning experience. Once you smell burned chocolate and retrace the careless steps that got it burned, you won't let that happen again.

13

HOME FOR THE HOLIDAYS

THANKSGIVING

CHRISTMAS

EASTER

PASSOVER

In a perfect world we would start making food for Thanksgiving on Halloween. In reality, even experienced cooks don't manage this. The crowds at the grocery store until midnight the night before prove my point that most of us cook just about the whole meal on Thanksgiving Day. This is certainly reasonable and achievable. Actually, it's kind of fun to wake up to a day you know you'll spend chopping and mixing and cooking and stirring, especially when you know the result is going to be great.

I definitely don't recommend that first-timers have this meal ready by noon. Many families eat Thanksgiving dinner at suppertime. Oh, and because Thanksgiving is such a customary gorging, don't feel that you have to have nibbles all over the house when people arrive. Get them something to drink and that's it.

THANKSGIVING

MENU

THANKSGIVING TURKEY

•

BREAD STUFFING

OR

CORN BREAD AND
OYSTER DRESSING

•

GRAVY

•

BOURBON SWEET
POTATOES

•

BROCCOLI ON THE SIDE

•

CRANBERRY SAUCE
FROM SCRATCH

•

"BUMPKIN" PIE

- *Cranberry Sauce* — Make up to 3 months ahead and refrigerate.
- *Bread Stuffing* — Make up to 3 months ahead and freeze in its casserole, covered with foil, or make up to 3 days ahead and refrigerate.
- *Corn Bread for Dressing* — Make up to 3 months ahead and freeze wrapped in foil. Thaw before making into crumbs for Dressing.
- *Corn Bread and Oyster Dressing* — Make up to 3 days ahead and refrigerate, but do not add oysters until just before baking.

3 DAYS AHEAD

- Put frozen turkey in refrigerator to defrost

1 DAY AHEAD
(if possible)

- Make cranberry sauce
- Prepare stuffing or dressing (no oysters) to bake tomorrow
- Bake pies
- Bake corn bread

(definitely)

- Set the table or buffet (remember hot pads)
- Get a good night's sleep

THANKSGIVING ONE STEP AT A TIME

✔ *Take one step at a time. Check off each step as you complete it.*

4 TO 5 HOURS BEFORE SERVING

__ Take turkey out of refrigerator
__ Preheat oven
__ Make corn bread (if not done ahead)
__ Make pies (if not done ahead)
__ Trim broccoli
__ Prepare stuffing or dressing (if stuffing turkey)
__ Prepare turkey and get it in the oven
__ Make cranberry sauce (if not done ahead)
__ Make sweet potatoes; put in oven with turkey
__ Make stuffing or dressing (if not done ahead); put in oven with turkey
__ Put big pot with steamer basket and salted water on the stove
__ Set up coffeemaker
__ Clean up

1 HOUR BEFORE SERVING
(guests begin to arrive)

__ Turkey's done; it can sit 1 hour
__ Pour juices off turkey, let fat rise in refrigerator
__ Make gravy
__ Stuffing and sweet potatoes done; will stay hot 30 minutes
__ Put wine and other drinks on the table
__ Carve the turkey
__ Boil broccoli water
__ Put cranberry sauce on the table
__ Put stuffing and sweet potatoes on the table

5 MINUTES LEFT

__ Cook broccoli
__ Bring broccoli to the table

MEAL TIME

__ Enjoy the meal
__ Flick on coffeemaker
__ Serve dessert

THANKSGIVING TURKEY AND TRIMMINGS

You are about to experience your first Thanksgiving behind the wheel—er, stove. You envision Perfect Turkey. But you recall turkey tundra, as dry in the mouth as it is to the touch, when someone's best efforts failed.

Lucky for newcomers, turkeys cook best by the easiest technique—roasting.

For what the American psyche knows as "the trimmings" (which I argue are not trimmings at all, but standard equipment) you will be making stuffing, gravy, cranberry sauce from scratch, and your first pumpkin pie. This menu has no fancy footwork and no weird ingredients. It's just a starting place for your own memories.

THE CLAMP

The drumstick clamp, almost unavoidable on fresh or frozen birds, is the meanest thing in cooking. It comes with no directions on how to handle it. I've drawn blood struggling with one. With the phone between my ear and shoulder, my hand stuck in a clamp, I called my butcher. He talked me through it like this:

With a towel, pull the upside-down "U" toward you. With your other hand, find the strength to lift the loosest drumstick up, over, and out of the clamp. Once the first drumstick is free, the second one will come over and out easily. To remove the clamp, squeeze its sides in, and push it away from you.

GETTING THE BIRD BROWNED

Nice brown color isn't an accident. It comes from vegetable oil. As a butter lover, I fought this concept. But butter will burn during the length of time a turkey spends in the oven. If you love butter, rub it all over the inside prior to roasting, then brush it on the outside as the cooking time nears an end.

No elaborate temperature schemes. Some recipes put the turkey in at 500°F and keep it there. The technique can produce crisp skin and tender flesh. But 500°F is insanely hot, causes

- Turkeys range in weight from the 6- to 8-pound category to as large as 26 pounds. Very small or very large turkeys are trouble. Small ones get blotchy. Big ones present food safety problems because their mass resists total heat penetration. The best range for roasting is a basic 11- to 16-pound turkey. If you're feeding a large crowd, roast two 12-pounders.

- Real home-cooked turkeys don't look like they just got photographed for a magazine. Some turkeys you see in magazines aren't even cooked, but smeared with coloring to make them appear evenly browned. The home-cooked turkey, to its credit, looks exactly like anything else that has sustained 350°F for many hours—legs splayed, irregularities in color, ripped skin. Don't worry. This is normal. It will probably happen to your turkey.

- The point of trussing is to form the turkey into a smooth round—no protrusions, no wings sticking out. This prevents burning of exposed areas.

- Giblets need long cooking. Get them going first. If you forget, it will be too late.

smoky kitchens and oven fires, and to me is a little overwhelming if you've never made a turkey before. Other recipes start at 500°F, then reduce the heat, raise the heat, and reduce it again. Forget it!

If your turkey weighs less than 14 pounds, it's 350°F all the way. If it weighs more than 14 pounds, it's a steady 325°F from start to finish.

TURKEY-ROASTING ESSENTIALS

Before you're ready to roast you might have to run to the store to pick up essential kitchen tools to make your turkey roasting easy and safe.

With enough celery, onion, and carrots on the bottom of your roasting pan, you don't need a roasting rack. But do you have the following?

A large roasting pan.

Vegetable oil and butter, salt and pepper.

A towel. You will have greater luck with the drumstick clamp if you grasp it and the slippery turkey with a towel.

An instant-read thermometer. This is your most important tool. With this, you don't need a roasting chart or a clock. You read the facts on the dial. If you don't have one, get one.

A turkey lifter. Some recipes ask the cook to flip hot turkey from breast to back during cooking, supposedly to distribute juices. Try this once and you'll let your future turkeys finish cooking in the same position they start. But you will have to lift the turkey out. I recommend a turkey lifter. The best ones look like snow chains but act like a sling. Two strands of metal chain-link lie over your bed of vegetables with handles draped over the side of the roasting pan. The turkey rests on top of the sling. You simply grasp both handles and heave. This device will put an end to burned hands, greasy potholders, and ripped drumsticks.

Foil. For great-looking turkeys, you may need to protect some areas from overbrowning. An hour or so into the roasting you might want to wrap foil booties around the drumsticks so they don't get dry and crunchy. Make the foil loose wherever you use it, or you'll steam the bird you're attempting to roast.

A Bulb baster (optional). This begs the question about basting. Is it necessary? New thinking discourages basting because it can streak the sheen on the skin. Turkey skin is so thick that basting really can't penetrate to the flesh. The one thing basting does is keep you very busy. I say baste if you like, but I've given it up.

A strainer. For straining clear juices for gravy.

WHEN IS IT DONE?

There is good news on this controversial front. It used to be that turkeys were cooked to suit food safety awareness—meaning overcooked to an internal temperature of 185°F. In response to complaints that this high finishing temperature was behind the Thanksgiving offerings of the dry, stringy meat we all dislike so much, new research was done.

Here's something that's not official, but it is safe.

In 1985 *Sunset* magazine and the University of California at Davis announced temperatures as low as 165°F for breast meat are safe. This lower figure is not an official turkey industry recommendation. It is simply safe to eat, but still too pink for some tastes. If you take the breast meat to 170°F the meat will be white and still nice and juicy.

With your instant-read thermometer in hand, here is the only roasting chart you'll need:

10- to 14-pound turkey: 1½ to 2¼ hours at 350°F
14-plus-pound turkey: 2½ to 3 hours at 325°F

- The giblets cook without much attention during the required 2 hours. Just put the pot on a back burner and work on the rest of your recipes. You only need to check that the liquid hasn't boiled off. If it looks lower than the level of the giblets, add a little more water, and keep simmering.

- Trussing keeps the bird round to prevent burning. But I assure you that your turkey will cook, trussed or not, and still be delicious.

- The turkey rests so juices can resettle inside the meat while making the meat easy to carve. The internal temperature will rise about 5 to 10 degrees.

- The turkey will stay hot for 1 hour.

TECHNIQUE — Roasting
BEST COOKWARE — Disposable aluminum roasting pan, or large roasting pan with shallow sides
BEST EQUIPMENT — Chef's knife and cutting board
HANDIEST GADGETS — Turkey lifter, instant-read thermometer

Remember to plan on serving the turkey 30 minutes to 1 hour *after* it's done cooking. You'll feel more relaxed about the post-turkey details, like making gravy and side dishes.

Serves 8 to 10

> ½ stick butter (4 tablespoons)
> 12- to 14-pound turkey
> 1 rib celery
> 3 large carrots
> 1 or 2 large onions
> Salt
> Vegetable oil
> White pepper

DO THIS FIRST:

1. Take out the butter. Preheat the oven to 350°F with a rack on the lowest notch. Keep it at this temperature through the entire cooking time.

2. Remove the turkey wrapping with scissors. Remove the clamp (see page 235). Find the paper bags that hold the giblets; they're in the cavities at the tail and neck.

3. Put the giblets, liver, neck, and heart in a pot on the stove with enough water to cover them. If you like, add a small onion and a carrot stick. Bring to a boil and cook, uncovered, over medium-low heat for 2 hours. You will use this liquid and the giblets later.

DO THIS SECOND:

1. Wash the celery and trim off the white part. Wash the carrots and cut off the ends. Cut both into 3-inch chunks and strew them in the bottom of a roasting pan.

2. Peel an onion and cut it in big chunks. Add it to the roasting pan.

3. If you're using a sling-type turkey lifter, lay it over the vegetables now.

DO THIS THIRD:

1. Wash the turkey inside and out in your sink with cool running water. Rinse several times. Pat dry. (If you don't pat it dry, oil or butter will slither off the skin.)

2. Rub inside the big cavity with the soft butter and some salt. If you've made stuffing, stuff the turkey loosely. It is only for effect.

3. Place any remaining stuffing in a lightly greased baking dish or casserole, covered, to be heated during the last hour the turkey roasts.

DO THIS FOURTH

1. *This trussing step is optional.* Twist the wing tips, which will burn first, under the wings. You'll have to use some force. Now run a single strand of string under the turkey's girth and up each side, catching the wings under the string. Continue the string over to the drumsticks. Tie them together, catching the fatty tail flap (Pope's Nose). If you have stuffed the turkey, close the skin flaps with small metal skewers or diaper pins.

DO THIS FIFTH:

1. Set the turkey breast side up (drumsticks pointing up) on the vegetables. Rub the turkey all over with vegetable oil, salt, and pepper. Let it sit 10 minutes, to let the seasonings soak in.

DO THIS SIXTH:

1. Place the turkey in the oven. In 45 minutes to 1 hour, check for overbrowned spots. If you find any, cover them loosely with foil.

2. At this point, add 2 cups of water to the roasting pan. Check the turkey's color again in 30 minutes.

Twist the wing tips under the wings

Catch the wing and draw the string over the drumstick

Tie the drumsticks together

3. *This is a good time to add to the oven the casserole of stuffing and the Bourbon Sweet Potatoes.* Slip them in over the turkey on a rack placed on the highest notch.

4. When 2 hours have elapsed, check for doneness. Remembering that dark meat finishes last, check the thigh first. There are two ways to check for doneness:

The most reliable method is to pull a drumstick away from the body. Where the skin has stretched, use a small knife to make a cut to expose the meat. Take a look. If you see red juices or pink meat, keep roasting. Check for doneness at 15-minute intervals. I like this method because no one will see the cut.

Another way to check for doneness is to stick an instant-read thermometer in the plumpest part of the thigh. It should register 175 to 180°F.

WRAPPING IT UP:

1. Remove the entire roasting pan from the oven and set it on a protective hot plate or board. Let the turkey sit 20 minutes to 1 hour. *This is important!*

2. If you have stuffed the turkey, remove all the stuffing with a big spoon; put it on a serving platter and keep it warm in a 200° oven while the carving takes place.

3. Finally, lift the turkey to a cutting board or platter for carving. Strain the juices from the roasting pan into a glass measuring cup (or a bowl). Discard the vegetables.

4. Make your gravy (see page 248).

5. To carve: With your hands, break off the two thigh-drumstick pieces at the natural place where the leg joins the body. Separate the thigh and drumstick, if you like. With your hands, break off the wings at the natural place where the joint cracks apart. Now, with a slender knife, take slices off the breast. (For more on carving, see page 78.)

BREAD STUFFING

TECHNIQUE—Sautéing, baking
BEST COOKWARE—Big skillet, at least 12", hopefully cast iron, a 9×13-inch baking dish
BEST EQUIPMENT—2 large bowls
BEST TOOLS—Chef's knife, cutting board, wooden spatula

Stuffing a turkey is really just for show. It is often discouraged by federal officials who believe we will poison ourselves if the interior temperature of the turkey doesn't rise high enough during roasting.

Why fight? Make the stuffing casserole-style on the side. It's easy, just as delicious, and makes this a classic make-ahead (which a raw, stuffed turkey definitely is not). You can make it weeks ahead and freeze it, or the night before and refrigerate it. Put the stuffing in the oven, along with the turkey, as the turkey nears doneness. If you don't have room in your oven for both, there is no problem waiting for the turkey to finish roasting. While it rests on the counter for an hour, use the oven to bake the stuffing and other side dishes. The turkey will still be hot inside—and even more juicy.

If you make this in a disposable aluminum baking dish, obey Elaine's Law: toss the pan and serve the stuffing in a decent-looking casserole or bowl.

Serves 8

1½-pound loaf firm white bread
2 cups milk
6 ribs celery
1 large onion
¾ pound fresh mushrooms
8 tablespoons butter (1 stick)
2 eggs
¼ to ½ cup chicken stock
2 teaspoons salt
Lots of black pepper

DO THIS FIRST:

1. Leave the bread out overnight, or for a couple of hours, to become stale. Pull the bread apart into clumps with your hands. Put the clumps in a large bowl.

2. Pour the milk over the bread. Push down on the bread to tuck it under the milk. If it doesn't go under immediately, give the milk a few minutes to soak in. If it looks like you'll need a little extra liquid to get the bread soaked, add 1 cup of water. To make sure it's all soaked, press down on the bread a number of times.

DO THIS SECOND:

1. Make long cuts down each rib of celery, then cut across the slices, to give yourself chopped celery. You should have about 3 cups. It doesn't have to be exact. Put the chopped celery in a large bowl.

2. Halve the onion through the poles. Chop each half. You should have about 3 cups. Again, it doesn't have to be exact. Add it to the celery.

3. With the mushrooms caps up, cut them in quarters. Add them to the celery. Have this bowl convenient to the stove.

DO THIS THIRD:

1. Get out your biggest skillet, about 12 inches across the bottom. Set it on a burner and turn the heat to high.

2. Add half of the butter. When it is melted, pour in the chopped vegetables.

3. Keep the heat high. Stir slowly all around the pan to coat the little pieces of vegetables. Sauté a good 10 minutes. You may want to turn the heat down to medium-high so you can leave the stove. (*This is a good time to do a little washing up.*)

DO THIS FOURTH:

1. Meanwhile, over the sink, pull off small portions of bread and squeeze out as much liquid as you can. Really press hard between your palms. Put these wet squeezed balls of bread in another

2. When the celery is soft and the mushrooms turn dark, add the bread.

3. Fry it, mixing and mashing with a wooden spatula, until it's well browned and all the liquid is absorbed. This will take another 10 minutes. Keep at it, even if it feels as though your arm will fall off. If it starts to stick and you find yourself scraping the bottom of the skillet, you've done it right.

DO THIS FIFTH:

1. Transfer the stuffing to a mixing bowl (you can use the same bowl the bread soaked in).

2. Crack the eggs on the rim of a little bowl. Beat them with a fork until they are solid yellow in color. Mix them into the stuffing.

3. Add the remaining 4 tablespoons of butter. Mix in enough stock to moisten the stuffing without making it soupy (or leaving it crumbly and dry). Add salt and pepper, and mix and mash with a big spoon. Taste. Does it need more salt? More pepper?

WRAPPING IT UP:

1. If you're stuffing the bird, do so when you are ready to roast.

2. If you're baking the stuffing on the side, smear a little butter in the bottom of an oblong baking pan (you may use a disposable foil baking dish). Spread the stuffing in the pan, cover it with buttered foil, and bake it during the last hour the turkey roasts. The oven temperature for turkey and stuffing is the same. How convenient.

3. After an hour, take off the foil and return the stuffing to the oven for 15 minutes to brown the top.

• The full recipe may not all fit in your turkey, so plan on baking all or some of it on the side.

• If you like the sound of this recipe because it's got oysters but you don't want corn bread, use a 1½-pound loaf of firm white bread instead.

• If you like the corn bread but not the oysters, you can replace the oysters with pieces of cooked bacon.

CORN BREAD AND OYSTER DRESSING

TECHNIQUE—Sautéing/baking
BEST COOKWARE—Large skillet
BEST EQUIPMENT—Large mixing bowl
BEST TOOLS—Chef's knife and cutting board, measuring cups, measuring spoons

Our tastes for stuffing vary based on what our families ate on Thanksgiving when we were kids. If your memories include corn bread stuffing, this recipe is for you. You can find corn bread mixes that are pretty good and ask only that you add eggs or a liquid, pour it in a pan, and bake. The corn bread recipe on page 246 is from scratch. It uses real cornmeal found in the flour section of a grocery store. I suppose it is more involved. It wants you to measure three things more than the mix does. This stuffing recipe also works with white bread.

Serves 8

1 corn bread (recipe follows)
2 tablespoons chopped fresh parsley
2 teaspoons dried thyme
1½ teaspoons salt
Lots of black pepper
5 ribs celery
1 medium onion
2½ cups frozen corn kernels
4 tablespoons butter (½ stick)
3 eggs
¼ cup chicken stock
1 pint oysters

DO THIS FIRST:

1. Turn the bread into crumbs (see sidebar). Put the crumbs into a big bowl.

2. Measure and add directly to the bowl the parsley, thyme, salt, and pepper.

DO THIS SECOND:

1. Make 3 lengthwise cuts down each rib of celery. Cut across the slices to get chopped celery. You should have about 2½ cups, but it doesn't have to be exact.

2. Peel the onion, halve it through the poles, and chop the halves. You should have about 2½ cups. Again, it doesn't have to be exact.

3. Measure the corn and have it ready near the bowl of crumbs.

DO THIS THIRD:

1. Get out a large skillet and set it on a burner. Add the butter and turn the heat to medium-high. Wait for the butter to melt.

2. Add the onion and celery and sauté until soft, a good 10 minutes. (*While the vegetables cook, you'll have time to clean up.*)

DO THIS FOURTH:

1. Add the sautéed onion and celery to the bowl of crumbs, stirring well to combine. Stir in the corn.

2. Beat the eggs and chicken stock with a fork. Pour them over the crumbs while mixing easily with the fork.

3. Add the oysters, juices and all. Use a big spoon to mix them in gently. (If the oysters are huge, you can cut them in half.)

WRAPPING IT UP:

1. Butter an oblong baking dish (or use a disposable foil baking pan).

2. Transfer the dressing into the baking dish. (You can set aside about 2 cups of it to put in the turkey, if you want.) Cover well with foil. Put it in the refrigerator until you're ready to bake.

3. Bake at 350°F (with the turkey) for 30 minutes. Take off the foil and bake 30 minutes more to brown the top.

HOW TO MAKE BREAD CRUMBS
You have the choice of using a blender, food processor, or your hands. Blender and food processor work equally well. Tear the bread (or corn bread) into rough pieces. Put a little at a time into your machine. Run the machine until you like the size of the crumbs. For stuffing don't let the crumbs get overly fine. Really fine crumbs make dressing rather pasty.

To make crumbs by hand, pull the bread apart with your fingers, over a bowl, until the crumbs are as small as you like. The truth is, this method will give your dressing the most interesting texture.

CORN BREAD

TECHNIQUE—Baking
MUST HAVE—10-inch cast iron skillet, mitt-style
   potholders that protect your arms
BEST EQUIPMENT—A big mixing bowl
BEST TOOLS—Measuring cups, measuring spoons,
   a big stirring spoon

This is the best way to get fresh corn bread for corn bread dressing. Corn bread is supposed to have a sharp taste, a kind of tang. You can make corn bread the day before you'll turn it into stuffing, or make it eons ahead (3 months!), wrap it in foil, and freeze it.

Makes 1 loaf

   4 tablespoons butter (½ stick)

   Dry mixture
   2 cups cornmeal
   1 teaspoon salt
   ½ teaspoon baking soda
   ½ teaspoon baking powder
   1 teaspoon sugar (optional)

   Wet mixture
   1½ cups buttermilk
   2 eggs

DO THIS FIRST:

   1. Preheat the oven to 450°F with an oven rack on the lowest notch. Put the butter into a 10-inch cast iron skillet. Set the skillet in the preheating oven for the butter to melt and for the skillet to get very hot.

DO THIS SECOND:

   1. Measure the ingredients for the dry mixture directly into a large mixing bowl.

   2. Pour the buttermilk into a second bowl and add the eggs. Beat with a fork until blended.

   3. Add the wet ingredients to the dry ingredients, stirring with the fork. Stop stirring the moment the mixture is evenly blended.

• The hotter the skillet, the browner and crustier the crust will be. Crust is the revered part of corn bread, particularly if you'll be using it for dressing.

• Whether you use yellow or white cornmeal depends greatly on where you're from and what you prefer. White cornmeal is ground finer and produces a creamier corn bread. Yellow cornmeal can be ground fine or gritty—as used in polenta—and produces a somewhat drier corn bread.

• Sugar is optional, again, depending on your upbringing and tastes.

• This is a recipe made routinely by home cooks with innate timing. They know they can get the dry ingredients measured, the wet ingredients beaten, and the two combined before the butter in the oven burns. If you are not this quick, have your measured ingredients ready on the counter before you insert the skillet into the hot oven.

• If you don't have a cast iron skillet (and why not, may I ask, after I've told you of their virtues for two books now) you can use an 8- or 9-inch square or round baking dish or a 9-inch round cake pan, of metal or glass. The browning will be less pronounced. Bakeware with a nonstick coating definitely will deprive you of the prized crust.

• Plain yogurt may be substituted for the buttermilk.

DO THIS THIRD:

1. Put on glove-style potholders that come up your arms. Open the oven door and pull out the rack holding the hot skillet. Lift the skillet, swirling so the bottom is fully coated with butter, and pour the rest of the hot butter into the batter. It will sizzle and pop.

2. Lower the coated skillet back onto the rack. Stir the butter and batter a few times, then pour the completed batter into the hot skillet.

WRAPPING IT UP:

1. Bake 20 to 25 minutes. The top should be nicely browned. Cool in the skillet on a wire rack.

2. To use in Corn Bread and Oyster Dressing, cool fully, then crumble. Otherwise, cut in wedges and serve from the skillet with dinner.

LET'S TALK

• Read the gravy-making tips that accompany Gravy and Sauce Workshop #2 on page 72.

GRAVY FROM THANKSGIVING TURKEY

TECHNIQUE—Boiling
BEST COOKWARE—Medium pot
BEST EQUIPMENT—Strainer, whisk

This is where the juices from the cooked turkey and the broth simmering around the giblets join together for inevitably tasty gravy. During the gravy-making you'll be able to adjust to make it as thick or as thin as you like.

Makes about 4 cups

> Pan juices from Thanksgiving turkey
> Liquid from the cooked giblets (see Do
>   This First, Step 3, page 238)
> Salt and pepper
> ⅓ cup flour
> ⅓ cup cold water
> Cooked giblets

DO THIS FIRST:

1. As your turkey roasts, it will give off juices to the roasting pan. After you take out the turkey to carve it, pour all the pan drippings into a strainer set over a big measuring cup (or a bowl).

2. Set the strained juices in the refrigerator. Wait about 15 minutes for golden fat, if any, to rise to the top. Spoon off as much fat as you can. A bulb baster will suck it up easily.

DO THIS SECOND:

1. Pour the de-fatted roasting juices into a medium-size pot.

2. Add the cooking liquid from the giblets. You should have 3 to 4 cups in all. This amount will vary every time you roast a turkey.

3. Bring the pot to a boil. Boil until almost one-fourth of the liquid cooks away. (If you like plain juices, add salt and pepper and serve. If you prefer thickened gravy, proceed.)

DO THIS THIRD:

1. Measure the flour and water into a cup and stir them together extremely well with a fork until you make a very smooth pourable paste.

2. Slowly pour and stir the flour paste, a little at a time, into the boiling juices until the gravy becomes as thick as you like. You may not have to add all of it.

WRAPPING IT UP:

1. Chop the cooked giblets and add them to the bubbling gravy. Taste. Is there enough salt and pepper? If not, add more.

BOURBON SWEET POTATOES

TECHNIQUE—Baking
BEST COOKWARE—Medium pot, 9×13-inch baking dish
BEST EQUIPMENT—Vegetable peeler, chef's knife, cutting board

This is another dish that can bake in the oven along with the turkey. Once the sweet potatoes are peeled, it goes together quickly and should demand little of you all the way through baking. But you'll be reminded of its presence when it starts to waft its sweet smell through your house.

Serves 8

4 pounds sweet potatoes or yams
1 stick butter (8 tablespoons)
1 cup brown sugar
½ cup frozen orange juice concentrate
⅓ cup bourbon

DO THIS FIRST:

1. Preheat the oven to 350°F (the same tempera-ture at which the turkey roasts). Smear a film of butter on the bottom, sides, and corners of an ob-long baking dish. Have the baking dish near your cutting board.

2. Peel the sweet potatoes. Cut them in half lengthwise. Then cut across the halves to make 1¼-inch chunks. Place the sweet potato pieces snugly in the baking dish as you go.

DO THIS SECOND:

1. Put the butter into a small pot or skillet. Measure the brown sugar (pack it into the measuring cup) and add it to the butter. Melt and stir over medium heat until bubbly.

2. Take the pot off the heat. Stir in the orange juice concentrate until it melts. Add the bourbon.

3. Pour the sauce over the sweet potatoes.

WRAPPING IT UP:

1. Cover the sweet potatoes tightly with foil. Bake 45 minutes.

2. Uncover and bake 30 minutes more, until you can pierce a sweet potato easily with a fork. The sauce should be bubbling and the tops of the sweet potatoes should be nicely browned.

• If you like cinnamon, add ½ teaspoon to the butter-brown sugar sauce.

• This dish is also good dusted with a faint amount of nutmeg after it comes out of the oven.

• It's very hard to overcook this dish. It can cook covered as long as 1 hour, and then uncovered up to 45 minutes. The sweet potatoes will still be fine.

• Once out of the oven this dish will stay hot for 30 minutes, covered loosely. (Use the same foil that covered the dish when it began to bake.)

BROCCOLI ON THE SIDE

- It would be great if you could wash the broccoli as well as trim it beforehand. Unfortunately, pre-washed broccoli gets soggy.

- Broccoli needs salt. Don't be too skimpy, because this is an amount of broccoli a little larger than what you'd normally make to serve 4.

- You can use the same recipe for cauliflower.

TECHNIQUE—Boiling or steaming
BEST COOKWARE—Dutch oven and flower-petal steamer rack, or large microwave-safe bowl
BEST EQUIPMENT—Paring knife, cutting board, colander

The fresh green vegetable that accompanies the Thanksgiving turkey will be the last thing you make. Have the broccoli completely trimmed and cut into florets before you even think about roasting the turkey. You have the choice of steaming or microwaving it. Because of the complexity of many of the other dishes on the menu, broccoli is welcomed plain.

Serves 8

2 to 3 heads broccoli
Salt

DO THIS FIRST:

1. Cut off the big broad stems, leaving only florets.

2. If some of the florets are big, slice through them lengthwise (rather than breaking them into smaller pieces) until they're mostly of uniform size.

3. Place all the florets into a freezer-quality zip-style plastic bag and press out all the air. Keep refrigerated until you're ready to cook it.

DO THIS SECOND:

1. When you're ready to cook the broccoli, rinse all the florets under running water in a colander.

TO STEAM:

1. Put 1 to 2 inches of water in a Dutch oven. Add 1 tablespoon salt. Set a steamer rack inside the pot.

2. Cover the pot and bring the water to a boil. Wait until you see steam escaping from the lid.

3. Add all the broccoli. Sprinkle lightly with salt. Immediately cover the pot again and steam, keeping the heat high, for 4 to 5 minutes.

4. Uncover the pot and transfer the broccoli to a serving dish. Serve hot.

TO MICROWAVE:

1. Put the washed broccoli into a large glass bowl. Add ¼ cup water and sprinkle all the broccoli with salt.

2. Cover tightly with plastic wrap. Microwave on High for 2 to 2½ minutes.

3. Uncover the broccoli, stir it, then microwave on High for 2 minutes more.

4. Serve immediately in the bowl it microwaved in.

• Pet-Ritz pie crusts are in the frozen food section of the grocery store. They come two ways, a 2-crust package for 9-inch pies, and a crust for one deep-dish pie.

• If you want to make one deep-dish pie, pour all the filling into the shell and bake 12 minutes at 400° then 45 minutes at 350°.

• Pumpkin is in the store's canned vegetable section. I've used Libby's canned pumpkin in these pies often.

• Look for the words "heavy cream" on the carton label. Try to avoid cartons of cream that contain elements other than cream.

• If you want to use electric beaters to mix the filling, beat only until blended. If you see bubbles and froth, stop immediately. That froth will bake, burst, and come out of the oven looking dull. The froth also toughens what you hope will be a creamy, custardy filling.

• The pie crusts have a certain machine-crimped look. To remove it, pinch the rim of the dough by hand in a pattern that you like. Make a rope, or pinch sideways V's all around the rim.

• The cookie sheet under the pies catches any spillover and adds an extra layer of insulation between the pies and the oven's heat.

"BUMPKIN" PIE

TECHNIQUE — Baking
BEST EQUIPMENT — Big mixing bowl
BEST TOOLS — Measuring cups, measuring spoons, whisk

The biggest surprise to beginning cooks is that canned foods usually avoided by purists aren't across-the-board offenses. One of the most reliable canned products is pumpkin pulp (often labeled as solid-pack pumpkin). I always recommend it because its consistency is standardized.

Without a real pumpkin to peel, boil, seed, or mash, these pies come together quickly. You don't even need a mixer. Here's a shortcut sure to horrify purists: Go buy a package of premade pie shells. Thaw them slightly. They'll be just soft enough to re-crimp the edges with your fingers so they look homemade.

Makes 2 small pies

> 2 9-inch frozen pie shells
> 1-pound can solid **pack pumpkin**
>   (or 1½ cups fresh **pumpkin puree,**
>   see page 48)
> 1 cup heavy cream
> ½ cup milk
> 4 eggs
> 1 cup light brown sugar
> 1 teaspoon cinnamon
> ¼ teaspoon ground cloves
> ½ teaspoon nutmeg
> ½ cup additional cream, for decoration

DO THIS FIRST:

1. Take the crusts out of the freezer to partially thaw. Preheat the oven to 400°F. Set a rack on the lowest notch.

DO THIS SECOND:

1. Open the can of pumpkin. Empty the can into a big mixing bowl.

2. Measure the cream and milk and add them to the pumpkin.

3. Add the eggs, cracking them into the pumpkin one by one.

4. Mix with a whisk. You don't have to whisk hard. Don't stop until the pumpkin is completely blended with the cream and eggs.

DO THIS THIRD:

1. Measure the sugar into another bowl. Measure the spices and add them to the sugar.

2. Add the sugar mixture to the pumpkin base. Whisk until completely blended and smooth.

DO THIS FOURTH:

1. The frozen pie crusts should be just soft enough at this point to re-form. With your thumb and forefinger, re-crimp the edges so they look homemade.

2. Place the crusts, still in their tins, on a cookie sheet.

3. Fill the crusts with pumpkin filling. (Each crust will hold about 2 cups filling.)

WRAPPING IT UP:

1. Place the cookie sheet holding the pies in the oven. Bake 8 minutes. Set a timer!

2. Turn the temperature down to 350°. Bake 30 to 35 minutes more. To test if the pies are done, insert a table knife into the middle of one. If it comes out clean, it's ready. If not, push them back into the oven for 5 minutes more and test again.

3. Whip the additional cream (see page 213) and use it to decorate the pies. Serve warm or cold.

• It isn't necessary to wash the cranberries.

• Don't worry about the light-colored berries. They'll pop and disappear into the rich, ruby sauce later.

• Disregard a pink foam halfway through the simmering. It will go away.

• Orange zest is what comes off an orange if you grate it on the smallest holes of a box grater. Just the colored, orange part, not the white, has the most intense flavor, like the orange's own extract.

• Use orange juice in its drinkable state. This is not a call for concentrate.

• If you don't have brown sugar, you can make this using all white sugar. If, for some reason, you are out of white sugar, you can make it using all brown sugar.

• Star anise, a licorice-tasting star-shaped pod, is one of the essential spices in Chinese 5-spice powder, and is very common in Mexican cooking. If you can't find it in the normal spice department, take a look at the Mexican or Chinese sections.

CRANBERRY SAUCE FROM SCRATCH

TECHNIQUE — Boiling
BEST COOKWARE — Medium-size pot
BEST TOOLS — Measuring cups, stirring spoon

Back in the introduction I promised no wierd ingredients. I lied. Star anise is a beautiful, fragrant star-shaped pod. I added it by accident to cranberry sauce years ago and now find cranberry sauce totally boring without it.

Makes 2 cups

> **12-ounce bag fresh raw cranberries**
> **½ cup white sugar**
> **½ cup brown sugar**
> **Zest of 1 orange**
> **½ cup orange juice**
> **2 whole star anise**

DO THIS FIRST:

1. Measure all the ingredients into a medium-size pot. Stir until everything is nicely blended.

2. Bring the pot to a boil over medium heat. Stir now and then so the cranberries won't stick.

DO THIS SECOND:

1. Once you see that the cranberries are boiling, turn the heat down to low (or medium-low, depending on your stove) and simmer for 20 minutes, lid off. This step will thicken the mixture into a sauce.

2. Stir a few times while it simmers. You don't have to babysit this.

WRAPPING IT UP:

1. Pour the cranberry sauce into a storage container. Cover and keep it in the refrigerator until you're ready to serve it. Just don't forget during the feeding frenzy that it's in the refrigerator.

There's always a lot more going on at Christmas than a meal. Even so, if you focus on the menu you'll see that it's easy—easier than Thanksgiving, in fact. If Christmas falls on a Sunday, you have all day Christmas Eve to get ready. If it's on a Monday, you have an entire weekend for planning and shopping. When Christmas falls on Tuesday, Wednesday, Thursday, or Friday, the last-minute crunch intensifies. Unless you've got the whole week off, you'll probably be shopping in throngs in a countdown mentality. The timetable on page 258 should help you relax and enjoy the cooking.

CHRISTMAS
MENU

SUGARED NUTS
(PAGE 51)
•
MULLED WINE
(PAGE 304)
•
PRIME RIB OF BEEF
•
HORSERADISH CREAM
•
MAPLE-ORANGE
WILD RICE
•
GARLIC MASHED
POTATOES
•
BUTTERED GREEN BEANS
•
FUDGE PECAN PIE

MAKE-AHEAD OPTION

- *Prime Rib of Beef —* Order from butcher any time after Thanksgiving, but at least 2 weeks ahead.
- *Garlic Mashed Potatoes —* Roast garlic up to 2 weeks ahead and refrigerate.
- *Fudge Pecan Pie —* Make up to 2 weeks ahead and freeze.
- *Horseradish Cream —* Make up to 1 week ahead and refrigerate.
- *Sugared Nuts —* Make up to 1 week ahead; store in airtight container.

1 TO 2 DAYS AHEAD

- Bring beef home

1 DAY AHEAD

- Set the table or buffet (remember hot pads)
- Stud 4 oranges with cloves (good job for a kid)
- Get a good night's sleep

CHRISTMAS ONE STEP AT A TIME

✔ *Take one step at a time. Check off each step as you complete it.*

4 TO 4½ HOURS BEFORE SERVING

— Take beef out of refrigerator
— Preheat oven
— Make pies (if not done ahead)
— Roast garlic for potatoes (in oven with pie; 350° okay)
— Prepare roast and get it in the oven
— Make wild rice; put in oven with roast
— Make mulled wine; keep warm on stove
— Make horseradish cream (if not done ahead); refrigerate
— Make sugared nuts (if not done ahead); set out in welcome area
— Wash and trim beans; have skillet on stove
— Set up coffeemaker
— Clean up

1 HOUR BEFORE SERVING

— Roast is done; it can sit 45 minutes to 1 hour
— Keep wild rice in oven a little longer, if necessary
    (guests begin to arrive; serve mulled wine and nuts)
— Make mashed potatoes; will stay hot, covered, 30 minutes
— Pour juices off roast; let fat rise in refrigerator
— Make gravy
— Put wine and other drinks on the table
— Carve the roast; bring it to the table
— Put gravy, wild rice, potatoes, and horseradish cream on the table

5 MINUTES LEFT

— Sauté beans
— Bring bowl of beans to the table

MEAL TIME

— Enjoy the meal
— Flick on coffeemaker
— Serve dessert

PRIME RIB OF BEEF

TECHNIQUE—Roasting
BEST COOKWARE—Oblong baking dish or disposable
  aluminum roasting pan
MUST HAVE—Meat thermometer
HANDIEST TOOLS—Long-pronged fork, long slicing
  knife, pot holders

If it doesn't seem like Christmas without a big-protein centerpiece, then your table is begging for the granddaddy of holiday classics, a stunning standing rib roast. The price per pound usually drops between Thanksgiving and Christmas, but be prepared to spend $50 to $60. Approach the butcher expecting personal service. You're going to need it.

Serves 6 to 8 (3-rib roast)
Serves 8 to 10 (4-rib roast)
Serves 14 to 20 (7-rib roast)

> **1 standing rib roast (7-rib, 4-rib or 3-rib)**
> **Salt and pepper**

DO THIS FIRST:

1. Take the roast out of the refrigerator for an hour.

2. Preheat the oven to 350°F, with the oven rack in your oven's lower third.

- Time-and-temperature charts don't work well. Today's meat is lean and roasts best at 350° all the way through the cooking. Recent popularized high-heat beginnings can cause shrinkage in your prized protein, and your house to fill with smoke. You will get a beauty of a roast using moderate, even temperature for the duration.

- If salt and pepper aren't added before roasting, the seasoning won't become part of the caramelizing on the crust.

- If you've got a 3-rib roast, estimate 15 minutes per pound for rare. For larger roasts, start thermometer readings after 2 hours.

- Buy an instant-read meat thermometer. Don't rely on thermometers that say Beef-Rare—140°. It will be medium.

- When the roast rests, the temperature will rise about 5 degrees. The resting is perfect for you and great for the roast. You can finish up side dishes, talk to guests, and think about the seating. The roast's juices will settle back into its flesh and the slices will be clean.

- If you want to make sauce from the pan juices, take the roast out of the pan, set it on a cutting board, and pour the pan juices into a glass measuring cup. Put the cup in the refrigerator for a little while so the fat can chill, solidify, and rise. While you wait the 5 or 10 minutes for this process to begin, turn to page 70 for directions on how to make the sauce.

DO THIS SECOND:

1. Place the meat, bones down, in a shallow roasting pan. Generously rub all the fat with salt and pepper.

2. Roast 15 minutes per pound. An 8-pound roast would take 2 hours to become rare.

3. Get a temperature reading with an instant-read thermometer. Continue roasting until the meat reaches the doneness you like:

Rare—120°F
Medium rare—130°F
Medium—140°F
Beyond medium—I will not be a party to this

WRAPPING IT UP:

1. Remove the roast, leaving the oven free for last-minute baking.

2. Cover the meat loosely with a big piece of foil, like a tent. Let the meat rest for 30 minutes. (Don't worry, it will still be hot.)

3. Carve (see page 80) and serve. Pour the pan drippings and juices collected during carving into a pitcher and put it on the table.

HORSERADISH CREAM

TECHNIQUE—Mixing
BEST EQUIPMENT—Bowl, fork

This is a 5-minute recipe you can adjust hotter or milder by varying the amount of horseradish.

Makes 1¾ cups

> 1½ cups sour cream
> ¼ cup white horseradish from a jar
> 1 teaspoon Dijon-style mustard
> ¼ teaspoon salt

DO THIS FIRST:

1. Measure all the ingredients into a bowl. Stir them with a fork.

2. Taste to see if it needs more salt.

WRAPPING IT UP:

1. Put the horseradish cream in a serving bowl. Cover with plastic wrap and keep in the refrigerator until serving. It will stay sharp for 2 days.

• Wild rice is compatible with anything smoky — cheese, poultry, game, pork — and also has a history of being mixed with foods that are naturally sweet, such as prunes, apricots, and raisins. Because really good quality wild rice has a definite nuttiness, it's also a good match with almonds, pecans, pistachios, cashews, or walnuts.

• Wild rice isn't a rice, but the seeds of an aquatic grass known as *Zizania aquatica*. It grows in water 2 to 4 feet deep.

• Always rinse wild rice well before cooking. Drain well.

• The ratio of wild rice to liquid is 1 to 3 (1 cup wild rice, 3 cups liquid), whether the liquid is water or stock. (Regular white rice is 1 to 2.)

• The extra liquid in this recipe from orange juice and maple syrup will be absorbed by the dried fruits as they plump during baking.

• Baking this dish frees a burner on the stove.

• By the time the wild rice has cooked, it will have expanded to 3 to 4 times its original volume.

MAPLE-ORANGE WILD RICE

TECHNIQUE — Sautéing/baking
BEST COOKWARE — Round or oval casserole with high sides and a lid (it should hold 6 cups)
BEST EQUIPMENT — Medium-size pot, chef's knife, cutting board, measuring cups

Wild rice and sweetness go together. That's why maple syrup and orange juice are the supporting flavors in this rich, creamy side dish. Also contributing some natural sweetness are golden raisins and chopped prunes. The outright crunch of deluxe pecan halves offsets the chewiness of the wild rice. This dish goes together quickly and bakes unattended and worry-free for 1½ to 2 hours.

Serves 8 (with leftovers)

4 or 5 tablespoons soft butter
1 cup chopped prunes
1 cup golden raisins
1 orange, for zest
¾ cup orange juice
¼ cup maple syrup
1 cup wild rice
3 cups chicken stock
2 teaspoons salt
½ teaspoon black pepper

Extra goodies: 1 cup deluxe pecan halves (or pistachios, walnuts, or slivered almonds)

DO THIS FIRST:

1. Preheat the oven to 350°F, with a rack on the lowest notch.

2. Smear 1 to 2 tablespoons of soft butter all over the bottom and sides of a 6-cup (1½-quart) casserole.

3. Chop the prunes, measure and place them in a bowl. Measure the raisins and add them to the prunes. Grate the colored skin off the orange on the finest holes of a box grater, or take off the zest with a zester, and add it to the prunes.

4. Measure the orange juice and maple syrup. Set both near the bowl of dried fruit.

DO THIS SECOND:

1. Measure the wild rice. Pour it into a colander or large strainer.

2. Hold the strainer under cold running water and wash the rice until the water runs clear. Leave the rice in the strainer.

DO THIS THIRD:

1. Put 3 tablespoons of butter in a medium-size pot. Turn the burner to high and wait for the butter to melt.

2. Pour in the washed rice. Turn the heat down to medium. Sauté the rice for fully 5 minutes. You know things are going well when some of the grains begin to burst and smell toasty.

3. Add the chicken stock. Turn the heat back to high, and bring to a boil.

DO THIS FOURTH:

1. As soon as the rice boils, turn off the heat and take the pot off the burner.

2. Add all the remaining ingredients—the dried fruit, juice, maple syrup, salt, pepper, and nuts. Stir it up gently.

WRAPPING IT UP:

1. Transfer the rice to the buttered casserole. Cover very tightly.

2. Bake for 1½ to 2 hours. It isn't done until the liquid is gone. Keep checking and stirring.

• The baking time is really a guess, and depends completely on the wild rice you bought. If it's cooked and cooked but stubbornly refuses to absorb liquid and remains crunchy—which it definitely should not—the rice might be old. Sometimes the harvest year is on the bag or box, so be sure to check. Also, make sure that the baking dish cover is a good fit. If too much steam escapes, the wild rice won't be able to completely cook. It should be chewy.

• If you have leftovers, you can freeze wild rice. It will hold up with just about the same quality as when you first made it. Stuff leftovers into a heavy zip-style plastic bag. Thaw on the defrost setting of your microwave.

• The potatoes are pre-mashed before the extras join in. This is to avoid lumps.

• If you want lumps, add the milk, butter, and garlic at the beginning of the mashing.

• It's okay if small nubs of soft garlic remain in the mixture. Once garlic has been roasted it isn't as strong as it is raw.

GARLIC MASHED POTATOES

TECHNIQUE — Boiling
BEST COOKWARE — Large pot and a lid
BEST EQUIPMENT — Potato masher or portable electric beaters, a big bowl
BEST TOOL — Potato peeler

In the case of roasted garlic in a batch of mashed potatoes, two heads are better than one. You can roast and refrigerate the garlic a week or so before you use it.

Serves 8 to 10

> 2 entire heads of garlic
> 5 to 6 big baking potatoes (russets)
> 2 teaspoons salt
> 4 tablespoons butter (½ stick)
> ¾ cup milk
> White or black pepper

DO THIS FIRST:

1. Preheat the oven to 400°F. Slice ¼ inch off the hairy root end of the heads of garlic. Wrap each head in foil. Put the foil packages on another piece of foil, as a temporary baking sheet.

2. Roast the garlic for 1 hour.

3. Unwrap the garlic heads and let them cool.

4. Squeeze the garlic cloves out of their skins and throw the skins away.

DO THIS SECOND:

1. Peel the potatoes. Cut each into 8 chunks.

2. Put the chunks into a big pot. Add enough water to cover them by a comfortable inch. Add 1 teaspoon of salt.

DO THIS THIRD:

1. Put the pot over high heat. Bring it to a boil.

2. When the water boils, cover the pot. Turn the heat down to medium and cook the potatoes, covered, for 15 minutes. *Meanwhile, put a colander in the sink and clean up the potato-peel mess.*

3. Pour the potatoes into the colander, then dump them back into their cooking pot.

4. Put the pot back on the turned-off burner, uncovered, for a few seconds to help the potatoes dry out.

WRAPPING IT UP:

1. Off the heat, mash the potatoes or whip them with a portable electric mixer in their pot.

2. When they are smooth, add the butter, milk, 1 teaspoon salt, and pepper, and mash or whip them again just to blend.

3. Add the squeezed garlic cloves. Mash or whip until the potatoes are as smooth as you like.

4. Put the potatoes in their serving bowl. Serve now, or cover with foil and keep warm in a 200°F oven up to 30 minutes.

BUTTERED GREEN BEANS

TECHNIQUE—Sautéing
BEST COOKWARE—10-inch skillet
BEST EQUIPMENT—Wooden spatula

Leave yourself 5 minutes at the end of all your efforts, including getting the roast carved and the pan juices on the table, to complete this simple dish. It's left plain on purpose.

Serves 8

> 2 pounds fresh green beans (or pea pods)
> 3 tablespoons butter
> ⅛ to ¼ teaspoon salt

DO THIS FIRST:

1. Get out a medium-size serving dish.

2. Wash the beans in a colander. Tear off the stem ends, dragging off the strings (if any) down one side of the length of the beans.

3. Bundle a few beans at a time on a cutting board and cut the bundles into 1-inch chunks. Get rid of the irregular ends. Put the beans in a bowl, and have the bowl convenient to the stove. You can do this at any point while the roast is in the oven. If you're using pea pods, tear off the strings but leave the pods whole.

DO THIS SECOND:

1. After the roast comes out of the oven and the pan juices are on the table, put the butter in a medium-size skillet.

2. Turn the heat to high. When the butter melts and loses its foam, add the beans.

3. Stir, wait for the heat to recover itself, then turn the burner down to medium. Sprinkle with salt—⅛ teaspoon to start. Stir and sauté 4 to 5 minutes. Taste, and add more salt if you think the beans need it.

WRAPPING IT UP:

1. Transfer the beans to the serving dish. Bring to the table hot.

• Fresh green beans include Kentucky Wonder, Blue Lake, Romano (a thick Italian bean), and other beans common to your area. Pick out the small tender ones from the grocery store display.

• Yes, you can use frozen green beans. Add them to the skillet while still frozen. I can't promise that you'll wow your guests with these, however.

• The strings are why green beans are called "string" beans, even though some varieties don't have strings at all. When you trim the beans you'll see if a string comes off with the stem cap.

• The sweetest peas of all are sugar peas, eaten pod and all. Don't confuse them with snow peas, which also may be used in this recipe in exactly the same amount. Sugar peas have their season in mid-spring, and a peaklet in November, so you may or may not see them by Christmas. Snow peas are available all year.

• The butter will actually thicken a little as the beans cook in it. By the time the beans are done, the butter will coat the beans nicely.

• The beans are done when they're still slightly crunchy but noticeably sweeter than when raw.

• Unsweetened chocolate is often called baking chocolate. Sometimes it comes as a wrapped rectangle, sometimes a square. Either shape implies 1 ounce, but check the package for equivalents. For more on chocolate melting see page 229.

• If you don't have a microwave, put the chocolate and butter into a small bowl, and set the bowl in a pan of water, such as a layer cake pan. Set this "water bath" arrangement over medium heat. Stir the butter and chocolate until both are melted. The moment all that's left is a small chunk of chocolate, take the pan off the heat. Keep stirring until the chocolate melts. This whole process will take about 8 minutes.

• Don't be alarmed when the pies sink as they cool. This settling enhances their rich texture.

• Each pie may be cut into six wedges even though they'll look small. This recipe is very rich.

FUDGE PECAN PIE

TECHNIQUE — Baking
BEST BAKEWARE — Pre-made frozen pie crusts
BEST EQUIPMENT — Mixing bowl, electric mixer or whisk
HANDY TO HAVE — Rubber spatula, cookie sheet

Easy and rich, this pie comes from mixing ingredients in one bowl, pouring the batter into two pre-made pie crusts, and baking them. My mom has made this for years and always to raves.

Makes 2 pies, for 12 wedges

2 frozen 9-inch pie shells
3 squares (3 ounces) unsweetened chocolate
3 tablespoons butter
4 eggs
⅔ cup sugar
1 cup dark Karo syrup
1½ cups nice-looking pecans halves
A batch of whipped cream (page 213)

DO THIS FIRST:

1. Take the pie crusts out of the freezer, unwrap them, and leave them on a cookie sheet while you make the pies.

2. Preheat the oven to 350°F with an oven rack in the middle.

3. Get out a big mixing bowl and your beaters.

DO THIS SECOND:

1. Unwrap the chocolate. Chop it into small pieces and put it in a microwave-safe bowl.

2. Measure the butter and add it to the chocolate. Microwave on Medium power for 2 minutes, uncovered. Stir the chocolate until it's all melted.

DO THIS THIRD:

1. Crack the eggs into the mixing bowl. Measure and add the sugar and Karo syrup, and the melted chocolate.

2. Beat on low speed, or whisk by hand, until you get a grainy batter.

3. Stir in the pecans.

DO THIS FOURTH:

1. Re-crimp the partially thawed pie shells so they look homemade.

2. Pour the batter into the pie shells. Scrape out the last drop with a rubber spatula.

3. Put the pies and their cookie sheet into the oven. Bake 40 to 45 minutes. The pies will puff while they bake but sink when they're cool.

WRAPPING IT UP:

1. Cool the pies completely. To serve, cut out wedges and top each serving with fresh whipped cream.

Easter dinner usually comes after church. Whether it's soon after church or prepared at a more leisurely pace for late afternoon is usually determined by family pattern. For people new to cooking such menus, when you eat is more a matter of buying as much time as possible to get everything ready. I've given you two timelines for Easter. One is for serving soon after you come home from church, at around 1 pm. The ham is baked the night before and served cold. The other timeline is for Easter dinner at 4 or 5 pm. The ham will be hot, or warm.

EASTER

MENU

CLASSIC BAKED HAM
WITH DIAMOND PATTERN
•
BREAD OR ROLLS (FROM
YOUR FAVORITE BAKERY)
•
PARSLEY RICE
•
ORANGE-FLAVORED
CARROTS (PAGE 292)
•
BRIGHT GREEN
ASPARAGUS
•
SUGARED STRAWBERRIES
WITH CREAM

EASTER
ONE STEP AT A TIME

✔ *Take one step at a time. Check off each step as you complete it.*

1 DAY AHEAD

__ Bake ham
__ Slice carrots and refrigerate
__ Chop parsley for rice and refrigerate
__ Prepare strawberries and refrigerate
__ Whip cream and refrigerate
__ Get a good night's sleep

TO SERVE BY 1 PM

EASTER DAY, AFTER CHURCH

__ Cook carrots
__ Cook rice
__ Boil asparagus
__ Warm bread or rolls
__ Slice ham
__ Set up coffeemaker
__ Clean up, if there's time
__ Put ham, bread, carrots, rice, and asparagus on the table

MEAL TIME

__ Enjoy the meal
__ Flick on coffeemaker
__ Serve dessert

4 HOURS BEFORE SERVING

__ Take ham out of refrigerator
__ Preheat oven
__ Prepare ham and get it in the oven
__ Prepare strawberries and refrigerate
__ Whip cream and refrigerate
__ Set up coffeemaker
__ Slice carrots

TO SERVE BY 4 PM

1 HOUR BEFORE SERVING

__ Ham is done; it can sit 1 hour or longer
      (guests begin to arrive)
__ Boil asparagus to serve at room temperature
__ Cook carrots
__ Cook rice
__ Slice ham
__ Put ham, bread, carrots, rice, and asparagus on the table

MEAL TIME

__ Enjoy the meal
__ Flick on coffeemaker
__ Serve dessert

1 TO 2 DAYS AHEAD
• Bring the ham home

1 DAY AHEAD
• Set the table or buffet (remember hot pads)

CLASSIC BAKED HAM WITH DIAMOND PATTERN

- Hams are easy to bake but confusing to buy. Most hams will be labeled "fully cooked." Despite what such a label seems to imply, the ham is not cooked in a way you'd like. While it was being smoked, it reached an internal temperature of 160°F, high enough for the USDA to qualify it as fully cooked. What hasn't happened to it is a nice baking at home.

- The salt/sugar curing process gives ham its pink color.

- It should be noted that modern American pigs are leaner than most of their brethren around the world.

- Your half ham will have come either from the butt (the shoulder) or the shank (the leg). Both have bones going through the middle of the meat, as would your own arm or leg. That's why a cross section of either of these looks kind of alike at the store. The shank is easier to carve and therefore preferable for this recipe.

- Look for ham that's still got some or all of its black rind attached. During initial baking it protects the fat from overcooking or browning. When it comes off later, the fat will still be undercooked enough to withstand more baking without withering up.

TECHNIQUE — Baking
BEST EQUIPMENT — Big roasting pan
BEST TOOLS — Paring knife, heavy aluminum foil

Ham is available in stores in many forms. The one we use here is the easiest to cook and one of the best. It's labeled "fully-cooked," but it still needs a couple of hours in the oven to be called "baked."

You may think this recipe is preoccupied with the ham's layer of fat. While you may not eat the fat, you've got to take care of it during cooking. Without the fat there would be no diamond pattern scored into your ham, no cloves stuck into the diamonds, and no visual replica of the hams that once made you happy.

Serves 10

> Half a "fully-cooked" bone-in smoked
> ham, about 5 to 7 pounds
> 6-ounce can frozen orange juice concentrate
> (don't add water!)
> 8-ounce jar apricot or peach jam
> 1 tablespoon ground cinnamon
> Jar of whole cloves (you'll need about 40)

DO THIS FIRST:

1. Plan to get the ham in the oven 4 hours before you'll serve it.

2. Take the orange juice concentrate out of the freezer.

3. Preheat the oven to 325°F, with an oven rack on the lowest notch. Get out a big roasting pan that has shallow sides. Unroll about 2 feet of heavy duty aluminum foil and line the pan.

4. If you have one, set a rack inside the pan. Set the ham on the rack, fatted side up.

DO THIS SECOND:

1. Bake the ham 1½ hours. While it bakes, clean up, mix the orange juice and jam into a glaze, and prepare other recipes for your meal. The ham certainly won't be done at this point.

DO THIS THIRD:

1. Take the ham out of the oven and set it on the kitchen table or counter.

2. If it has any rind, cut or peel it off now, but please leave a nice, thick, even layer of fat.

3. Use a small knife to cut lines in one direction through the fat, but not all the way into the meat. Now cut lines in the opposite direction, to make a diamond pattern all over the fat.

4. Rub the cinnamon all over the ham and fat. Stick a clove in the center of each diamond.

5. Dab or spoon orange juice-jelly glaze all over the ham.

DO THIS FOURTH:

1. Return the ham to the oven, still at 325°F, for about 45 minutes more.

2. Every 20 minutes or so, dab more glaze on the ham.

3. Bake the ham until it reaches an internal temperature of 140°F. Check with your instant-read meat thermometer.

WRAPPING IT UP:

1. Cool the ham well before slicing, 30 to 45 minutes. Don't worry, it will still be warm when you eat it.

2. To carve, cut straight down to the bone near the small end, then make a diagonal slice a few inches beyond to connect with the first cut. Keep slicing diagonally all the way across the ham. Turn the ham over and slice the same way. (See Carving, page 77.)

• Bone-in or boneless? Cooking is rife with trade-offs, and this is a big one. This recipe uses a bone-in ham because it gives you the most rind and fat to work with. In boning a ham and rolling it back up, processors lose much of that fat layer. If you're nervous about carving, you can buy a boneless ham. But don't be tempted to cut diamonds in it; you'll nick the meat, you'll lose juices, and the ham may be dry. Do put glaze on a boneless ham anyway. To carve a boneless ham, just slice it like a loaf of bread.

• The price of ham drops to something like 99 cents a pound during the weeks before Easter. This is an incredible buy for a piece of meat that can cost $3 a pound and more during the rest of the year.

• Sometimes hams are given away free as store promotionals during the pre-Easter season. Don't be afraid. Take the ham home.

• You don't have to add water or cover the pan.

• Hams can be sweetened with brown sugar, cider, bourbon, or maple syrup, or given hotness from mustard or horseradish.

• You'd be amazed what you can smear over a ham. A friend thinks of baked ham as a chance to use up nearly-empty jars of strange and wonderful food taking up space in the refrigerator. A recent ham was amazing with kiwi-apricot jam (obviously a gift) mixed with soy sauce, Dijon mustard, orange juice, and white horseradish.

• Flat-leaf parsley, also known as Italian parsley, is stronger and more aromatic than regular curly parsley. Try to use it in this rice. In spring Italian parsley is easier to find.

• Rice cooks in the classic 1-to-2 ratio. One cup of rice cooks perfectly in 2 cups of liquid. Remember that and you won't need a recipe again.

• The amount of salt is really up to the chicken stock. If you've bought unsalted or one of those "lite" chicken stocks, or are using water, you'll still have to add salt. I assure you, you won't like rice without salt. It's flat.

• If the rice sticks a little, it isn't ruined. It will have more flavor. But there's a big difference between a little stuck-on and burned. If it sticks a lot, it's probably burned. I doubt this will happen in the time frame in this recipe.

• If you want to be sure the rice won't stick, don't cook it in a cheap, flimsy pot. Go out and get a pot with a thick, heavy bottom and you'll never burn rice — or most any other food for that matter.

• This method works for regular long-grain rice, basmati, Texmati, and medium-grain rice such as Calrose.

PARSLEY RICE

TECHNIQUE — Sautéing/steaming
BEST COOKWARE — Medium saucepan
BEST UTENSIL — Measuring cups
BEST TOOL — Cutting board and chef's knife

Once finished, in its serving bowl and covered, the rice will stay hot a surprising 30 minutes.

Serves 8

¼ cup minced fresh parsley
1 medium onion
2 cups raw long-grain rice
3 tablespoons butter
4 cups canned chicken stock or water
1 teaspoon salt

DO THIS FIRST:

1. Have ready a serving bowl and serving spoon.

2. Mince the parsley, measure it, and put it in a small cup. Peel and halve the onion. Chop the halves into nice-looking ¼-inch dice. Leave it on the cutting board, and set the board near the stove.

3. Measure the rice, butter, and chicken stock and have them all convenient to the stove, too.

DO THIS SECOND:

1. Put the butter in a medium-size saucepan. Turn the heat to high.

2. When the butter sizzles, push the onion off the cutting board and stir it around in the butter for a minute.

3. Now add the raw rice and stir it around quickly for another minute. The rice should smell toasty and become coated with butter.

DO THIS THIRD:

1. After the rice and onion are coated with butter, pour in the chicken stock, which will sizzle. Add the salt. (Use less salt if the stock is salty; you'll have to taste it.)

2. With the heat still high, bring the rice to a boil, uncovered.

3. When it boils, cover the pot and turn the heat down to low. Simmer 20 minutes. (*This a good resting place to clean up the cutting board and knife and check on other kitchen details.*)

WRAPPING IT UP:

1. Uncover the pot and add the parsley. Stir it around until it's evenly distributed.

2. Cover and simmer 2 more minutes. Taste. If the rice is still too crunchy, cover the pot again and simmer 2 more minutes.

3. Remove the cover, give a couple of stirs, and pour the rice into the serving bowl.

BRIGHT GREEN ASPARAGUS

TECHNIQUE—Boiling
BEST COOKWARE—Your widest skillet, 10 to 12 inches (not cast iron)
BEST UTENSIL—Tongs

As green vegetables go, asparagus is the most forgiving about when it's made. That's because the tender fresh stalks are just as good warm or cold as they are hot. In spring, there's nothing wrong with room-temperature asparagus. If this helps you time the courses in your meal, take this option.

Serves 8

> 3 bunches fresh asparagus
> 1 tablespoon salt

DO THIS FIRST:

1. Have a long serving dish, such as a slender oval, ready for the finished asparagus.

2. Wash the asparagus. To get rid of the tough bottoms, bend each asparagus stalk where it looks like the toughness begins—about an inch from the bottom. The tough part will snap off at a natural spot.

3. Have the asparagus ready near the stove.

DO THIS SECOND:

1. Fill your widest skillet (12 inches, preferably) with water to within ½ inch of the rim. Add 1 tablespoon salt.

2. Bring the water to a boil over high heat, covered. When you see steam escaping from under the lid, uncover the skillet and add the asparagus.

3. Keep the heat high and wait for the boil to come back. In all, cook the asparagus about 4 minutes, uncovered.

DO THIS THIRD:

1. To test if the asparagus are done, stick the point of a knife into a spear. If it goes in easily, it's done. Or, hold a spear out of the boiling water with tongs. If it droops just slightly, it's done. Or, best, pull a spear out of the water. Take a bite. If you like the way it feels and tastes, it's done.

WRAPPING IT UP:

1. Pull the asparagus out of the water with tongs.

2. Either serve them immediately in the long dish or let them cool in the dish and serve them at room temperature within 30 minutes or so.

• Cast iron can discolor asparagus.

• When the asparagus go into the skillet, they will retard the boiling. You'll have to wait for the boil to come back.

• There are lots of theories on cooking asparagus. They can cook standing up in a special asparagus holder. They can also be microwaved. I find that boiling lying down in a skillet gives them the best flavor and gives you the most control over their stages of doneness.

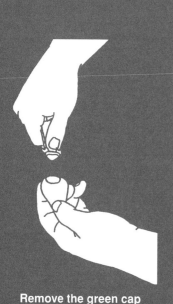

Insert the tip of the knife into the strawberry

Remove the green cap and the core

SUGARED STRAWBERRIES WITH CREAM

TECHNIQUE—Slicing, whipping cream
BEST EQUIPMENT—Big mixing bowl
BEST TOOLS—Measuring cups and spoons

Strawberries and cream is as fine a treat for company as it always is for the family any day during strawberry season. Here it is dressed up with a touch of liqueur.

Serves 8

> 4 pint baskets whole strawberries
> ½ cup sugar
> 1½ cups whipping cream
> 1 teaspoon vanilla
>
> *Optional: ¼ cup liqueur (Cointreau, Cognac, Amaretto)*

DO THIS FIRST:
1. Put all the strawberries in a colander and rinse them really well. Let as much water drain away as possible. It's okay if they still have a few droplets of water clinging to them.

DO THIS SECOND:
1. The real way to take the green caps off strawberries is to dig out a cone-shaped section, which will get you the cap and the core in one maneuver. Hold a paring knife in your dominant hand, a strawberry in the other. Press your thumb on the top of the strawberry near the point of the knife so it can steady both the knife and the green cap.

2. Insert the tip of the knife into the strawberry. Turn the strawberry in one direction and your thumb and the knife in the other. Make the point of the knife go in a circle while your thumb holds the cap steady. When the circle is complete, the green cap and the core will come out. You'll have to practice a few times.

DO THIS THIRD:

1. Slice the capped strawberries and place them in a bowl as you go.

2. Sprinkle the strawberries with the sugar. If you're using liqueur, add it now. Stir once or twice, and leave the strawberries alone for about 30 minutes.

WRAPPING IT UP:

1. Whip the cream with the vanilla (see page 213).

2. Serve the strawberries in wine glasses (or dessert dishes) layered with whipped cream, starting with strawberries and ending with cream.

3. Drizzle some of the strawberry juice left in the bottom of the strawberry bowl over the whipped cream. Wow!

MAKE-AHEAD OPTION:

1. Cover the sugared strawberries and put them in the refrigerator.

2. Whip the cream up to 24 hours ahead. (It won't separate if you don't overbeat it.) Put it in a bowl just large enough to hold the whipped cream and cover with plastic wrap. Refrigerate.

3. At serving, remove the strawberries and cream from the refrigerator. Use a slotted spoon to get the berries out of the bowl.

The traditions of Passover actually benefit the cook. Any number of dishes can cook unattended while the Seder, the telling of the biblical story of Moses leading the Israelites out of Egypt, is going on. If you preplate everyone's helpings of the food they'll need during the telling—such symbols as salt water for dipping, charoses, parsley, and horseradish—and have it on the table when everyone arrives, your Passover will have a smooth and relaxing start.

PASSOVER MENU

CHOPPED LIVER
·
CHAROSES
·
CHICKEN SOUP AND MATZO BALLS
·
LEG OF LAMB
·
ORANGE-FLAVORED CARROTS
·
BRIGHT GREEN ASPARAGUS (PAGE 276)
·
HONEY PEARS

PASSOVER
ONE STEP AT A TIME

✔ *Take one step at a time. Check off each step as you complete it.*

3 TO 4 HOURS BEFORE SUNSET

__ Trim asparagus; have skillet of water on stove
__ Prepare carrots for cooking
__ Set up coffeemaker
__ Arrange individual seder plates and put on table
__ Preheat oven
__ Make crumb crust; press on lamb
__ Clean up
__ Put chopped liver, extra charoses, and horseradish on table
__ Put plate with 3 matzos near host's setting
(guests begin to arrive)
__ Get lamb into oven
__ Start soup reheating

DURING THE SEDER
(about 1 hour before serving)

__ Cook matzo balls in soup
__ Cook carrots; keep warm in pot, covered
__ Get up from the table a few times to check on things
__ Lamb is done; it can sit up to 1 hour

AFTER THE SEDER

__ Serve chicken soup, matzo balls
__ Cook asparagus
__ Carve lamb and bring to the table
__ Bring carrots and asparagus to the table

MEAL TIME

__ Enjoy the meal
__ Flick on coffeemaker
__ Serve dessert

MAKE-AHEAD OPTION
- *Chicken Soup* — Make up to 3 months ahead and freeze.
- *Charoses* — Make up to 1 week ahead and refrigerate.
- *Hard-cooked eggs for Seder Plate* — Make up to 1 week ahead and refrigerate.
- *Leg of Lamb* — Order from butcher 1 week ahead.

1 OR 2 DAYS AHEAD
- Bring leg of lamb home
- Make chopped liver and refrigerate
- Make honey pears and refrigerate
- Make charoses (if not already done) and refrigerate
- Make chicken soup (if not already done) and refrigerate
- Make hard-cooked eggs (if not already done) and refrigerate
- Set the table; everyone gets a wine glass
- Get a good night's sleep

- Notice there's no mayonnaise, no expensive ingredients, no herbs and spices. A classic doesn't come any simpler.

- The longer the onions cook, the sweeter they'll make your chopped liver. This is a good thing. People will take a bite and exclaim "it's nice and sweet!"

- Chicken livers are sold in the poultry case in plastic tubs and are almost never sold frozen.

- It doesn't matter if you add the livers without draining off their liquid. It all cooks away anyway.

- The longer the livers cook, the easier they'll be to mash. My grandmother got her mashing done using only a fork. Well, perseverance and a fork.

- The most mechanical you can get is an immersible blender. Otherwise, machinery will take chopped liver way beyond chopped.

- Start your own stash of livers by saving them every time you buy a whole chicken. Wrap each one in plastic wrap, then store in a zip-style plastic bag in the freezer. When you've saved enough to make chopped liver, it will seem like it's free. This is what Dan Aykroyd meant when in his '70s impersonation of Julia Child on "Saturday Night Live" he said, squirting fake blood, "Save the liver!"

CHOPPED LIVER

TECHNIQUE — Sautéing
BEST COOKWARE — Wok or big skillet
BEST EQUIPMENT — Mixing bowl
BEST TOOL — Potato masher

For such a simple recipe, this comes with lots of secrets. Four that come immediately to mind are: lots of onions cooked a long time; cooking the livers very well-done without scorching them; getting your hands on some real schmaltz (rendered chicken fat); and not overmixing, by which you'll go too high on the gastronomic scale and end up with paté.

Makes 3½ cups

> 2 large onions
> 4 tablespoons rendered chicken fat (schmaltz)
> 1 pound chicken livers
> 3 hard-cooked eggs
> 2 teaspoons salt
> Lots of black pepper

DO THIS FIRST:

1. Peel the onions, then slice them into rings. Put the onions in a big skillet or a wok. Add 1 tablespoon of schmaltz.

2. Turn the heat to medium. Cook the onions until they're soft and golden. This will take about 7 minutes.

DO THIS SECOND:

1. Add the chicken livers. Cook over medium heat, stirring now and then, until they're very well done, dark, and sitting in a skillet gone nearly dry. This will take probably 15 more minutes.

2. Meanwhile, you can peel the eggs. Mash them with a fork in a separate bowl.

3. Take the liver and onions off the heat and let them cool a little.

DO THIS THIRD:

1. Transfer the cooled liver and onions to a wide bowl. Mash with a potato masher or fork until you've got small chunks of even size.

2. Add the mashed eggs and mash some more.

WRAPPING IT UP:

1. When the mixture is fairly even, add the remaining 3 tablespoons of schmaltz and the salt and pepper. Stir and mash until smooth.

2. Cover with plastic wrap and keep in the refrigerator until serving. Serve from the bowl with a spreading knife, surrounded by matzo pieces (or crackers).

WHAT IS SCHMALTZ? Schmaltz is rendered chicken fat, with an explanation. If you put 6 to 8 ounces of raw, yellow chicken fat in a medium-size pot and smother it with an entire chopped onion, then set it over medium-low heat until the fat melts into a liquid, you'll get rendered chicken fat. But it won't be schmaltz—not yet.

If you keep cooking until the onions get black-brown and the yellow of the liquefied fat deepens, which could take 2 to 3 hours, only then will you have schmaltz. Strain out the solids. That's schmaltz coming out the other side.

- Save the excess chicken fat on whole chickens. Or ask the butcher to save about a pound of fat for you.

- Chopped liver looks nice sprinkled with parsley, but it isn't a requirement.

- It's always best served cold.

- Schmaltz is identified with Eastern European Jewish cooking because it was difficult there to obtain any other kinds of cooking oil. But rendered chicken fat is used extensively in stir-frying in China.

- A non-animal product called Nyfat made by Rokeach (Roh-KAY-achk) is a stand-in for schmaltz.

• Pecans are a good substitute for walnuts.

• Peanuts can't be used because they're legumes, which are avoided during Passover.

• Sweet red wine would be the Concord grape wine made by Mogen David or Manischewitz. Lots of kosher wines from California are available now. If you use a dry red, such as a Cabernet Sauvignon or Zinfandel, add 1 teaspoon of sugar to the charoses.

CHAROSES

TECHNIQUE—Chopping
BEST EQUIPMENT—Chef's knife and cutting board

Charoses is a mixture of finely chopped apple and nuts that when mashed together symbolizes the mortar slaves laid between the bricks in Pharoah's Egypt. It is eaten at a particular point in the service before the meal. The type of apple doesn't matter. By spring, you'll be buying last fall's cold-storage apples anyway, unless they're coming in fresh from Down Under. I've used at times combinations of York, Empire, Rome, Fuji, Gala, or Granny Smith, to name a few.

Makes 2 cups

> 3 or 4 apples
> 1 cup walnut halves or pieces
> 1 teaspoon cinnamon
> ½ cup sweet red wine

DO THIS FIRST:

1. Peel the apples. Cut the flesh from the cores and throw the cores away. Chop the apples as finely as you can, which is pretty finely.

2. Chop the nuts finely and add them to the apples.

DO THIS SECOND:

1. Add the cinnamon and wine and stir to blend everything well. Cover and refrigerate one or two days.

WRAPPING IT UP:

1. Before serving, stir the charoses well to mix in any wine that sank to the bottom.

2. If the nuts were dry and absorbed the wine, you might have to add more wine to moisten the mixture just enough so it holds together.

CHICKEN SOUP

TECHNIQUE — Boiling
BEST COOKWARE — Tall stock pot or big pot, such as a Dutch oven
BEST EQUIPMENT — Colander, strainer, big bowl
BEST UTENSILS — Chef's knife, cutting board, big stirring spoon

This is all-purpose homemade chicken stock. But add the Eastern European effect of dill, and it becomes the familiar bowl of chicken soup for matzo balls. Either version can be used instead of canned stock in making rice, other soups, and in skillet recipes for chicken. Homemade stock also yields a few helpings of boiled vegetables, and enough boiled chicken to use back in the soup or in other dishes. This stock is very rich because the bones and skin from the cooked chicken return to the stock for more cooking. This pulls out the bones' gelatin while intensifying the flavor.

Somewhere a law is written that says chicken soup tastes better the next day. The extra night in the refrigerator also gives any fat a chance to rise to the top so you can take it off and throw it away (or use it like schmaltz).

Makes 3 quarts, plus

> 1 whole chicken, about 4 pounds
> Water
> 1 big onion
> 3 carrots
> 4 ribs celery
> Few sprigs fresh parsley
> ½ teaspoon white pepper
> 1 tablespoon salt
> Matzo Balls (recipe follows)
>
> *Optional Jewish ingredient: 1 large sprig fresh dill, or 1 teaspoon dried dill*

DO THIS FIRST:

1. The day before you want to serve chicken soup, pull out the package of giblets from the chicken's cavity. Wash the chicken and put it in a big soup kettle or tall stock pot.

LET'S TALK

• The best stocks are made with hens. These can be as heavy as 6 pounds, although some fryers are being bred to weigh 4-plus pounds.

• Liver turns stock gray. Cook it separately.

• Keep the liver for Chopped Liver. Wrap it in plastic and put it in the freezer if it will not be used immediately.

• Use a very large onion. Believe it or not, the onion lends a subtle sweetness to the stock.

• Buy 3 bulk carrots. There's no point buying a whole bag.

• Fresh parsley used with stems and all is easier to strain. Save yourself the hassle of chopping it.

• White pepper is used because it's invisible. Flecks of black pepper, for stock purists, are unsightly.

• Unsavory as it sounds, "scum" is the impurities in the chicken coming to the surface. The more of it you catch, the clearer your stock will be.

• The scum will get whiter and hold its shape in big bubbles after boiling begins.

• An "askew" lid covers three-fourths of the opening of the pot.

- During the uncovered cooking, the level of the stock will begin to lower; the stock will thicken and become a rich, green-gold color.

- The stock should be free of particles.

- If you don't have a strainer—and I don't mean the little ones used for tea—please buy one. You won't be sorry, because you can also use it for washing vegetables and fruits under running water. Get one a good 8 to 10 inches in diameter with a long handle, so the strainer can sit across your biggest bowl without falling in.

- You may also use an inexpensive plastic colander placed in a very wide, large bowl. But unless the holes are very tiny, expect more particles to come through. You can solve this problem by lining the colander with a clean dish towel. It will catch everything.

- The stock is refrigerated soon to retain quality. It is covered loosely to let steam escape. If covered too tightly when hot, condensation forming under the covering can give the stock an early rancidity.

- The fat will congeal in a solid layer on the surface. It will be easy to lift off and discard. Or, save it and use it in your matzo balls.

- If your stock gels somewhat when chilled, you have made it perfectly.

2. You can add the giblets to the soup—the gizzard, heart, and neck—but not the liver.

3. Fill the pot with enough cold water to completely cover the chicken. Place the pot over high heat, uncovered, and wait about 20 minutes until it boils.

DO THIS SECOND:

1. During this time, you can prepare the vegetables. Peel the onion and leave it whole. Wash the carrots and celery and cut them in thirds.

2. Wash the parsley. Tie the stems together with a little string.

DO THIS THIRD:

1. Checking back on the chicken, skim off grey scum as it rises to the surface. Do this with a big metal spoon in one hand, to remove the scum, and a coffee cup in the other, to receive it. Keep skimming periodically during the first 10 minutes of actual boiling.

2. When the scum subsides, add the prepared vegetables and pepper. Keep the heat high and return the liquid to a boil. At the boil, cover the pot with the lid askew. Turn down the heat and simmer 1½ hours. *This is more than enough time to clean up the vegetable mess and set up a colander in a big bowl near the stove.*

3. During last 30 minutes of simmering, add the salt.

DO THIS FOURTH:

1. Use tongs to lift the whole chicken out of the soup and into the colander. Keep simmering the soup, uncovered.

2. When you can touch the chicken without burning your fingers, peel off the skin with your hands or tongs and pull out the bones.

3. Put all the skin and bones back in the pot. Also pour back any juices that dripped through the colander. (You can serve the chicken meat in the finished soup or use it for another dish.)

4. Keep simmering on low heat, uncovered, 30 minutes more. Set up the same big bowl and cleaned-out colander arrangement for the final draining. Have ready another bowl or storage container for the cooked vegetables.

WRAPPING IT UP:

1. Use tongs to withdraw the carrots, celery, and onion to their bowl.

2. Pour the stock through the colander. Use pot holders! Throw away the skin, bones, and parsley pieces.

3. Cool the strained soup and bowl of vegetables about 30 minutes on the countertop. Cover each loosely with foil and put them in the refrigerator overnight.

4. Next day, skim the soup of all the fat but a tablespoon. Pour the soup into a pot and reheat it on medium-high heat, uncovered, until it boils. Serve with Matzo Balls.

MAKE-AHEAD OPTION:

1. To freeze stock, pour it into 2-cup freezer containers or pint-size heavy-duty locking freezer bags. If you use bags, be sure to force out extra air. I prefer this method because the bags take up little room in an already packed freezer.

2. Avoid freezing in large amounts. Large quantities take longer to freeze and longer to defrost, and force you to use more stock than you may need at one time.

3. Place the containers in the freezer quickly, leaving them open slightly to prevent condensation from forming inside. In a few hours, when cold, seal securely.

4. Defrost bags of frozen stock in a pan of hot water or in a bowl in the microwave. If thawing in a microwave, open the bag.

- This is a double recipe. To make less, divide the ingredient amounts in half.

- Schmaltz is rendered chicken fat. You can use solid vegetable shortening, such as Crisco, instead. Or, if you've already made your chicken soup and given it a chance to get very cold in the refrigerator, chances are you've got a thick layer of congealed fat lying across the surface. Skim this off to use as part of the fat requirement.

- To cook this amount and to allow the matzo balls to expand, you might need the boiling soup *and* a pot of boiling water, depending on how much soup you've made and how large the soup pot is. Once served in the soup, a matzo ball boiled in water is indistinguishable from one boiled in soup.

- A fork is all you need to mix this batter.

- The refrigerator time is important. The egg and water slowly drink in the matzo meal, and the fat solidifies, making the batter thick enough to roll into balls.

- The cooking time of matzo balls coincides with the duration of a short Seder—about 45 minutes prior to eating.

MATZO BALLS

TECHNIQUE—Boiling/steaming
BEST COOKWARE—Soup pot or Dutch oven
BEST EQUIPMENT—Mixing bowl, hands

Don't make the mistake of assuming that you get feather-light matzo balls by adding more and more eggs. The secret to light matzo balls is the volume of water and fat. The more liquid, the lighter they are. You can tell by how the batter behaves. If it's stiff, you'll get hard matzo balls. If it's loose, they'll be light. Please give yourself time for the batter to chill. You can boil the matzo balls once all have arrived and the Seder reading begins.

Makes 10 huge or 16 to 20 medium matzo balls

> 4 eggs
> 1 cup schmaltz (see page 283)
> 2 cups matzo meal
> 1 tablespoon salt
> 1 cup water or chicken soup

DO THIS FIRST:

1. Get out a big mixing bowl. Crack in the eggs. Add the schmaltz and beat with a fork until the fat and eggs are blended.

2. Add the matzo meal, salt, and ¾ cup of the water. Stir with a fork until thick. If the batter is a tad loose, don't add any more water. If it's thick, add the remaining ¼ cup.

3. Put the bowl in the refrigerator, uncovered, for 1 to 2 hours.

DO THIS SECOND:

1. Have a big pot three-fourths full of water boiling hard on high heat. Or, if the chicken soup has been refrigerated, take it out of the refrigerator, set it on high heat, covered, and bring it to a boil.

2. Take out the bowl of matzo ball batter.

3. Wet your hands. Use a ¼-cup measuring cup to portion out a scant ¼ cup for each matzo ball. Roll each into a ball with your wet hands. They'll be a little smaller than golf balls.

WRAPPING IT UP:

1. Drop the balls gently into the boiling water or soup. When they're all in, immediately cover the pot.

2. When you're certain the water is boiling at a clip, you can turn the heat down to medium. Cook 45 minutes. Try not to peek.

• You can find leg of lamb in the fresh meat case of any supermarket. It will probably be shrink-wrapped.

• Lamb is at its best price in the weeks before Passover and Easter.

• New Zealand and American lamb are the most common. New Zealand lamb is slightly gamier than American, but both are delicious.

• If you buy your lamb from a human, such as a real live butcher, you can request that the membrane, "fell," be pulled off before you walk out of the store.

• The crumb mixture made from matzo meal is a little rougher than the exact same recipe using bread crumbs. It bakes very crunchy.

• The beauty of leg of lamb is that the thickest parts will suit the medium-rare lovers while the thinner ends where the bone protrudes will give well-done slices.

• This is another example of meat that is big, but easy.

LEG OF LAMB

TECHNIQUE—Baking
BEST COOKWARE—Cookie sheet, cooling rack
BEST EQUIPMENT—Mixing bowl, hands

The crust in this recipe is reminiscent of the French herb-crumb crust so often baked onto the top of a leg of lamb, but it uses matzo meal instead of bread crumbs. It takes about 15 minutes to make the crumb mixture and press it onto the lamb. Then you put it in the oven and forget about it for the next two hours.

Serves 10 to 12

> 6- to 8-pound whole leg of lamb, with bone
> 1 tablespoon minced garlic
> 1 tablespoon fresh chopped parsley
> 1¾ cups matzo meal
> 1 tablespoon Dijon mustard
> ½ teaspoon dried rosemary or thyme
> ¼ cup olive oil

DO THIS FIRST:

1. Preheat the oven to 350°F, with an oven rack in the lower part of the oven.

2. Unwrap the lamb. If there is "fell," a thin membrane tugging tightly over its fat, slit it with a sharp paring knife and peel it off. You'll probably want to wash your hands.

3. Get out a cookie sheet and a cake cooling rack. Set the rack on the cookie sheet, and place the lamb on the rack.

DO THIS SECOND:

1. Get out a mixing bowl. Mince the garlic as finely as you can and ~~put~~ it in the bowl.

2. Chop the parsley and add it to the bowl.

3. Measure the matzo meal into the bowl. Add the remaining ingredients and stir with a fork, then with your hands, until the mixture loosely holds together. It helps if you grab the mixture into your fists and squeeze.

4. With your hands, press a thick layer of crumbs all over the lamb. Pat and press until it all stays on.

WRAPPING IT UP:

1. Bake 1½ hours, then start checking its temperature. Figure 15 minutes per pound for medium-rare, 20 minutes per pound for medium. An internal temperature of 135°F in the thickest part means it's rare; 140° to 145°F is medium-rare.

2. Let the leg of lamb cool about 15 or 20 minutes.

3. To carve, slice diagonally through the crust and across the top of the meat, drawing the knife down the length of the leg, which is the same direction as the bone.

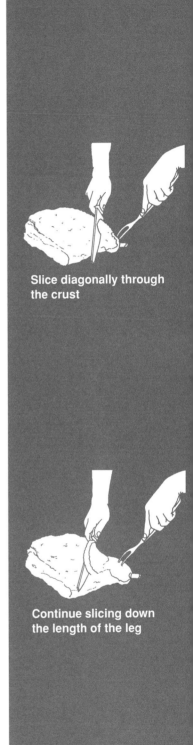

Slice diagonally through the crust

Continue slicing down the length of the leg

ORANGE-FLAVORED CARROTS

TECHNIQUE—Sautéing/boiling
BEST COOKWARE—Medium-size pot with a lid
BEST TOOLS—Vegetable peeler, chef's knife and
  cutting board

Think of this as a partial make-ahead—if
you slice the carrots early. Once the carrots are
sautéed, mixed with the rest of the ingredients,
and on the stove with the lid on, you can walk
away.

Serves 8

> 3 pounds carrots
> ½ cup frozen orange juice concentrate
>   (not diluted)
> ½ cup brown sugar
> 2 tablespoons vegetable oil
> 1 teaspoon salt

DO THIS FIRST:

1. Cut the end off each carrot. Peel the carrots
with a vegetable peeler. Cut them into ½-inch-
thick slices—not too thin. Put them in a work-
bowl as you go, then take the bowl to the stove.

2. Measure the orange juice concentrate and
sugar and have them convenient to the stove.

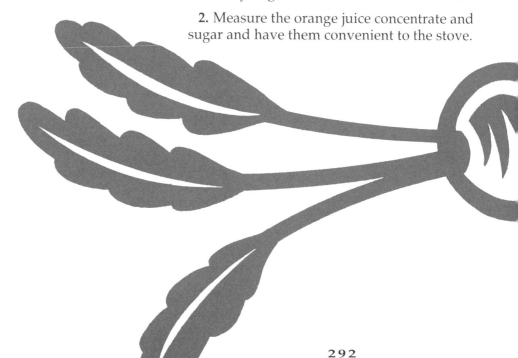

DO THIS SECOND:

1. Put the oil into a medium-size pot. Turn the heat to high.

2. When the oil is very hot, pour in all the carrots. Stir over high heat for 1 minute.

3. Add the orange juice concentrate, brown sugar, and salt. Stir the carrots so they're completely coated and glazey.

4. Cover the pot, turn the heat down to low, and cook, covered, about 20 minutes. Take the lid off now and then and give a couple of stirs.

WRAPPING IT UP:

1. By the end of the cooking time the carrots should be nice and soft.

2. Serve them in a pretty bowl. Once cooked, they'll stay hot, covered in their pot or serving dish, for 20 minutes.

• Pears turn dark quickly. That's why we go to the trouble to make the lemon-water. Having it handy buys you a lot of time so you can do a good job of peeling the pears and concentrate on not nicking the stems.

• The more you boil the poaching liquid the thicker and syrupier it becomes.

• Pears poached in cast iron will turn gray.

HONEY PEARS

TECHNIQUE—Poaching
BEST COOKWARE—Very large skillet, about
   12 inches wide (no cast iron, please)
BEST UTENSILS—Vegetable peeler, melon-baller,
   slotted spoon

If you've always secretly loved canned pears, you'll love the way pears come out after poaching (boiling lightly) at home in water sweetened with honey. They're easy to cook and, because they taste best nice and cold, demand to be made ahead for an easy dessert after a major meal.

Serves 8

   1 lemon
   8 pears (Bartlett or d'Anjou)
   3 cups water
   1½ cups honey
   1 teaspoon cinnamon
   4 whole cloves

DO THIS FIRST:

1. Fill a big bowl with water. Cut the lemon into quarters, squeeze each section into the water, then drop the spent pieces into the water, too. Have this bowl near your pear-peeling area.

2. Peel the pears with a vegetable peeler. Leave the stems! Drop each peeled pear into the lemon-water.

DO THIS SECOND:

1. Halve each pear lengthwise. This is tricky, but try to cut the stem in half, too, so each piece gets a little stem.

2. Scoop out the cores with a spoon or, better yet, a melon baller. Put the pears back into the lemon-water.

DO THIS THIRD:

1. Get out a big wide skillet. Pour in the 3 cups of water. Measure the honey and scrape it from the measuring cup into the pan with a rubber spatula.

2. Add the cinnamon and cloves.

DO THIS FOURTH:

1. Bring the water to a boil. When it boils, add the pears, flat sides down. Lower the heat to medium-low and poach the pears 20 minutes. *Clean up the pear-peel mess and get out a cookie sheet and a container to store the finished pears.*

2. The pears are done when the point of a sharp knife glides into the thickest part.

WRAPPING IT UP:

1. Remove the pears with a slotted spoon and let them cool on the cookie sheet.

2. Crank up the heat and boil the poaching liquid until you've got about 1½ cups of syrup. This will take 8 to 12 minutes.

3. Transfer the cooled pears to a big storage tub. Pour the syrup over the pears.

4. Chill the pears until you serve them. Serve them in bowls with some syrup spooned around them.

THE SEDER PLATE
At Passover symbolic foods are discussed and eaten. Every family has its own way of going through the Seder, but most Seder plates have certain basic items.

PLACE-SETTING SEDER PLATE
(For each guest)

Hard-cooked egg on lettuce leaf
Sprig of parsley or leafy piece of celery
Dollop of horseradish (red or white)
Spoonful or two of charoses
Small cup of salt water for dipping

(Host's Seder Plate)

Hard-cooked egg on lettuce leaf
Sprig of parsley or leafy piece of celery
Dollop of horseradish (red or white)
Roasted shank bone
Spoonful or two of charoses
Small cup of salt water for dipping
Plate of 3 matzos

14

DRINKS BY
THE PITCHER

BLOODY MARYS
BY THE PITCHER

TECHNIQUE — Shaking
BEST EQUIPMENT — 2-quart juice pitcher with a lid
BEST TOOLS — Measuring cups

Serves 6

Garnish
6 ribs celery
2 limes or lemons

Bloody Mary mixture
1½ cups vodka
4 cups tomato juice
⅓ cup lemon juice
1½ tablespoons Worcestershire sauce
A few drops Tabasco
⅛ teaspoon celery salt
Ice

DO THIS FIRST:

1. Trim and wash the celery, to be used as "swizzle" sticks.

2. Cut the limes or lemons into small wedges.

DO THIS SECOND:

1. Get out a 2-quart juice pitcher with a lid.

2. Measure all the Bloody Mary mixture ingredients except the ice into the pitcher. Cover and shake very well.

WRAPPING IT UP:

1. Fill 6 tall glasses with ice. Pour the Bloody Mary mixture over the ice. Tuck in a celery stick, and float a piece of citrus on top.

MAKE-AHEAD OPTION:

1. You can mix and chill all the ingredients except the vodka 2 to 3 days in advance. Keep the container tightly closed. To keep things extra cold, put the vodka in the refrigerator or freezer.

2. Add the vodka and shake well just before serving.

3. To serve, transfer the mixture to a serving pitcher filled with ice.

A pitcher of one cocktail or another is the easiest way to mix a batch of drinks that a bartender would make one at a time. You may find yourself pouring often, but you'll mix only once. You can prepare the drinks in any old plastic container, but serve them in a nice pitcher. The best serving pitchers for mixed drinks are plain glass or glazed ceramic, for two reasons. One, these are good-looking without being expensive; and two, they keep liquids cold longer than plastic. Get a 1-quart pitcher for drinks portioned out in small glasses (such as martinis) and a 2-quart pitcher for drinks with more volume, such as lemonade or Bloody Marys.

If the refrigerator is full with the food for your party, get two large ice chests. Use one for alcoholic beverages, such as wine and beer, the other for non-alcoholic. Twenty pounds of ice will chill down two chests.

• Sugar-water is known in classic cooking as Simple Syrup.

• Simple syrup is a good thing to know how to make. Boiling sugar in water is the only way to get a sweetened liquid absolutely smooth, with not a trace of sugar granules.

• Simple syrups vary in thickness and the intensity of their sweetness. The more sugar, the sweeter and thicker the syrup will be.

• Fresh mint is obtainable at grocery stores, but perhaps not such a large amount. If you have a friend or neighbor who grows mint, they'll gladly give you what you need. Mint is a garden terrorist; loaned mint is hardly missed.

• If you don't have the time to steep mint in simple syrup overnight, give it 6 to 8 hours. It will be fine.

• Crushed ice is the one required julep item most often ignored. That's because most home-freezer icemakers don't give crushed ice; you've got to buy it. Crushed ice is prettier and keeps the drink cold longer.

MINT JULEPS BY THE PITCHER

TECHNIQUE — Boiling
BEST COOKWARE — Dutch oven
BEST EQUIPMENT — Strainer

The Kentucky Derby is always run the first Saturday in May. No Derby party is complete without large batches of mint juleps. The best ones are started 2 days ahead.

Makes slightly less than a gallon

> 4 cups water
> 7 cups sugar
> About 4 cups packed fresh mint leaves and stems
> 10 cups bourbon (about 3 fifths)
> Crushed ice
> Fresh mint sprigs

DO THIS FIRST:

1. Measure the water into a large pot. Measure the sugar into the water.

2. Turn the heat to high. Cover the pot and bring it to a boil.

3. When you see steam seeping out from under the lid, uncover the pot and boil the sugar-water for 5 minutes. Give it one or two stirs.

4. Turn off the heat.

DO THIS SECOND:

1. Wash all the mint under running water. You don't have to dry it.

2. Add all the mint to the sugar-water. Bury it under the surface of the liquid.

3. Cover the pot. Let the pot sit out at room temperature overnight, or at least 6 to 8 hours, so the mint can flavor the sugar-water. Stir it up now and then if you're passing through the kitchen.

DO THIS THIRD:

1. Place a strainer with a long handle across the rim of a big bowl.

2. Pour the liquid through the strainer. Throw the mint away. That's the mint base coming out the other side.

3. Measure 4 cups of the mint liquid and pour it into a juice pitcher that holds 1 gallon.

4. Add the bourbon. Chill overnight, or a few days. It's got to be very cold when you serve it.

WRAPPING IT UP:

1. Set out julep cups on a serving tray. Use plastic or paper disposable cups, or tall or short glassware.

2. Fill each cup with crushed ice nearly to the rim.

3. Pour the cold mint-julep mix over the ice. Now go back and stick a fresh mint sprig into each cup.

4. If you really want to be proper, also stick a short straw into each cup beside the mint, the better to draw in the mint's essence.

MARTINIS BY THE PITCHER

TECHNIQUE — Shaking
BEST EQUIPMENT — 1-quart juice pitcher with a lid
BEST TOOLS — 2-cup measuring cup, strainer
HANDY TO HAVE — Toothpicks

The world's classiest cocktail at its most traditional is a simple ratio of one-to-two. That's two parts gin to one part dry vermouth. It's easy to make martinis ahead of time or to make a batch as guests watch and wait. The secret is that everything has to be cold. These martinis are served "up" in the classic stemmed and flared martini glass.

Serves 6 to 8

> Ice cubes
> Small olives stuffed with pimientos
> 1⅓ cups gin
> ⅔ cup dry vermouth

DO THIS FIRST:

1. Have ready a bowl of ice cubes. Have the olives handy near some toothpicks.

2. Line up all the martini glasses. If you like, put a few ice cubes in them to chill the glasses while you do the set-up.

3. Get out a juice pitcher and its lid, a 2-cup measuring cup, and a small strainer.

DO THIS SECOND:

1. Measure the gin and pour it into the juice pitcher.

2. Measure the vermouth and add it to the gin.

3. Add about 6 big ice cubes. Cover and shake very well.

DO THIS THIRD:

1. Let the martini mixture sit a moment or two. This is when you dump the ice out of the glasses and stick olives on toothpicks.

2. Remove the lid. Cover the opening with a strainer, upturn the container and pour the martinis into the glasses.

3. Put an olive in each glass.

MAKE-AHEAD OPTION:

1. You can store the gin-vermouth mixture in the juice pitcher, closed tightly, up to 2 to 3 days. Do not add ice.

2. To serve, add a few ice cubes, shake, then strain the martini mixture into martini glasses, or strain it into a nice-looking serving pitcher and pour it into the glasses right away.

• The simplicity of this cocktail shows flaws easily. Use a good vermouth (Cinzano) so when you taste the vermouth you'll enjoy it.

• Don't skimp on the gin, either. When buying gin look for the term "London Dry Gin" on the label. You can't go wrong with Beefeaters, Gordon's, Bombay, or Tanqueray.

• For the coldest martinis, pre-chill the bottles of gin and vermouth in the refrigerator. You can also keep these spirits in the freezer, where they won't freeze.

• The bigger the ice cubes, the less they'll melt. Crushed or shaved ice melts quickly and before you know it will water down the martini.

• The shaken martini mixture sits a few moments on the ice to get the mixture as cold as possible.

• Strainers designed specifically for capturing ice in such situations are regulation bar ware. If you'd rather not use your tea strainer to hold back the ice in your martini, go to any restaurant supply store (look up Restaurant Supply in the Yellow Pages) and pick up a stainless steel strainer.

• The salt can be regular table salt or coarse kosher salt.

• Tequila ranges from such stand-bys as Jose Cuervo to incomparable greats such as Herradura.

• Cointreau is an orange-flavored liqueur. It is absolute regulation in margaritas made by Pancho Morales. Trust me, Triple Sec is just fine.

MARGARITAS

TECHNIQUE — Shaking
BEST EQUIPMENT — 1-quart juice pitcher with a lid
BEST TOOLS — 2-cup measuring cup, strainer

It might surprise you that a real margarita isn't a snow cone in a glass caked with salt. Its flavor is a mystical balance between smoky tequila, sweet orange, and tart lime. There are lots of stories about the birth of the margarita, but I always put my money on Francisco "Pancho" Morales of El Paso, Texas, whose claim that he invented and named the margarita when he was a bartender in Juarez, Mexico during World War II is pretty hard to dispute. He used Mexican limón which has a delicate flavor nearly matched by mixing lemon and lime juices together. After you squeeze the lemon and lime, you'll run the squeezed piece around the rims of the glasses, just as Pancho did.

Serves 6

¼ cup salt
1 lemon
1 lime
1⅓ cups white tequila
⅔ cup Cointreau or Triple Sec

DO THIS FIRST:

1. Have ready a bowl of ice cubes. Get out a shaker container with a lid, a 2-cup measuring cup, and a small strainer.

2. Measure the salt and pour it onto a plate. Have ready six 4-ounce tumblers.

DO THIS SECOND:

1. Cut the lemon into quarters. Squeeze enough juice out of the pieces to measure ⅛ cup. Pour the juice into a shaker jar.

2. Cut the lime into quarters. Squeeze enough juice out of the pieces to measure ⅛ cup, and add it to the jar.

DO THIS THIRD:

1. Rub the squeezed pieces of lemon and lime around the rims of the glasses.

2. Dip each wet rim into the plate of salt. Shake off as much excess salt as possible. You won't use all the salt on the plate.

3. If you want the margaritas "on the rocks," add a few ice cubes to each glass.

DO THIS FOURTH:

1. Measure the tequila and pour it into the jar.

2. Measure and add the Cointreau.

3. Add about 6 big ice cubes. Cover and shake very well. Let the margarita mixture sit for about 30 seconds.

WRAPPING IT UP:

1. Remove the lid. Cover the opening with a strainer, upturn the container, and pour the margarita mixture into the glasses.

MAKE-AHEAD OPTION:

1. You can store the tequila-Cointreau mixture in the juice pitcher 2 to 3 days. Do not add the lemon or lime juice, and do not add ice.

2. When you serve, add the lemon-lime combination and a few ice cubes, cover, and shake it up, then strain the margaritas into the tumblers, or strain the mixture into a nice-looking serving pitcher and pour it into the glasses right away.

• The best time to stick about a hundred cloves into oranges is one night when you're watching television.

• Stick the cloves into the oranges in some kind of pattern, or fit them tightly all over the rind.

• It's okay if the cinnamon sticks go into the vat of cider along with the boiled cider mixture.

• Use light rum. Dark rum overwhelms this mellow mixture. Believe me, I know.

• You can also keep the mulled wine warm throughout the party in a crock pot or in a large electric coffee maker.

MULLED WINE

TECHNIQUE — Baking, boiling
BEST BAKEWARE — Cookie sheet
BEST COOKWARE — Huge pot, small pot

Hot baked oranges dropped into warm wine and cider make the house smell like you invented the concept of hearth and home. Busy yourself with sticking lots of whole cloves into oranges the day before to avoid any sense of being rushed the day you make and serve the wine.

Serves 12

> 4 oranges
> Bottle of whole cloves
> 1 gallon jug apple cider
> 3 cinnamon sticks
> 1½ cups light rum
> 4 cups red burgundy jug wine

DO THIS FIRST:

1. *The day before* you'll serve the wine, or early on the day of your party, stud the oranges with the whole cloves. Just stick them in like little nails.

2. Two hours before you'll serve the wine, put the oranges on a cookie sheet and bake them in a 350°F oven for 2 hours.

DO THIS SECOND:

1. Meanwhile, measure 2 cups of cider into a small pot. Add the cinnamon sticks. Bring the pot to a boil, uncovered. Turn down the heat and simmer for 5 minutes.

2. Pour the rest of the cider into a very big pot that you can serve from. Put it over low heat. It will stay here for the rest of the recipe and for serving.

DO THIS THIRD:

1. Pour the boiled cinnamon-cider into the big pot.

2. Pour in the rum and burgundy. Keep warm while the oranges finish baking.

WRAPPING IT UP:

1. Drop the hot oranges into the warm wine. They should sizzle, then continue to add flavor as long as the wine mulls on low heat.

2. Set out cups and a ladle and let guests serve themselves.

• Notice: no cinnamon, no soft drinks. This isn't punch. And be sure to use inexpensive wine. The concept and intent will be all but ruined if you use the good stuff.

• To be truly Spanish, look for inexpensive red wine from La Mancha.

• Sangria can also be approximated with any California red table wine, such as Gallo Hearty Burgundy, or an inexpensive Syrah from Australia.

• The sugar acts as a smoothing element—the sangria shouldn't be really sweet.

• Sparkling water makes the sangria lively and reduces the alcohol a little, so you can keep on drinking.

• Big chunks of ice is the tradition.

SANGRIA

BEST EQUIPMENT—Chef's knife and cutting board
BEST TO HAVE—Clear glass serving pitcher

This is one of the all-time great drinks by the pitcher—ice cold, beautiful, and always refreshing. Sangria is a Spanish mixture originally made to take the rough edge off a full-bodied dark red wine. A sangria comes to life when the wine is used to macerate (soak) thin slices of orange and lemon overnight.

Serves 12

> 2 lemons
> 2 oranges
> ½ gallon jug red table wine
> 2 tablespoons sugar
> ½ cup brandy
> 1 quart sparkling water (Calistoga or Perrier)
> Ice (big chunks are best)

DO THIS FIRST:

1. *The day before your party,* slice the lemons and oranges into thin rounds. Put them in a pitcher.

2. Pour the wine over the fruit.

3. Cover the pitcher with plastic wrap and set it in the refrigerator overnight.

WRAPPING IT UP:

1. Just before serving, add the rest of the ingredients and stir.

VARIATION: WHITE WINE SANGRIA

This is popular in Seville. Use jug Chardonnay or any generic white table wine, even California mountain chablis. Instead of soaking lemons and oranges overnight, soak fresh slices of peeled peaches in the white wine. Finish with the same amounts of sugar, brandy, and sparkling water, then the ice chunks.

LEMONADE
BY THE PITCHER

TECHNIQUE—Shaking
BEST TOOLS—Citrus reamer, paring knife and cutting board, wire-mesh strainer or colander
GREAT TO HAVE—Electric citrus reamer

Lemons are a year-round crop. When they're selling at 5 for $1, that's the time to make lemonade.

Makes about 7½ cups (a scant 2 quarts)

> 6 to 7 lemons (or 1 cup lemon juice)
> ⅔ cup sugar
> 6 cups (1½ quarts) ice water

DO THIS FIRST:

1. Cut each lemon in half across its girth. Squeeze the juice out of each half. You should get about 1 cup, but it doesn't have to be exact.

2. Set a big wire-mesh strainer, at least 8 inches across, over a mixing bowl. Pour the juice through the strainer to catch the seeds and pulp. (If you *like* pulp, pour the juice into a bowl through a colander, which will catch seeds but let some lemon matter through.)

DO THIS SECOND:

1. Pour the strained juice into a 2-quart juice pitcher. Add the sugar, cover, and shake really hard.

2. Add the water and shake well again.

WRAPPING IT UP:

1. Pour the lemonade over ice in tall glasses, or refrigerate it. Shake every time you pour from the container.

• The amount of lemon depends on your taste. Add more lemon juice if a tarter, heightened lemon taste is what you like. Add more sugar if this lemonade isn't sweet enough for you.

• The general rule is that 6 lemons will give you 1 cup of lemon juice. Of course, nature doesn't always cooperate with such specifics. Some lemons are juicier than others, and some lemons are tart while other varieties are sweet. This food thing is imprecise, so you'll have to forgive the inexactness of this recipe.

• You'll get more juice out of a lemon if you roll it firmly on the countertop under your palm. This loosens the skin and, uh, gets the juices going. You'll get up to 2 teaspoons more than if you hadn't rolled the lemon.

• If you have a citrus reamer (juicer) powered by electricity or just human energy, this is the time to use it.

APPENDIX

MENUS

MENUS AND HOW THEY GO TOGETHER

People new to cooking tell me that they're most likely to try cooking for company during a holiday. This is when they've got a few days off from work, they have time to plan and shop, and they have the feeling that there's even time to fix a mistake.

Successful menus balance time. While one recipe bakes inside the oven, you're free to sauté something else. Plan your menus according to the activity the recipes require of you. The balance of flavors will follow.

This book is full of recipes that company loves. Sometimes a single recipe is the menu; at other times you'll group up to three recipes together. Remember that not everything has to be made or ready at the same time. Not every recipe has to be served hot. In summer, food can be made ahead and served cool. In winter a hearty casserole with salad makes a fine dinner for any number of people.

To help you plan, in the following list an asterisk (*) appears next to the recipe you start last.

One-recipe menus for six
1. Greek Salad
2. Beef Stew and Airy Light Dumplings
3. Seven-Layer Salad
4. Risotto That's an Entire Meal

Two-recipe menus for six
5. *Big Piece of Roasted Fish
   Corn Salad
6. Spinach Quiche
   *Simple Salad with Walnuts
7. Thick White Bean Soup with Chicken Thighs
   *Broccoli on the Side
8. Lasagne
   *Simple Salad with Walnuts
9. *Beef Stew and Airy Light Dumplings
   Honey Pears
10. Texas Crowd Chili
   *Spinach Salad with Ham, Eggs, and
      Mustard Dressing

11. Beer-Cheese Soup
     *Spinach Salad with Ham, Eggs, and
       Mustard Dressing
12. Grilled Coconut Chicken
     *Cherry Tomato Salad
13. Pasta with Improved Tomato Sauce
       from a Jar
     *Simple Salad with Walnuts
14. Yucatan-Flavor Roast Pork
     *Orange-Flavored Carrots
15. Tomato Bisque
     *Caesar Salad
16. Flank Steak Marinated in Beer
     *Garlic Mashed Potatoes
17. Spaghetti in Substantial Meat Sauce
     *Simple Salad with Walnuts
18. *Grilled Peppercorn Steak
       Potatoes au Gratin
19. *Clam Chowder
       Spinach Quiche

Three-recipe menus for six
20. Yucatan-Flavor Roast Pork
     *Orzo
       Honey Pears
21. Grilled Coconut Chicken
     *Sautéed Greens
       Sugar Cookies
22. Stuffed Artichokes
       Leg of Lamb
     *Buttered Green Beans
23. *Deviled Eggs
       Simple Israeli Diced Salad
       New Potato Salad
24. Cold Cucumber-Buttermilk Soup
     *Big Pot of Ginger Chicken Wings
       Blue Cheese Cole Slaw
25. Potato Soup
     *Yucatan-Flavor Roast Pork
       Your First Cheesecake
26. Lasagne
     *Broccoli on the Side
       Big-Batch Brownies and Frosting

OTHER EXCUSES TO PUT
RECIPES TO USE FOR COMPANY

A Saturday or Sunday afternoon
"California" Onion Dip Without Using a Mix
*Chile con Queso
  Soused Shrimp Cocktail
  Big-Batch Brownies and Frosting

For Children
  Deviled Eggs
*Things on Toothpicks (Cheese and Fruit)
  Vanilla Pudding, or Birthday Cake,
    or Jelly Cookies

Valentine's Day
  Sugared Nuts
*Risotto That's an Entire Meal
  Chocolate Truffles

Two Menus for Any Monday "Grill" Holiday
(Memorial Day, 4th of July, Labor Day)
  Flank Steak Marinated in Beer
  Cherry Tomato Salad
*Grilled Corn on the Cob
  Sugared Strawberries with Cream

*Grilled Peppercorn Steak
  Corn Bread
  Marinated Mushrooms
  Blue Cheese Cole Slaw
  Sugared Strawberries with Cream

Come for Cocktails
  Marinated Mushrooms
  Ricotta Cracker Spread
  Sugared Nuts
*Martinis by the Pitcher

It's Hot Outside
(Completely made ahead)
  Cold Cucumber-Buttermilk Soup
  Cherry Tomato Salad
  Tabouli
  New Potato Salad

RECIPES IN *NOW YOU'RE COOKING* THAT YOU CAN SERVE TO COMPANY

The following recipes in my previous book, *Now You're Cooking: Everything a Beginner Needs To Know To Start Cooking Today,* are great company fare.

Nachos
Hummos
Guacamole
Beer and Cheddar Spread
Boiled Shrimp with Cocktail Sauce
Gazpacho
Potato Salad
Cole Slaw
Chicken Salad
Pot Roast
Basic Grilled Steak
Steak in Cabernet Sauce
Chicken That Makes Its Own Sauce
Wine Sauce Chicken
Broiled Lamb Chops in Garlic-Mint Marinade
Chocolate Sauce for Ice Cream
Chocolate Birthday Cake with Chocolate Frosting

INDEX